Ski Randonnée_!

AAC 2009
Jean Vives

by

Dr. Jean Vives Ed.D.

Forward by Brian Litz

Ice Box Books
Fraser, Colorado
www.SkiRandonnee.com

Library of Congress Cataloging-in-Publication Data

Vives, Jean, 1949-
    Ski Randonnée / Jean Vives.
        p.   cm.
    Includes bibliographical references and index.
    ISBN1-4243-0789-9   ISBN 13 978-1-4243-0789-0
    1. Skiing.   2. Mountaineering.   3. Skis and skiing.

ISBN: 1-4243-0789-9   ISBN 13 978-1-4243-0789-0

Graphic Design: Tina Wilson, Firebird DesignWorks; Illustrations: Marjorie Leggitt, Leggitt Design and Illustration; Copy Editor: Amy Leavitt, Page by Page Copy Editing. InDesign software, Mac G4 System v.10.

Printed in Hong Kong by Regal Printing Ltd.
Ice Box Books
P.O. Box 280
Fraser, Colorado 80442 USA
www.SkiRandonnee.com
jean@SkiRandonnee.com

Notice of Caution

Backcountry Skiing is Dangerous.
Every effort has been made to find state of the art information, however–

This book is not a substitute for professional instruction and practice using appropriate equipment and techniques.
Ski Responsibly and Use Your Brain

Thank You

Front Cover:
Upper Left: Jeff Russell photo, high above Winter Park, Colorado.
Upper Right: Brian Litz photo, skiing above Durrand Glacier, British Columbia.
Lower left: At the fracture line above Silverton, Colorado. Courtesy of Colorado
                    Avalanche Information Center.
Lower Right: Ski guide Reudi Beglinger leading above Golden, British Columbia.

Back Cover:
Photo by Marc Gallup, Skier scouting drop in above Fernie, British Columbia.

For All Backcountry Skiers

Contents

Contents

Preface

In 1996, I completed the first and still the only American scientific research into Alpine Ski Touring or what is increasingly being called Ski Randonnée after its French roots. In my doctoral dissertation, at the time I stated that there was a growing shift to wider skis in the backcountry. I also pointed out that the Randonnée binding was superior in its mechanical efficiency compared to the cable Telemark binding. Now we are seeing more Telemark bindings shifting to the mechanical pivot design. What will the future bring? Read on.

Why is this backcountry ski book different? Because it was written after reading all the ones before it! And this is not another book on Telemarking! Randonnée from the French literally means to "walk about". The term "Ski Randonnée" is used more in Europe whereas the terms "Alpine Ski Touring" or "AT" skiing and "ski mountaineering" are used more in America. My goal in writing this book was to provide a catalog, if you will, of backcountry ski techniques geared for the parallel skier. While there are several books out on Telemark skiing there are none available for Randonnée skiing. While there are numerous magazine articles describing expeditions or exploits of extreme skiers, there is no source of practical information for the everyday skier. Randonnée skiing is not just about extreme skiing or repelling down cliffs, it's also about skiing to a hut for a night out or having lunch on top of a peak during a beautiful Spring Day. It's about skiing from one resort to the next. It's about skiing untouched powder!

Ski Randonnée! is not just about skiing technique – it is also about adapting to winter. It presents an objective and analytical look at the world of backcountry skiing through concise technique descriptions and over 100 photographs and illustrations. Whether you're a resort skier who is looking to expand your horizons or a cross-country skier who wants to go higher, you'll find this book packed with clear, usable information – including techniques borrowed from ski guides, mountaineers, ski patrollers, and snow rangers – that will make you an effective, knowledgeable wilderness skier.

Chapter 1 will bring you up to date on the most recent advances in cold weather clothing, while chapter 2 does the same for Randonnée ski touring equipment, including skis, poles, boots, and bindings. Chapter 3 talks about climbing techniques on skis and on foot using climbing skins, crampons and ice axe. Chapter 4 goes into skiing techniques that the resort skier already knows and how they can be used in the backcountry. Chapter 5 looks at mountain terrain hazards specific to skiing and includes glacier skiing and crevasse rescue techniques. Chapter 6 provides readers with descriptions of how to use altimeters/barometers as weather forecasting tools and includes a helpful sequence of photos showing the major stages of storm development. Chapter 7 covers the all-important skills needed to navigate safely in the backcountry, using maps, altimeter, compass and GPS devices. Terrain recognition skills are vital, and this chapter also contains a unique opportunity to cross-reference mountain terrain features to a photo and map of the same terrain. Chapter 8 describes how to recognize and then ski and climb around avalanche hazards and helps you determine what information about the route and snow conditions is important to obtain before leaving home.

Chapter 9 covers winter camping, expedition planning, and overseas travel. Finally, chapter 10 covers the critical components of surviving an emergency, focusing on the basic idea that if each individual is prepared to survive alone if necessary, the whole group becomes stronger. I advocate defensive skiing and equipment preparation. I've also included a complete survival equipment list and encourage all skiers to learn winter bivouacking techniques. The Technical Appendix is loaded with information about conditioning, nutrition, and ski route grading. The Colorado Haute Route is outlined for the first time in any publication.

Backcountry skiing is exciting and fulfilling, but as with any sport some aspects can be potentially dangerous. I've used the techniques in this book for over 30 years in both mild and extreme weather conditions and found them to be safe and effective. If you're new to the backcountry, I recommend practicing all of these techniques in good weather conditions and on easy terrain before moving into less forgiving situations. No book is a substitute for instruction from a qualified guide or instructor. But it does help to form an intellectual foundation of principles and concepts for correct action on the mountain and for that a book can be valuable.

Good Skiing!

Dr. Jean Vives EdD., Fraser, Colorado

Advisors-Reviewers

Every effort has been made to make this book technically accurate. The following are some of the reviewers and advisors who have help to edit the material so that it reflects the state of the art of Randonnée Skiing. This book would have been much more difficult to do if it had not been for their help for which I am greatly indebted.

- Peter Hackett, MD, Wilderness Medical Society
- Peter Cliff, UIAGM, Mountain Guide, Writer
- Louis Dawson, Ski Mountaineer, Writer, Historian
- Ethan Greene, Director, Colorado Avalanche Information Center
- Scotty McGee, PSIA, Jackson Hole Mountain Sports School
- Charlie Gray, PSIA, Winter Park, Colorado
- Bruce Edgerly, Backcountry Access Inc.
- Denny Hogan, Silverton Avalanche Center
- Rod Newcomb, American Avalanche Institute
- Dale Atkins, Colorado Avalanche Information Center
- MSgt. Jack Loudermilk, retired, U.S. Army
- Bill Clemens, MD, National Mountain Rescue medical director
- Gary Neptune and staff, Neptune Mountaineering
- Laura E. Seitz, ACR Rescue Electronics
- Julie Ann Lickteig, MA, associate professor of nutrition
- Todd Kipfer, Big Sky Institute, Montana State University
- Petzl of USA

Foreword by Brian Litz

Growing up in the foothills of Colorado's Rockies I have been able to experience the mountains in all seasons, though the snowy months of winter and spring cast a particularly strong spell on me. Thinking back over all the days spent wandering around the mountains - it is both humorous and sobering to think of all the ski-bound trials and alpine errors that my gang and I have survived as we morphed from green horns, to dare I say it, experts.

Looking back however, there is no point along the upward trajectory of my ski career, where I can't say that a book like Jean Vives's exhaustive "Ski Randonnée" would not have been a welcome instructional tool to shortcut the learning process (and copious number of near misses). As with any lifelong mountaineer, my education continues. I still learn something new about myself, my abilities, my gear, and the mysteries of the mountain wilderness each time I set ski to snow. This process however will now benefit from the trove of information, hints and tips crammed between the covers of this fine book.

Weather, ski techniques, avalanche safety, equipment, and clothing, are but a few of the many topics that are covered in Vives's succinct, erudite and easy to understand fashion. Over the years, his life spent living in, working in and playing in the mountains of the world from Colorado to Khathmandu have bestowed him with a wealth of knowledge. Whether you methodically crunch through "Ski Randonnée!" from start to finish, underlining passages and dog-earing pages, or if you nibble away at it bobbing in and out of the pages as the spirit moves you, you'll be hard pressed not to find information that will greatly enhance your metal-edged adventures.

Of course, most importantly, when the ski day is done and you're sitting in a bar enjoying that aprés brew, I guarantee you can easily win the price of the book back many times over via bars bets - with all the fun and fascinating factoids you'll have garnered from each page! Sure, the book technically is aimed at the Randonnée or AT skier, but every skier including cross-country, Telemark and today's big-mountain free riders will find this book a most helpful, if not essential, tool for their trade.

-Brian Litz

Kosha Rigby and company climbing unknown couloir on Baffin Island during a North Face factory trip to Sam's Fjord. See - crampons and ski poles are a nice way to climb! Photo by Whit Richardson.

Clothing 1

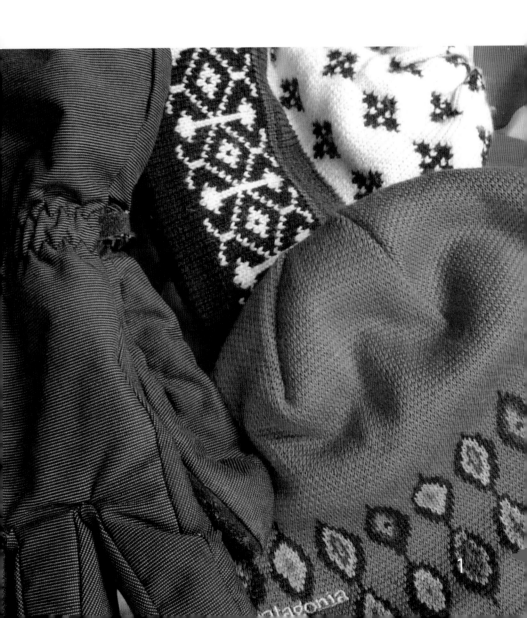

Ski Randonnée!

We live in a Golden Age of garment technology where there is "body mapping" and "sonic welding of seams". Sewing machines are so 2004! Experienced mountaineers and skiers know that good winter clothing makes winter outings all the more pleasurable and safer. In the end, your clothing is your primary shelter.

Buying Clothing

Clothing is most cost-effective when it can be used for several sports. For instance, storm jackets and pant shells can function as rainwear in the summer for instance. Because good raiments are expensive, consider building up your wardrobe selection over a few ski seasons while you are improving your skills and increasing the scope of your ski activities. Insuring your ski gear under a homeowner or renter insurance plan is an absolute must. Having your equipment stolen is a terrible experience!

How Clothing Works

The climate in the mountains is one of extreme cold and heat. Garments must serve two purposes: repel external moisture and allow sweat to evaporate from the garment. Therefore, breathability, wicking, and venting are three very important functions to consider when purchasing clothing. Choosing the proper clothing for the conditions can make the difference between an enjoyable ski tour and a damp and freezing experience.

Interacting With the Environment

As you ski, heat and sweat in the form of vapor exert an outward pressure against the inside of the garment. Whether this vapor can escape depends on the materials that the garment is made of and the prevailing weather conditions. Heat and moisture flow from areas of high temperature and/or humidity to areas of lower temperature or humidity. For example, when air inside the garment is warm and moist and the outside air is cold and dry, heat will escape more quickly. Conversely, when the temperature outside the garment is higher than the temperature inside, as during spring skiing or when snow is mixed with rain, the hot air inside the garment escapes more slowly, making it more difficult to maintain a comfortable temperature

Cover 1.1: Cold weather clothing is more colorful and warmer than ever before due to advances in garment technology. Vivesphoto.

Fig. 1.1: Charlie rubbing on wax before a downhill run above Breckenridge, Day Three of the Colorado Haute Route (CHR). He's wearing soft shell pants from Mountain Hardwear and a soft shell jacket from Cloudveil. Vivesphoto.

inside the garment. If it is raining outside (100 percent humidity), will sweat still escape? Yes, but not as well as when the outside weather is dry.

There are four thermal processes describing how the body interacts with clothing and the environment: Convection is the process by which heat is pulled or taken away from the body by the air currents whether inside or outside the garment. In Conducton heat is drained from the body when it comes into contact with something cold such as snow, rock, ice, or moist air. Cold, humid air is able to wick heat away from the body faster than cold, dry air. This is why the damp maritime climates of coastal ranges such as the Sierras and Cascades feel colder than the Continental climates of interior ranges such as the Rockies.

Radiation is another thermal process when it comes to controlling the amount of heat inside a garment. The warmth of the sun is actually short wave solar radiation. Most sunlight is reflected back into space, but dark-colored garments will absorb more of this energy than light-colored ones, even on a cold day. For example, it can be 90 deg.F. (32 degrees Celsius) on the surface of a red ski jacket while the air temperature is only 40 degrees Fahrenheit (4 degrees Celsius). Skiers who wear dark-colored garments can have more trouble staying cool on warmer days, but this can be remedied by undoing a zipper or taking a layer off. Since dark garments absorb so much radiation, the skier stays warmer with less clothing weight and bulk.

Thermal Density and Loft

Thermal density describes the amount of heat that clothing captures within its filaments, fibers, or feathers. When air is captured in a still area of clothing, its temperature is raised by body heat. This warm air is conserved around the body and remains stable if protected from convection or conduction forces from the outside. This is the concept behind the idea of dressing in layers.

The thickness of the insulation in a garment or a sleeping bag is called loft. Loft is especially important when goose or duck down are the insulating materials. Unfortunately, when down gets wet the loft collapses, losing all its insulation properties. When a typical garment is wet, the microspaces between the fibers are full of water and thereby cannot hold warm air. Fantastic new Hydrophobic (water-hating) fibers such as synthetic fleece (Polartec™, etc.) do not absorb any water at all from the inside (sweat) or the outside (snow), and are fast-drying as a result.

Shape of Garment

The shape and fit of a garment determine its ability to hold heated air around the body. Microconvection air currents can enter a garment, wicking heat off the body. The closer the garment is to the body, the less convection currents occur. This is one of the attractions of newer soft shell designs. Underwear is close-fitting to eliminate drafts. Be sure that all underwear and shirts are long enough to fit snugly below your belt line to keep heat in. New concepts in tight fitting underwear such as UnderArmor™ are used by professional athletes to increase one's awareness of the body in space (ie, kinetic sense), in addition to reducing convection currents. I can attest that it is excellent for eliminating sweat dripping down my back. It also keeps me warm on cold days and strangely doesn't overheat me on warmer days. People often use Stretchy Lycra and biking tights subconsciously as a de facto replacement for UnderArmor™ type material which can be used during warmer conditions.

As already stated, you need to capture and keep air in your clothing so that it is heated by your body. Dressing in layers is an efficient way of capturing air and heating it. Each layer has a purpose. In the following sections we will see how each layer of clothing works.

Layer One: The Base Layer

Underwear keeps you dry and warm. Polypropylene and Capilene™ materials, when directly against the skin, delay the condensation of sweat vapor so that it can evaporate. Underwear usually comes in light, medium, and expedition weights. A lightweight layer can be used under an expedition weight layer during colder conditions, and then used separately during warmer conditions. Newer wool blends (Devold™, Smartwool™) are getting more attention from skiers who normally prefer traditional materials.

The underwear layer is usually made up of two separate pieces, top and bottom. One-piece underwear (long johns) might seem like a good idea at first. Most have a drop seat for toilet use, and the one-piece design prevents bunching. However, the top part can't be used by itself, making it less versatile in changing conditions.

The top should be long enough to tuck in, and have a turtleneck with a zipper for maximum temperature adjustability. Cuffs at the wrists keep your wrists warm and prevent from escaping (some even have thumb holes!). The bottom garment should have cuffs at the ankles, and for men, a fly in front. For maximum comfort when snow camping or hut skiing, you can rotate two sets of expedition and/or medium weight underwear, changing into a second set at night for pajamas and leaving it on to become the first layer of your ski clothes the next day. In winter,

Fig. 1.2: Jean skinning up in comfort! The base layer thermal wear can double as lounge wear around the hut. Add some down booties for max comfort! The Skinner Hut, Day Two of the Colorado Haute Route (CHR). Charlie Gray photo.

Ski Randonnée!

your underwear becomes an integral part of your sleeping insulation system. A short-sleeved, quick-drying, nylon jogging T-shirt (made of a Dacron™ polyester blend) worn right on the skin keeps you even dryer than a long-sleeved undershirt by itself. It also works great during spring touring when you just want something on your skin to protect you from the sun.

Layer Two: Insulation

The insulation layer should be hydrophobic and (see figure 1.3) usually consists of a heavy expedition-weight thermal underwear and a vest (which can be fiberfill, pile, or gortex- goose down), or any combination

Fig. 1.3: Dressing in layers makes clothing more flexible when conditions turn warm or when you get heated from climbing. Enroute to the Jackal Hut, 10th Mountain Hut System, near Leadville, Colorado. Vivesphoto.

thereof. A vest helps to maintain core temperature, and can be used with the base layer alone during warmer conditions. A full jacket (fleece, down, or Primaloft™) is used less often due to the heat generated in ski touring. However, an insulated jacket can be used if it is cold enough. A fleece vest with an outer nylon shell works best, since it is not snowproof and windproof when used by itself. Pile pants teamed with a storm pant can be used in very cold conditions, while stretch Lycra, biking tights, or stretch pile can be used during warmer conditions.

A jacket, sweater, or shirt should be long enough to stay tucked into your pants during exercise. A good test when buying these items is to reach for the sky with each arm to see if the bottom of the garment comes over your belt or if sleeves pull away from your wrists. If either of these things happen, buy the next size up. Be sure your clothing has high collars for protection from wind. Always keep your receipts and don't be afraid to take an item back if it doesn't feel right.

Many types of insulating materials have been used over the ages. Fur was the first insulator, and in many regions of the world, it is still the material of choice. Let's review some of the contemporary materials used for insulation.

- WOOL – The wool industry hasn't been resting during the synthetic revolution. Today's wool underwear feels luxurious and doesn't shrink (or stink!) like it used to. Wool is not hydrophobic though, and can absorb up to 30 percent of its weight in water. Powder snow sticks to woolly knickers like glue, so they should always be worn with a nylon shell for increased water resistance.

- GOOSE DOWN – Goose down is a great insulator and has a high thermal density as long as it's dry. When down gets wet it loses all insulation, and it is very difficult to dry, even over a raging campfire. To protect down from moisture, it must be paired with Gore-Tex™ either as a garment or a DryLoft™Gore-Tex™ in sleeping bag form. Goose down comes in different grades or power of fill with corresponding increases in prices: 500, 600, and even 800 loft is sold.

- PILE FLEECE GARMENTS – Pile fleece (Polartec™, among others) is actually made of a fine polyester plastic. It comes in several grades of thickness from lightweight to expedition weight, with corresponding 200, 300, and 400 weights. The plastic is spun into a wool-type material that has a very high thermal density. It is hydrophobic, which makes it a good insulator even when wet. The newer versions seem to get more luxurious with each passing season. You can even get stretchable windproof fleece garments for added warmth.

- POLYESTER FILLS – The best polyester fill comes in the forms of Polar-guard™ HV and Primaloft™, (the names fluctuate almost yearly) which consist of a long continuous filament that resists shifting during use, allowing the garment to stay warmer longer. This filament can also be shredded in its Primaloft™ form which is used in place of down as stuffing for vests, jackets, and sleeping bags. Dacron materials are less expensive and easier to maintain than down, and unlike down insulate even if wet. The main drawback is that they don't compress as easily as down (although Primaloft™ is better), and take up more room in your pack. A compression sack can help remedy this.

- COTTON – Cotton is an absolute no-no in the backcountry. It fails completely as a cold-weather insulator because it absorbs water and sweat and conducts heat away from the body. Jeans or cotton T-shirts (not to be confused with nylon jogging T-shirts) should not be worn when skiing. Jeans can get very wet after a few falls in the snow and won't dry. Many ski patrollers have had to cut and peel wet or frozen jeans off skiers who had broken their legs while skiing – a painful process to say the least.

Layer Three: Wind Protection

The insulation layer helps trap air around the body and keep you warm. The outermost layer, the storm suit (see figure 1.5), will further help maintain body temperature. This layer consists of pants and a jacket, and is vital because it protects all the other layers from the environment. It should be waterproof, breathable, and easily ventable. "Water resistant" is not the same as "water proof". Getting wet doesn't cut it. That's why I prefer garments made of Gore-Tex™ fabric that is "guaranteed" not to allow water in (I'm not being paid for the endorsement). The outer layer must breathe. Sweat vapor must be allowed to escape if your clothing is to remain dry. Don't ever believe that you'll be able to dry your clothing with body heat. You'll need it yourself to stay warm. You also can't assume that the weather will be warm enough to dry clothes, or that you will be able to find enough wood for a fire. In the meantime, your cold clothes will be wicking heat away from your body while you are looking for firewood!

You should envision yourself in the worst weather conditions possible when choosing your outer-layer garments. With proper care, outer-layer garments should last at least five years with moderate weekend use. Most manufacturers make both lightweight and expedition-weight garments. Although expedition-weight gear is nice, it is also heavier. Unless you are a beginner who falls a lot, you will be able to get away with the lightweight version. Check to see whether lightweight jackets and pants have reinforced knees, elbows, and seats, all of which are necessary for handling abuse.

Materials

The shift in backcountry clothing has been to breathable, waterproof materials, and it is often more important to look for what garments are

Fig. 1.4: Clothing has to take on many roles in order save weight and time in the backcountry. Jean is wearing his insulation layer vest and pant shell. Shrine Mountain Inn, Vail Pass, Colorado. Charlie Gray photo.

made of than what company makes them. The two most effective materials for this outer layer are coated nylon and Gore-Tex™.

- GORE-TEX™ – Gore-Tex™ gear may be the biggest breakthrough in outdoor clothing today. This material allows sweat vapor to escape from the garment and keeps moisture out. Evaporation of sweat keeps the body drier – a critical factor in staying warm. Gore-Tex™ is Teflon™ that is specially laminated to the inner shell of the garment. Some Gore-Tex™ clones such as HellyTech™ work well while others don't. You have to do your research. It really depends on the name behind the garment. Studies have shown that Gore-Tex™ brand materials are superior to any other material in terms of breathability and water resistance. Gore-Tex™ can remain waterproof after 500 hours of continuous water exposure while allowing body moisture to escape. Gore-Tex™ comes in three-ply and two-ply versions which are used on separate parts of garments – three-ply is more abrasion proof and is usually used on the shoulders and elbows, while two-ply is often used on the body of the jacket.
- COATED NYLON – Coated nylon skiwear is far less expensive and lighter than Gore-Tex™, and works well if vented properly. However, it can be similar to wearing a plastic bag – your sweat can't escape, so your clothing can get wet. Goose down should not be used under coated nylon since it will get wet. Wool and Primaloft™ are better choices for such a clothing system. Adding zippers at the underarms ("pit zips") and using them religiously will help to get your clothing dry.

Storm Jacket

A Gore-Tex™ jacket is best, but as mentioned a jacket of coated material can be used if it is well-vented. The jacket should have pit zips and large pockets for warming hands or storing a camera. It should also have a large hood with an elastic cord big enough to fit over a ski hat and able to be adjusted snugly around the face. The wrist closures should be Velcro™ or elastic and must be expandable enough to fit over gloves. Elbows should be reinforced. A Velcro™ wind flap over the main zipper is a good idea in case of the event of a zipper failure

Storm Pants

The pants should have full-length zippers so that you can put them on over your skis and boots. Reinforcement at the knees and buttocks is also a plus. Snaps and elastic closures at the waist make for easier toilet use. Pants or bibs with built-in suspenders will allow you to drop the seat without taking off the front of the pant, which is helpful in terrible weather.

Get suspenders if you can't find pants with built-in ones, since pants always slide down during touring. The inside of the pants should be heavily reinforced to prevent cutting of the pant material by ski edges. In addition, there should be a built-in gaiter or tight closure to keep snow out.

One-Piece Ski Suits

One-piece ski suits can be insulated or noninsulated. But you must have a butt zipper – without a zipper, you need to take off all your clothes to relieve yourself – a real hassle.

One-piece racing suits are very lightweight and used for track skiing, but are difficult to use when nature calls. They are made of Lycra and are not very warm, so they can only be used during very good weather. One-piece downhill ski suits or Alpine climbing suits are insulated, making them too warm for all but the very coldest ski tours.

Fig. 1.5: See – Randonnée skiers and Telemarkers do get along after all! Both have wind/waterproof clothing and are ready for exercise on a great powder day. Jackal Hut, Leadville, Colorado. Vivesphoto.

11

Ski Randonnée!

The traditional two-piece jacket and pant system seems to be the best for all-around use. Bib knickers are great if they have a seat zipper for toilet use.

Soft Shell Technology

Soft shells have been the big "buzz" over the last few years due to their tailored look and trim "sexy" appearance. Traditional clothing systems consist of three layers: wicking, insulation, and protective layers. The soft shell system attempts to combine two layers (insulation and protective) into one to reduce bulk and weight. Additionally, they are more fitted to the body to reduce convection currents inside the garment in order to reduce chilling and are made with lycra or spandex so they move better with the body. Due to Polartec Power Shield fabric they are 98% windproof and are very water repellant, but not completely waterproof unless they contain Gore-Tex™ (a wet ski lift chair might get you wet). In drier climes they work extremely well, but on wetter days or in maritime climates, they beg an overshell.

Clothing Color

The color of the clothing used in wilderness skiing is very important. Clothing must dry quickly, so black is a popular color for outerwear because it dries so well. Unfortunately, in warm weather it can be very hot and uncomfortable. From a rescue standpoint, storm suits should be brightly-colored (yellow, red, or blue) for maximum air-to-ground visibility. Tests have shown that contrasting colors such as black and yellow or black and red are more visible than single colors.

Accessory Clothing

Don't neglect the details! In the following sections, I'll discuss some of the accessories you'll want to add to your basic outerwear to get the most out of backcountry skiing: gaiters, gloves and glove liners, socks and sock liners, and hats. Each of these items will add to the comfort and safety of your trip. For example, your hat and gloves cover areas of the body where your blood comes closest to the weather (wrists and head). If those areas are not protected, you'll still be cold! An extra hat or pair of gloves weighs little but adds greatly to your enjoyment of the sport.

Gaiters

Gaiters are not as popular now since most backcountry ski pants have built in gaiters, but some don't and some people just like to ski with knickers. High-top gaiters (16 inches [41 centimeters] high) are mandatory for skiing off the track. Gaiters keep your legs and feet warm by keeping snow out of your boot liners. They can also protect your expensive pants from getting cut by skis edges, rocks, or crampons.

Coated nylon gaiters are not ideal – they accumulate body moisture on the inside of the gaiter, which means wet clothing. But if that's all you have, just unzip your gaiters occasionally at rest stops to vent the moisture out. Naturally, Gore-Tex™ gaiters are best because they vent moisture and are warmer as a result. Gaiters with Velcro™ closures are preferred over those with zippers, which can break. If you do have gaiters with zippers, installing zipper pulls will also make it easier to open and close your gaiters with cold fingers. Newer gaiters have replaced the usual nylon cord in the instep with a strap-and-buckle. The buckle should always placed on the outside of the leg for easier access.

Overgaiters and Overboots

An overgaiter is just a bigger version of a gaiter that covers the whole boot. It is especially good when using leather boots. Newer, warmer, plastic boots have eliminated the use of these coverings. Overboots are different only in that they cover the bottom of the boot as well. They are great for skiing in very cold conditions or for those whose feet tend to get cold. They keep your boots drier, and as a result warmer. Overgaiters and overboots also protect your boot from sharp rocks, crampons, and ski edges. Those made with Gore-Tex™ are preferred, as they keep the boot drier. They usually seal around the welt of the boot using an elastic rubber cuff (which must be replaced occasionally, depending on use – replacements will be more frequent when one walks on pavement or rocks).

Gaiters for Alpine Ski Touring Boots

Most gaiters open on the front and back, but rarely on the side where your ski buckles are. Alpine ski touring gaiters that have an extra-long strap to go under the plastic boot have remedied this. Some people use this gaiter for their high-performance telemark boots as well.

Ski Randonnée!

Gloves and Mittens

Many people prefer the warmth of a mitten over a glove, but people with warmer hands prefer to have the dexterity of the glove. Some newer designs using removable pile liners offer the warmth of a mitten with the convenience of a glove. People with extra-cold hands (or feet) shouldn't be afraid to get electric hand and boot warmers that use rechargeable batteries for day touring. Chemical heat packs are better to have along on longer tours since electric hand warmers need to be recharged. Spraying antiperspirant on the hands (and feet) adds warmth by keeping them dry. I discuss gloves, mittens, and glove liners on the next page.

- SKI TOURING TRACK GLOVES – Leather cross-country track gloves have a tendency to get wet from sweat and snow. Better gloves are now made completely of synthetic materials and are more water resistant.

- DOWNHILL SKI GLOVES – If you are a downhill skier already and own some of the newer downhill gloves, they will be warm enough for occasional off-trail skiing. Look for gloves with Thinsulate™ or Primaloft™ insulation and a Gore-Tex™ shell. Newer ones have a long forearm covering (a "gauntlet") that has an elastic closure.

- MOUNTAINEERING GLOVES – These gloves are fitted with a long sleeve and rubberized material and are used with a removable inner pile liner. These gloves usually have articulated fingers that are premolded in a grip position so that it takes less effort to flex them. They are very tough and warm, and last forever. Skiers should buy them in a size larger than they normally wear so that a liner can fit inside.

- MITTENS AND MITTEN SHELLS – Wool mittens absorb snow and turn into a wet mess very quickly, causing freezing hands – so they should always be used with a nylon shell. The shell should be reinforced in the palm area to minimize wear to the material, and should have an elastic or Velcro™ closure. A shell made for mountaineering is the most durable.

- GLOVE LINERS – Glove liners are a must in very cold weather. They keep the hands warm when you take your gloves off to work on clothing or take a photo. They also protect the gloves' insulation material from getting wet with sweat, which would lessen their insulation effectiveness. They are usually made of polypropylene or Capilene™. Look for liners that have a cotton-like finish, are not slippery, and allow for increased finger dexterity.

Fig. 1.6: It is important to have clothing that can easily be adjusted for extreme heat as well as extreme cold. Ventilate your clothing before you get too hot. Heat can increase energy demand by a significant degree. Spring skiing on a closed trail, Loveland Ski Area, Colorado. Vivesphoto.

Ski Socks and Liners

Many people wear rag wool socks out of tradition; however, today we have many varieties of socks made out of superior materials. The problem with rag wool or fleece socks is that they allow your foot to be loose inside the boot, negatively affecting performance. Nylon-Dacron™ and polypropylene wool blends are always more durable than wool by itself. Modern ski boot socks retain dead air space even when compressed. Polypropylene helps keep the sock dry because it is a solid fiber and doesn't absorb moisture. Dry skin is warm skin, and is less prone to blistering because the skin-sock interface develops less friction.

Ski Randonnée!

Liner socks are more often used with hiking boots than with ski boots. Most boot fitters would agree that the fewer layers between you and your ski boot the better. While the randonnee boot is used for some hiking the emphasis must be kept on ski performance. Most modern ski socks afford excellent insulation and padding.

Snow Hats

We have often heard that 40 percent of our body heat is lost through the head. But that is from a dry head! When the head and hat are wet, that figure can rise to 75 percent, not including the windchill factor! Hats should be warm, windproof, and water resistant. Your hat should fit comfortably under your storm jacket hood. Choose a knitted hat with a smooth finish that sheds snow, since those with a rag or fleece finish can collect snow and get soaked during heavy snowfalls. A wool/synthetic blend ski hat is a good choice for both resort and backcountry skiing. It's wise to spray hats with a waterproofing material like Scotchgard™ to maintain water resistance. It's hard to beat a waterproof Gore-Tex™ nylon-shelled, pile-insulated hat in bad weather. Face masks and balaclavas are also very useful in windy, cold conditions. Windproof fleece is softer on the face than neoprene, which can hold moisture. Always bring an extra hat – it's light insurance!

Sun Hats

Your body needs protection from sun as much as from the cold. Sun is a potent force in the mountains. Skin cancer is a real threat, so always wear some type of hat to keep the sun off your face and neck on warmer days . The old-fashioned cotton baseball cap works just fine. I have experimented using a knitted ski cap and baseball cap in rotation. The hat not being used should be stuffed inside the jacket for fast access. It seems that mountain weather changes almost changes minute to minute.

Caring for Clothing

Remember that you are maintaining expensive gear – so make it last. Always follow the manufacturer's instructions on garment care. If in doubt, call the shop where you bought the garment for cleaning advice or check out the manufacturers web site.

Cleaning and Waterproofing

Clothing and sleeping bags insulate better when they are clean. When clothing fibers hold dirt instead of air, there is less dead air space and loft, resulting in a reduced ability to insulate and keep you warm. Clothing should be clean, dry, and kept at room temperature before applying a spray or liquid waterproofing to protect garments against grime. Many new high-tech cleaning-waterproofing products use water-repellent polymers to help remove dirt and body oil and give down jackets and sleeping bags an increased degree of water resistance.

Sealing Seams

Seam leaks are becoming less common as many garments and tents today are presealed electrostatically at the factory. Seams appear mostly on storm jackets and pants, and on tent floors and roofs. They also appear around the welts of boots. If the seams on your garments have not been presealed, purchase the appropriate seam sealer and apply to dry, warmed surfaces only in a heated, well-ventilated room. Apply one coat and let it dry for a few hours, then apply another.

Zippers

Zippers seem to have a mind of their own, and can break at the worst possible moment. Lubricants such as silicon or Teflon help maintain easy-pulling zippers, and suntan lotion even works in a pinch. Be sure you can work all of the zippers on your clothing and other gear quickly by adding pull loops (see page 18). The newer rubberized zippers are tougher and more waterproof. Every time you have to take off your gloves to use a zipper, you lose body heat and your hands may get colder. In the field, carry some safety pins in your repair kit just in case a zipper breaks. Dental floss can be used for emergency mending, so place a sewing needle in your repair kit.

Making Zipper Pulls

Most zippers are too small to use with large gloves or mittens in the middle of a blizzard, so each zipper should have a pull loop. Go down to your local mountain shop and buy about 20 feet (6 meters) of round 4 mm Perlon™ accessory cord, which is easier to grip than flat webbing. Twelve-inch (30-centimeter) pieces of cord work best for clothing. Use 14-inch

Ski Randonnée!

(36-centimeter) cord on sleeping bags, backpacks, and tent zippers. Burn the ends of each piece with a butane lighter after cutting, or have the shop cut them electronically. Tie the ends with a square knot, stick one end through the loop and loop through the knot, and you've created a zipper pull. You'll be happy you had them!

Fig. 1.7: Zipper Pulls are a must in the backcountry. Nothing is more frustrating than trying to pull a zipper open with big gloves or mittens! Vivesphoto.

Conclusion

Clothing can make the difference between enjoying backcountry skiing and hating it. Investing in good clothing is the first smart thing you can do to ensure your enjoyment of the sport and your safety in bad weather conditions. In the ultimate sense, your clothing is your first shelter, and good winter clothing provides the foundation for all your outdoor exploits. You can spend more time skiing and less time heading indoors to warm up. You'll have more patience and endurance, which will help you make good decisions in bad weather. Mountain rescuers have often found survivors with only their clothing to keep them warm. Think about it.

Fig. 1.8: Skiing up the scenic Bachelor Gulch area near Berthoud Pass, Colorado. Vivesphoto.

Gear 2

Ski Randonnée!

Can you have too much equipment?? Are you crazy?? No way!! While ski clothing will keep you warm and dry, good ski equipment will help you ski faster and farther while using less energy. In fact, good ski equipment can lift your skiing ability to a whole new level of performance. The applications of space age materials and construction technologies are providing skiers with a whole new range of ski equipment and clothing that is more effective and fun in backcountry conditions.

Merging of Equipment

It is getting harder to see the differences between Telemark and Randonnée equipment. Telemark boots are more frequently being used with adjustable-release bindings, a feature once unique to AT bindings. Today, only one characteristic separates advanced Telemark and AT equipment, besides the ability to latch the binding down, the pivot point. Randonnee bindings incorporate a plate and a machined metal pivot for heel lift during locomotion. Telemark bindings generally use the boot's own flex for heel lift. That is about to change as some Tele bindings such as the Karhu™ and Bomber™ are moving to a metal pivot system.

Which is more efficient in uphill climbing? The steeper it gets, the better Randonnée equipment works. My research has shown that the two modes are identical in energy expenditure, even though the AT gear tested was

Cover 2.1: It must be Diamir™ heaven! No, just The Dix Haute on The Haute Route, between Zermatt and Chamonix. Why so many Diamirs™? Because it's the biggest rental backcountry binding in Europe, attesting to its durability and flexibility. Vivesphoto.

Table 2.1

COMPARING TELEMARK TO RANDONNÉE

Mfg.	Model	Weight/pair	Cost
TELEMARK BINDINGS (NONRELEASABLE)			
Black Diamond	O2	50 oz.	$189.00
Bomber	BishopT1	64 oz.	320.00
Rottefella	R8	62 oz.	160.00

Mfg.	Model	Weight/pair	Cost
TELEMARK BINDINGS (RELEASEABLE)			
Karhu	7tm Power	50 oz.	$275.00
Voilé	CRB	57 oz.	175.00
RANDONNÉE BINDINGS			
Diamir (Freeride)	Fritschi	60 oz.	$425.00
Dynafit	Classic	24 oz.	299.95
Naxo	SL	80 oz.	475.00
TELEMARK BOOTS			
Garmont	Ener-G	65 oz.	$679.95
Crispi	X-R	61 oz.	620.00
RANDONNÉE BOOTS			
Dynafit	TLT	56 oz.	$469.95
Lowa	Rodeo	69 oz.	550.00
Scarpa	Denali	62 oz.	598.00

Mfg.	Model	Profile	Weight/pair	Cost
TELEMARK SKIS				
Black Diamond	Frantic	105-73-93	826g/100cm.	$499.00
Dynafit	FR 8.0	113-75-99	794g/100cm.	499.95
AT SKIS/WIDE TELEMARK				
Goode	Carbon 116	139-116-123	694/100cm	$990.00
K2	Sahale	120-70-89	688/100cm.	420.00
Volkl	SnowWolf	113-76-100	799g/100cm	650.00
SKI POLES				
Black Diamond	Traverse	2 sections	21 oz./pr	$49.95
Leki	Classic	2 sections	24 oz./pr	109.95
Black Diamond	Self Arrest	2 sections	28 oz./pr	159.00

Ski Randonnée!

35% heavier! This shows how efficient a mechanical pivot is compared to the bending of a boot as a pivot. Some newer AT gear is even lighter than newer Telemark equipment. The prices for the two forms of equipment have reached parity over the years (see table 2.1).

Randonnée Equipment Use Increases

Renting equipment is a great way to determine which ski/binding setup is best for you. Unfortunately, not every ski shop is renting Randonnée equipment so be sure to call ahead. More shops are adding Randonnée equipment as the sales of the equipment grows. During the winter of 2004-5, Randonnée sales grew by 400% according to Couloir Magazine. Ski magazines are increasingly including Randonnée gear in their ski tests since the same skis used at the resort are being used in the backcountry. Studying the latest equipment reviews can help you stay current on new ski models. Beginners shouldn't be afraid of so-called high performance equipment; it will help them ski better with less effort. Additionally, a ski

Fig. 2.2: Skis-skis-skis! Renting or demo-ing can be the best way to get the best skis for you. Call ski shops ahead of time to be sure they carry Randonnée gear. Vivesphoto.

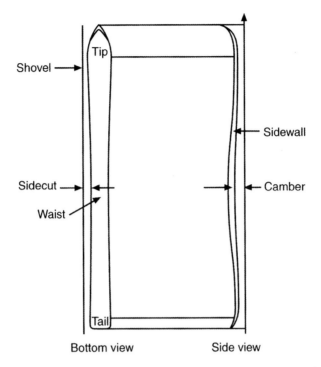

Fig. 2.3: Parts of the ski. Adapted, by permission, from J. Yacenda, 1998, High-Performance Skiing, 2ed. (Champaign: Human Kinetics).

doesn't have to say "backcountry" on it to be used there; many people ski the backcountry with "resort" skis. Whatever you choose, use the same equipment for both resort and backcountry skiing. This will help you get used to your equipment faster.

Randonnée Skis

I have some good news and I have some bad news. The good news is that there are a lot of beautiful skis out there. The bad news- there are a lot of beautiful skis out there! In the recent 2006 gear issue of Couloir magazine there were 100 different models available! How can a person choose? First, I'll tell you what I have and why and then I'll offer some ideas. I use 178cm Rossignol™ Bandit XXX's with Diamir Fritschi™ bindings for my deep powder set up. I use 171 cm Black Diamond™ Crossbows with Dynafit™ Tour Lite bindings for spring and summer skiing (more about the bindings later). The Rossi's are a little heavier but they really perform in deep powder where I actually like a little extra weight and stability. I can also use them for high speed cruising at the resort and feel very comfortable at speed since the

23

Ski Randonnée!

Diamirs™ release so well even with my Scarpa™ rubber soled AT boots. The Crossbows are great in the Spring for ski tours and peak descents because they are so lightweight and packable. Tele skis can be used by parallel skiers and visa versa (although some Tele skis have a softer flex pattern for telemarking only).

Choosing Skis:

Know thyself and get a ski that will lift your performance to a higher level. Find your weaknesses and get a ski that will fill in the gaps. Problems turning in powder and crud? Get a ski that will turn for you. People think that backcountry skiing is all about powder skiing. Powder is only part of the story. It could be powder, hardpack, crud and ice, all in one run. I highly recommend getting a non-specialized backcountry ski. Ski testers often use adjectives like "all mountain", "all terrain" and "versatile" to describe these skis.

Marketing and Ski Hype

We all watch backcountry ski films and Warren Miller movies. Guys jumping off rock faces and skiing that perfect powder in Alaska. But let's get real. Yes, they are making great turns. That is because: a.) the powder is perfect because they waited 7 days for those conditions!; b.) the skier is skiing perfectly because they are professional skiers! – that's all they do every day! c.) as a professional they can ski test many skis and custom tune them for that day's snow condition. I would love to see a ski company design a ski not with a professional skier/mountaineer's advice but with an intermediate backcountry skiers advice. The ski you use needs to ski everything, not just powder.

Going Fat

Skis have been getting fatter with each passing season for good reason, it makes it easier to ski untrack snow whether it be powder or crud. Width isn't as critical on ice where a narrower ski might work better. Many skiers (myself included) own two pair of skis: one for powder and deep winter conditions and then a ski for spring and early summer skiing. Skiing can be twice as hard with equipment that is not suited to your strength or the snow conditions, so it is imperative that you choose the ski(s)that works best for you. With that in mind, consider the following characteristics when

24

looking for skis (for ski anatomy see figure 2.1).

- WIDTH – It is impractical to sideslip or turn in thick, mucky snow or wear a heavy pack if you are using narrow skis. For skiers used to AT gear, anything over 90 mm is considered a wide ski. Both AT and Telemark proponents would agree that a wider ski has distinct advantages. It offers more flotation than a narrow ski in powder, crud, slush, and sun crust – especially when wearing a pack – because of its increased skiing surface area. A shorter, wider ski has as many cubic centimeters touching the snow as a very long, narrow ski, but distributes body weight sideways as well as forward and backward, which reduces sinking into deep snow. Because wide skis are easier to turn, beginners will fall less and learn faster.

- LENGTH – Skis used to be measured by touching your palm to the tip of the ski. Today this sounds quaint. Now, since there are so many ski models out you must trust your ski shop to pick the right length for you. A ski must be matched to the ability level, aggressiveness, and weight of the skier. In the past, skiers of higher ability tended to have longer skis. Today that is not the case...ask the US Ski Team members who now race on 165's ! When is short too short? The now defunct Trak Ski Co. made a unusual ski called the Bushwacker in the early 70's. It was 153 cm long and 100 mm wide and it had a fishscale bottom on it for climbing. A neat idea but it could not stay on top of deep snow. It simply did not have enough surface area of flotation to handle my 170 pounds. They're were so short that the tails buried themselves into the snow causing backward falls. You really do need some length; not just for skiing but for climbing as well.

Skis are measured in two different ways: cord length and running length. Cord length is measured by running a tape measure along the ski's top surface from the heel of the ski to the tip of the ski. The running length is a measure of the surface of the ski that actually touches the snow. On a 195-cm ski, this may amount to 177 cm. of actual surface area on the snow. Shorter skis are lighter, increasing endurance, reducing travel time, and making packing easier.

- WEIGHT – Heavier skis tend to carve through heavy snows better. Not a good enough reason to use them all the time. Long-haul backcountry skiing involves hours of touring and climbing between relatively short moments of downhill skiing. Always get the lightest ski available.

Fig. 2.4: Lightweight equipment is truly worth the extra investment. Remember – not only may you ski on your gear – you may end up carrying all of it on your body. Day 2, Colorado Haute Route (CHR), Copper Mountain. Notice the "S-K-Y" couloirs on the peak in the background. Vivesphoto.

- SKI CORE – Skis are generally built from sandwiched combinations of four materials: foam, wood, metal, and now carbon fiber. Foam and fiberglass are used for flexibility. Wood adds stiffness and dampening. Metal adds torsional stiffness, and durability. Wood and metal skis may hold binding screws better than a pure foam core. The latest buzz is about carbon fiber that is now being used to replace wood in some cases to increase torsional stiffness and reduce weight. Most skis have a reinforced midsection called a binding plate that gives binding screws solid anchorage into the ski (see discussion on ski bindings, page 35). Speaking of strength, you don't see skis breaking in half like they used to. But delamination can occur occasionally-more later.

- TORSIONAL STIFFNESS – This is the amount of flex or twist the ski has along its long axis. The ski should be stiff enough to hold on ice and hard snow. Performance on ice is important, because a fall on ice can cause more serious injury than a fall into fluffy powder. There are many types of skis that work well in all conditions, but metal skis work the best on ice due to their superior torsional stiffness. Cap skis, also made of the foam-wood-metal combination, use a top cap of fiberglass which is heat molded to a torsion box construction making it torsionally stiffer. They are popular due to their increased edging power.

- VIBRATION DAMPENING – When a ski vibrates it is spending more time in the air and not on the snow, holding an edge. To maintain control on hard snow and ice, the ski must be able to dampen vibration. To test this, hold the ski vertically with your fingertips, then lightly drop the ski down from an inch above the floor. Does the ski vibrate? The less it vibrates, the better it will be on hardpack and ice.

- FLEX – Generally, the ski should have a predictable, even flex, tip to tail, for skiing powder and crud. However, the tip of the ski may flex a little more than the rest of the ski, allowing the ski to deflect off crud or rocks to minimize the effect on the ski's tracking. An aftbody, or rear of the ski, that is stiffer than the front of the ski is good for edging on ice and finishing turns in all conditions.

- SIDE CUT – Side cut is the amount, in millimeters, that the waist of the ski differs from the tip, or tail, of the ski. This measurement determines the ease with which the ski can be turned. Maneuverability in tight spaces among trees and rocks is important in the backcountry. So-called shaped skis with 30 mm of side cut (parabolic or hourglass skis) do speed turning response. However, the downside is that a waist that is too narrow allows the ski to collapse in the middle when skiing powder or crud. So-called fat skis with 20 mm of side cut are better suited for backcountry conditions, since these combine increased flotation and turning ease. When purchasing skis, sidecut information is normally listed by the manufacturer on the ski or its packaging, and it can also be obtained from magazine ski tests and or from ski shop personnel.

- SIDEWALLS – The side of the ski is prone to damage from rock and ice, so it must have a proven record of durability.

- CAMBER – Camber is the amount of spring or life that a ski has, which allows the ski to spring back after being compressed on the snow. Traditionally, backcountry skis had a double camber, allowing the ski to be unweighted slightly and thus enabling forward gliding, which was important for using wax or skins. Today, most modern backcountry skis do not have a double camber, as downhill performance has been given a higher priority than trail performance.

When buying skis be sure that they don't have too much camber – your body weight should be able to compress the skis fully. There is an old Nordic ski test to verify this. Lay the skis down on a flat, hard floor, and slip a piece of paper under each ski. Then, step on top of both skis together, making sure your weight is equally distributed on both skis. Have a friend pull the pieces of paper out from under the skis simultaneously. If he can pull the paper out from under the skis, those skis are not the right length – go to the next longer length. If he cannot pull both pieces of paper out, then those skis are the correct length for your weight. The idea is to be able to make contact with the snow as well as float on top of it. This is an essential attribute for touring and climbing.

- BASES – There are two methods of base processing for ski bottoms. A sintered base is made from melted plastic chunks, while extruded plastic bases are made from preformed sheets of P-tex™. Sintered bases are porous, so they hold wax better. Bases come in different levels of hardness. A level 2,000 P-tex™ base is very hard, so it won't get damaged by rocks. The flip side is that it is really hard to tune the skis yourself since the base material is so hard to file.

- COLOR – A dark-colored ski bottom won't melt snow any faster or slide better than a light-colored ski. But bright-colored skis are easier to find if they get away from you. Base color may be significant in ground-to-air signaling, according to French tests in which yellow fluorescent bases were visible by helicopter from three miles (5 kilometers) away.

Ski Tuning

Backcountry skis get beat up because they are used on ungroomed slopes, but they still need to be maintained at a high level. Sharp edges and good bases are a basic requirement for good turning. Ideally, it would be great if you could have your skis tuned before each day of skiing. However, in a less than perfect world we must make some concessions. Should you tune your own skis? With harder base materials and metal edges, you'll find that it takes more time and effort than you care to spend. Certified technicians with professional tools do a great job, and many of them are backcountry skiers themselves. Besides, isn't the $30-$40 you spend to get your skis tuned a small price to maintain a $700-$900 investment? At a minimum,

Fig. 2.5. Ski boot liners should always be removed at the end of the day to dry, even if they are a Gor-Tex™ or Thermofit™ liners. On the Haute Rotue. Vivesphoto.

get your skis tuned just before the ski season starts, when many ski shops have tuning specials. Then get your skis tuned right before spring skiing so they will be sharp on morning ice. Some people put a storage wax on their skis for the summer. If you do enjoy tuning your own skis there are some good books on ski tuning and professional grade tools are available to do the job right (see bibliography). In the field you can take out nicks in the edges of your skis with a small sharpening stone. But leave the heavy files at home – overzealous attempts at tuning can ruin your new skis. Carrying a small piece of glide wax comes in handy if skis get sticky due to sudden temperature changes.

Randonnée Boots

Boots are the most important piece of equipment you will buy since they make the vital connection between ski and body. Good-fitting boots mean increased strength, endurance, and comfort, and can reduce falling by transmitting turning forces quickly and forcefully to your skis. This is vital

29

on ungroomed backcountry snows. Poor-fitting boots mean cold feet, blisters, pain, and reduced endurance.

Boot Construction

Randonnée Boots are essentially double boots with a plastic shell and insulated inner boot. This inner boot can be removed and dried by hanging above a hut fireplace or inside a sleeping bag during winter camping. Good inner boots have a durable bottom, allowing the boot to be worn around the hut. Worn inner boots can be replaced with factory made replacements or a custom heat molded inner such as the Raichle Thermofit™. Both work well but the advantage goes to the heat molded inner boot since it saves weight, eliminates lacing completely, and is custom fitted to your foot and ankle.

All AT boots have been plastic for some time and prefaced the development of the plastic Telemark boot. These boots also have a removable inner boot for warmth while skiing. The ski boot itself has a Vibram climbing sole, so it can't be used with regular downhill bindings (see figure 2.4). AT boots lack a flexible footbed (except for Randonnée racing models), making the boot uncomfortable for extended walking or downclimbing. Bring running or trail shoes if extended walking on pavement (over 2 miles [3 km]) is required. For skiing and touring, forward and rear flex is arrested by a lock on the rear of the boot that can be manipulated easily. Randonnée boots basically are available with either two or three buckles. Four buckles can double as resort ski boots whereas three buckles are lighter and usually more com-

Fig. 2.6: Randonnée boots from left: Garmont, Scarpa Verdict 2, Crispi 3-Buckle and Dynafit Racing.

fortable for hut touring
and general backcountry
use. (I use the three buckle
Scarpa boots.)

Boot Fitting

Larger ski shops that deal
with backcountry equip-
ment carry more Randon-
née equipment than ever
before. Don't expect to
just walk into the first
shop you visit and buy a
pair of boots. Talk with
the shop's boot-fitting
expert and try a couple
of pairs. Fit boots using
the socks you normally
wear while skiing; prob-

Inner Boot

Stiffening
Strap

Cuff
Release
(hike mode
adjustment)

Hiking sole

Fig. 2.7: Anatomy of a boot.

ably a medium-weight ski sock. Wear the boots around the house for a
few hours after you make your purchase to check the fit. Return them if
they don't feel good. There are a lot of good boots out there, so it's the
fit that counts, not the brand. If $50 to $100 separates you from the boot
you need, make yourself buy it – you will save money and time in the long
run. Remember that a pair of boots can last for a few years, making for a
minimal yearly investment over the long term.

Fitting Problems must be Fixed

The inner boot is generally comprised of two pieces. The inner boot shell
usually has laces and a walking sole for around the hut. It will also has a
generic foot bed to provide the wearer with basic arch support. Additionally, the plastic shell itself can be heated and "punched out" to conform
to wider feet. Any or all of these components can be customized to solve
fitting problems.

If you are bowlegged or knock-kneed, you will have a harder time turning
your skis. Most boot shells have canting adjustments that can be used to
adjust for these conditions. A ski boot specialist can replace the factory

31

footbed with a custom-molded orthotic footbed that will hold the foot in a neutral position and spread body weight over the whole foot bottom evenly. This makes weight changes and edging easier and more precise. Be sure to ask the shop about this and if they don't know, find a ski shop that does. It's very important to have your feet aligned in the boot which is then aligned with your binding which is then aligned with your ski. Everthing works together and if one part is not working properly you will experience discomfort and expend extra energy needlessly. Another problem relates to socks: If you are constantly getting blisters, you might be wearing too many socks to make up for a cold boot. This allows your foot to swim around inside the socks causing friction between the skin and the sock. In that case you should definitely consider new boots or heat molded Thermofit™ liners. Avoid hard plastic orthotics, which do not flex with the foot.

Using Downhill Resort Boots for the Backcountry

There is a growing number of resort boots that come with "walk mode". However, most resort ski boots keep the skier in a constantly forward flexed position, making flat skiing or walking miserable. This can be remedied somewhat by unbuckling the top two buckles. For a peak ascent, it's easier to pack your downhill ski boots and hike up in trail boots during Spring conditions (see Ascent).

Randonnée Bindings

Adjustable-release Randonnée plate bindings (see figure 2.6) have been in constant use in Europe for over 40 years. They allow the foot to be locked down during downhill mode. During climbing or walking mode they can be released or "free-heeled". All have standardized DIN release settings. By the way, "DIN" stands for "Deutsch Industrial Normal", a standardized engineering measure used throughout the ski industry related to torque and force applications. The release setting is a function of DIN. All Randonnée bindings have some type of heel elevation system for climbing efficiency. Some Randonnée plate bindings also accept plastic climbing boots (Silveretta™), allowing them to be used for approaching winter climbs. The Fritschi Diamir™ used to be the only true step-in binding available that can speed mode changes during "transitioning" due to its fast step-in features. Now, however, Silveretta™ and Naxco™ have joined the market in the last few years with their versions.

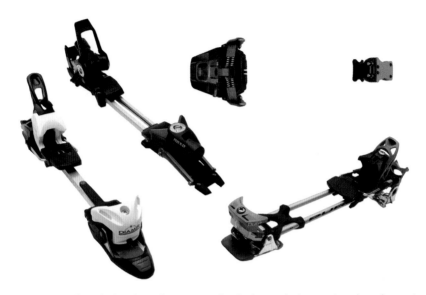

Fig. 2.8: Randonnée bindings have a mechanical metal pivot point that dramatically increases its mechanical efficiency over the Telemark binding, which relies on a cable/spring/boot hinge combination. In fact, the steeper the climb, the more efficient the Randonnée binding becomes. Vivesphoto.

AT bindings are becoming more sophisticated in design each year. For example, the Dynafit™ binding (see Fig. 2.8) consists only of a heel and toe piece, using the boot itself for the plate function. This saves weight, making them lighter than most Telemark bindings. While they lack the higher heel elevators of some bindings like the Fritschi, you can't ignore the pleasure of a light binding. However it can clog with snow easily, which some patient people don't mind. Others prefer to use them in the Spring, where deep powder is not a problem.

The Bindings Pivot Point

The bindings pivot point has become a sales point for some binding manufacturers by exploiting an often overlooked design feature of Randonnée bindings. The exact distance between the ski boot toe and the pivot point of the binding plate creates a lever arm. When that lever arm is eliminated it creates a more natural feel during diagonal striding. Naxo™ and Silveretta™ have made a point of moving the pivot point under the boot's toe. Reducing the lever arm of the pivot mechanism also increases work efficiency (see equation in the Nutrition chapter) and reduces the energy required to lift the binding plate thereby increasing

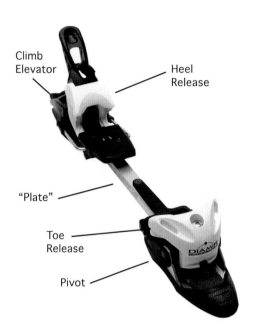

Climb
Elevator

Heel
Release

"Plate"

Toe
Release

Pivot

Fig. 2.9: Anatomy of a Randonnée binding.

energy efficiency during touring. Is this enough to buy the binding? In my opinion, the energy savings are marginal.

Randonne Bindings and Release Considerations

Simply stated, bindings should hold the boot to the ski when desired and release the boot when desired. Basically, a Randonnée binding uses a plate that is attached to a metal hinge. The boot then fits within a modified toe and heel piece allowing for an adjustable release. Some bindings, like the old Ramer binding adjusted the release at the pivot point itself. All AT bindings have a release function. How about cross compatability between Telemark and Randonnée bindings? Overall, some plastic Telemark boots can fit into AT bindings if needed. This is not recommended since the box like toe of the Telemark boot will not work properly with the adjustable release Randonnée toe. However, AT boots will not work with Telemark bindings.

Binding Release Calibration

AT bindings are DIN calibrated and can be adjusted by using tables that compare your body weight and ski ability. Don't set the screws and forget about them. Experiment with your own individual strengths and weaknesses. Have a binding technician show you how to adjust your own bindings.You should know how to adjust your bindings by yourself in the field and you should always carry the proper tools to do so. The following variables can affect how your binding may need to be adjusted:

- DIFFICULT TERRAIN AND SNOW – The binding should be elastic enough so that it doesn't pop off with every little vibration or with additional

Fig. 2.10: Randonnée Scarpa boot with Diamir binding. Vivesphoto.

pack weight. Experience with your own binding will guide you on whether to increase or reduce its setting depending on the snow you are skiing. On extreme ski descents, where a premature release can be dangerous, skiers can eliminate the binding release altogether by locking the binding, as on the Dynafit™. Binding manufacturers have staged "DIN" wars lately, pushing the DIN higher and higher. The Naxo™ nx21 has a DIN 13 release setting!

- PRIOR HISTORY OF LEG INJURY – Beginners, younger and older skiers, and people with previous history of leg injuries should use a lower setting. The skier should make the shop aware of past injuries or a history of knee weakness.

- SNOW CONDITIONS – Heavy spring snow requires a lower setting on some bindings due to the increased incidence of slow, twisting falls. Ask the ski shop about any needed adjustments under these conditions. It's a good habit to have the shop check your bindings at the same time you get your skis sharpened.

Stacking

Stacking increases the distance between the boot and ski with plastic spacers (available at ski shops). By increasing this distance, the more aggressive skier is able to increase the mechanical advantage of the leg over the ski, increasing the crank (the power the leg can apply to the turn).

It also keeps the boot from hitting the snow during radical turns. This is rarely used in Randonnée skiing since the binding itself acts to elevate the boot over the ski.

Touring Adapters

There are several AT binding adapters that fit into the bindings of downhill skis. This eliminates the need to purchase new equipment, which would be a compromise for the person who just wants to backcountry ski occasionally. Problems don't arise with the adapters themselves. Don't forget that downhill skis and bindings are very heavy by themselves. Some downhill boots do have a walking mode which does help but it can still be uncomfortable.

Binding Noise

AT bindings are notorious for making a clacking noise during touring. Even Telemark bindings squeak due to friction between binding and boots. This can be remedied by spraying silicon on the boot edges where they meet the binding. AT clack can be softened by covering heel elevators or ski surfaces with rubber electrical tape. Plastic boot noise can also be helped with silicon spray at the cuff and hinge parts.

Runaway Straps

Runaway straps prevent losing a ski to terrain (such as a crevasse) where walking out may be impossible, forcing a bivouac. The wire clip (used on many Telemark bindings) that is attached to the skier's boot is a ski retention device meant for resort use only and is difficult to use with gloves. String or cord is not a substitute because knots can freeze up, preventing release during an avalanche emergency. Many resort skiers avoid runaway straps because they can cause the ski to "windmill" during high-speed crashes, causing head injuries. However, backcountry ski speeds rarely approach resort speeds. I prefer ski brakes myself but I have seen skis with ski brakes disappear down very big slopes because the slope was icy and steep. In deep powder, the ski can submarine under the powder for many feet before stopping. The most effective solution is to use runaway straps that are attached to the binding. Runaway straps are best constructed of nylon webbing with a velcro or metal clip closure that can be released or attached quickly. Any attachment should be released before crossing a suspected avalanche zone. A powder cord (a four foot piece of brightly colored webbing) also works well during deep powder conditions.

Ski Crampons

Sometimes snow is too hard for skins to adhere. It could be a patchy situation where adhesion comes and goes. On very hard snow or ice, ski crampons – metal teeth that can be pushed into the snow – can be helpful for climbing while ascending low-angled traverses. They come in two styles, with advocates for each: one attaches to the binding (see figure 2.11), while another model attaches to the ski. The binding type allows the ski edges to remain in contact with the snow while you advance the ski to the next crampon placement, but if this type of crampon is used with heel elevators while climbing, the elevators will prevent the teeth from reaching the snow – not a problem for the ski-mounted type. But, ski-mounted types can make you feel like you are on stilts if they don't penetrate the snow, making you feel very unbalanced. The trend is currently going for the binding mounted ski crampon.

Ski Poles

The ski pole is to the skier what an ice axe is to the mountaineer. Think of it as an extension of your hand. It can be used to maintain balance, initiate

Fig. 2.11: Ski Crampons are a necessity on very icy slopes where freeze melt cycles have made the snow porous. This is often the case in Spring skiing in marine climates. Vivesphoto.

turns, and prevent falls. During bushwhacking, it can be used to beat down face level branches, and at night you can use it to anchor your tent. You can use it to probe for crevasses on glaciers or to determine the strength of ice on ponds and rivers. When crossing a stream or log, you can use your ski pole for support. On the approach hike you can use it for walking support. It can also be used to probe for weak layers when digging avalanche pits. The ski pole has many uses – so buy some good ones! Some qualities to look for:

- SHAFT – The use of Nordic bamboo or fiberglass track ski poles for backcountry skiing is a mistake. The Nordic track pole was designed to have a certain flex and propulsion effect on the skier during track skiing, but in the backcountry, strength has priority over flex. Spend the extra money and buy adjustable-length metal ski poles. They are double walled, thereby twice as strong as a single pole. You can adjust your ski pole length at will for uphill, downhill, level skiing or long traverses where you may make the downhill pole longer than the uphill pole. There are two general methods that allow the pole to be adjusted: a twist adjusted bushing-washer mechanism and a "flicklock" lever that has been borrowed from camera tripods. Neither is perfect. Occasionally check for fractures in the plastic parts (see Maintenance). Ski poles can be made into avalanche probe poles-some easier than others. More people are opting for having a set of probes instead of spending precious minutes for the conversion.

- LENGTH – To measure your pole in the classic manner, stand on the ground in your ski boots. With the pole upside-down and touching the ground, grip it under the basket. With the proper length, the forearm should be 15 degrees above parallel to the ground. An adjustable pole makes these measurements unnecessary since you can adjust the pole at any time to any length that is comfortable. Sometimes we like longer poles for longer strides on flat terrain. It's also good to have a longer pole for balance if you need to walk downhill in your ski boots for any distance. On long traverses, you can make the uphill pole shorter for comfort. This also allows the shoulders to stay "square" to the traverse and minimizes the feeling of being pushed outwards, away from the slope. Its always good idea to collapse poles during auto transport to prevent tears to the car's interior.

- TIPS – Tips should be kept sharp and replaced if damaged. Dull ski pole tips can cause you to miss pole plants and self-arrests! Ask your ski shop about the best method of sharpening your ski pole tips.

- BASKETS – Large traditional Nordic ski baskets cause several problems: snow loads on the baskets during trail breaking in deep powder, greatly increasing fatigue and arm strain. They snag tree limbs, causing falls during downhill skiing. They also prevent fast self-arrests because the basket gets between the pole tip and the snow. A standard diameter Alpine ski pole basket of four inches is sufficient.

- GRIPS – Old leather ski pole handles used to soak the leather gloves of skiers; freezing hands and causing frostbite. Today, leather has been replaced with durable plastic and rubber composites. Standard Alpine ski pole handles are best for backcountry skiing because they offer a definite platform for the hand during skiing and help to dissipate shock and reduce fatigue to the arm and the shoulder joint. Other handles have a self-arrest blade built in so you can self-arrest on steeper slopes (see Fig 2.12).

- STRAPS – The strap is an important part of the propulsion system because you push back on it during the latter part of the stride. Straps should be adjustable in length and wide enough to disperse stress over a wider area of the hand for better comfort. Ski poles' straps should

Fig. 2.12: From left-Black Diamond™ self arrrest grip pole, Black Diamond™ standard grip and a Life Link™ avalanche probe pole. Vivesphoto.

39

Ski Randonnée!

Fig. 2.13: You don't have to be an extreme skier to use an ice axe. Spring summit skis often reguire an early morning approach climb and having an ice axe can add a greater sense of security and therefore speed. Vivesphoto.

be removed during tree runs to reduce unwanted falls and hand, arm, and shoulder injuries.

Improving Your Grip

A ski pole is no good if you can't hold onto it. Wool gloves or mittens ball up with snow, allowing your hand to slide off the pole. Rubberized electrical tape wrapped around the ski pole shaft can increase your grip during icy conditions. You can also rub ski touring wax along the length of the shaft. Your emergency duct tape supply can be wrapped around the ski pole, 12 inches below the handle for use as a lower grip during long traverses.

Self Arrest Ski Poles

I know this book is not about extreme skiing per se. However, self arrest ski poles are good to have if you are just skiing up or across steep, exposed terrain where a slip can prove injurious. I was coming back from a ski descent near Aspen one Spring morning and I had to cross a snow bridge across Independence Creek during a high Spring run off. I knew the bridge was soft but I had to get across (and I knew it wouldn't hold). I was almost across when the whole thing went. My feet were in the water but my old Ramer self arrest grips went straight into the newly exposed snow wall as I fell–I was glad I had them! While the Ramer is no longer available, the Black Diamond™ Self Arrest Grip is.

Ice Axes

Both ice axes and crampons are used on ski tours in the Alps, but they are rarely used in the United States in a widespread manner. This may be changing as skiers start to explore higher mountains and more difficult ski routes in the states and in Canada. Lightweight ice axes and crampons are great to have when one is climbing long, icy slopes during early morning spring ascents. There are many new, lightweight ice axes available. Length is determined more by function than by a person's height. A general use ice axe that is approximately 70-75 cm long is the most versatile for climbing and for belaying on snow.

Crampons

Lightweight crampons with front and rear wires and with an arch retaining strap go on the fastest. Be sure to spend some time with them at home adjusting the crampons so they fit tightly to the ski boots you intend to use (Fig. 2.14). They should be tight enough so they stay on the boot without the retaining strap. Crampons can be used together with ski poles to climb slopes much faster than with ski boots alone (see Ascent). There are models made specifically for ski tourers which are lightweight and fully adjustable to one's ski boot. Ski boots make great crampon

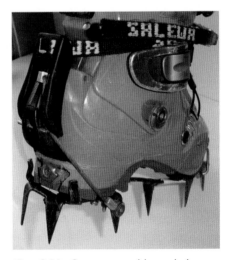

Fig. 2.14: Crampons add a whole new dimension of security for spring ski tourers who are going over steep passes or up steeper slopes on early morning climbs. Notice yellow tape marks right crampon. Vivesphoto.

41

Fig. 2.15: Typical contents of a daypack heading for the backcountry. Ropes, ice axes and crampons are optional depending on route. Vivesphoto.

boots since they are plastic and stiff. Using crampons instead of just slamming your ski boot toe into hard snow can save you some toenails – that I know. Ski boots alone are acceptable for short climbs, but if long climbs are anticipated carry the extra weight of the crampons. The climbing will be faster, surer and more fun.

Day Packs

Packs make skiers look so "backcountry". But seriously, as with shovels - the model doesn't matter – the thing is to use one. The day pack is one of the most important pieces of equipment you will buy. You should carry enough gear to survive (uncomfortably) a bivouac out in the snow. A complete gear list of what to have in your pack is in the appendix. Newer packs come with a lot of great ideas. It has to be able to carry a pair of skis either on the sides or diagonally on the pack. Ice axe-shovel loops are mandatory. Hydration systems are more popular than ever. Freezing of the water supply tube has been a problem which has been solved by storing the hydration tube in a zipper compartment in the shoulder strap. There are many great packs out there. Just look at the equipment issues of the latest skiing magazines.

One trouble with packs is that they're black, some of your gear is probably black as well. Things disappear in your pack and then when you really need them you can't find them. Take your day pack more seriously and organize it. Put things into color coded stuff sacks: Headlamp into a yellow sack (since it will be dark outside); First aid into a red sack, etc. Get creative. It's good to see more packs that are using more visable colors such as yellow or red. Always carry a few equipment straps along just for tying down skis and other gear such as ropes and crampons. These accessory straps come in different dimensions of width and length. They're also good for sudden binding repairs as well.

Maintenance of Ski Equipment

Good equipment doesn't stay that way by itself. At the beginning of the ski season and before especially cold ski tours, lubricate all sliding parts of the ski pole with silicon spray so they don't freeze together. A shotgun cleaning kit with a ramrod is very effective in cleaning the inside of the ski pole tubes. There are several systems used to adjust ski pole length, and some use a nylon bushing inside the pole. When the bottom part is twisted, a screw within the pole shaft expands the bushing within the pole, allowing adjustment of the pole length. These nylon bushings have a tendency to break with wear and tear at low temperatures, so always keep spare bushings in your repair kit. The biggest mistake is to overtighten the mechanism. Once it engages, twist the pole only once more to make it tight.

A few other things: avalanche beacon batteries should be checked frequently if you are an active skier, ski edges and bases should be tuned, ski binding screws should be checked for tightness, bindings should be lubricated and tested for function, and packs should be check for rips and tears.

Repair Kit

You must know how to fix your equipment out in the field, since problems always seem to happen when it's cold and you're exhausted. Find out from your ski shop what spare parts you should carry to repair your ski bindings and poles. A suggested list of items for a repair kit appears in the equipment list in the appendix.

Ski Randonnée!

Common Equipment Emergencies

- BINDING TEARS OUT OF SKI – Duct tape won't keep a wet binding on a wet ski. Even if the ski is warm, the tape will be cut by the metal edges within a few miles. With a multipurpose knife, you can drill new holes with the leather punch. Now insert drywall expansion sleeves that are used with larger screws. You will find that this is so strong you might not even need to fix it once you get home.

- JAMMED SKI POLE SLEEVES – If the two halves of an adjustable ski pole get jammed together and refuse to come apart, heat the poles in a hut or over a camp stove so that they are just warm, not hot. Find a sturdy tree branch or hut roof beam. Tie Prussik knots around each part with shoelaces. In the Prussik knot, shoelaces are wound around the ski pole and threaded through themselves twice. The Prussik knot is prevented from sliding up or down the ski pole by duct tape holding it in place. Tie the upper Prus-sik knot around a tree branch, then stick your foot through the lower knot and put your body weight on it slowly until the poles come apart.

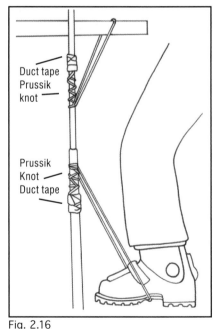

Duct tape
Prussik
knot

Prussik
Knot
Duct tape

Fig. 2.16

- BROKEN SKI POLE SHAFTS – Find a stick just big enough to fit inside the two halves of your broken shaft, and trim it down with your knife (don't use old wood, it could break). Once you have joined the two shaft pieces, wrap the whole thing with duct tape. Use additional wood pieces if one is not enough.

- BROKEN BASKETS – A ski pole shaft without a basket is especially dangerous to those around you, and you won't be able to push off the snow without a basket anyway. Make a temporary basket with duct tape and small sticks – be creative.

- BROKEN SKIS – With today's skis, it is very rare to have a ski break in half, but I have seen it happen. The best fix is to mount the binding on the tip half of the ski, so that the ski shovel will stay on top of the snow. Skis will more often delaminate. Duct tape might work if the skis are very dry. Another fix is to use a leather awl and drill two holes through the ski sandwich material so that a piece of wire can be threaded through to hold the layers together.

Conclusion

The purchase of effective ski equipment can greatly help you learn how to ski backcountry snow conditions. Good equipment can also increase your travel speed in changing snow and weather conditions. Durable, worry-free equipment doesn't stay durable and worry-free all by itself. Skis, bindings, boots and poles must all be maintained for best results and maximum performance. In addition, skiers must be prepared for equipment breakdowns – both with their own equipment as well as the equipment of others.

Fig. 2.17: Europeans are more aquainted with ice axe and crampon use than their North American counterparts – although that trend may be changing. On the Haute Route. Vivesphoto

Ascent 3

Climbing is an integral part of backcountry skiing. Instead of dreading the climb, anticipate what you're going to see once you reach the top! While skiing on the flats is not as exciting as going downhill, skiing the flats can be a pleasant experience if you learn to relax your mind and go with it. If you're expedition skiing, you'll need to cover a lot of ground between those downhill sections. Skiing or climbing up the slope you intend to ski down is a good practice, and lets you inspect snow conditions. Climbing in the backcountry is all about technique and equipment. It's not all muscle!

Why Climbing Skins?

Climbing skins and Nordic wax provide the basic snow locomotive force in skiing: the ability to grip and glide over the snow. Traditionally, wax was used for long-distance ski tours on rolling or low angle terrain. Most skiers now use skins for flat skiing and climbing because for the most part the glide available with wax is negated when you carry a heavy pack or break trail in deep snow. Additionally, compared to skins, wax is impractical due to its lower adhesion qualities on steeper climbs of varying snow conditions. The idea is to save energy. Climbing skins climb snow that wax doesn't handle well. Skins make steeper climbing faster and safer. Finally, they can be left on for skiing downhill to reduce speed when the skier is fatigued or is carrying a heavy pack.

Cover 3.1: A dramatic alpine backdrop during an early morning climb en route to the Vignette Hut from the Dix Hut, day four of the Chamonix-Zermat Haute Route. Vivesphoto

Fig. 3.2: Advancements in skin adhesives have rid the skier of skins which used buckles and straps that often interferred with traversing steeper slopes quickly. Vivesphoto.

Climbing Skins

Climbing skins were originally made out of actual seal skin. Strips of seal skin were fastened to the bottom of the skis with adhesive or buckles, enabling the ski to grip snow while allowing for glide (see figure 3.2). Seal skin was used because its fur has a "nap" (that is, the fur is slanted, so these skins allow you to slide skis forward but not backward because the skin bristles up, gripping the snow). Most modern climbing skins are mohair, nylon, or plastic. Nylon skins are preferable because they absorb less water, ice up less, and have better glide than mohair or plastic skins.

Climbing skins use an adhesive that can be reapplied after it has worn off. Older skins had several buckles that allowed snow to accumulate between the skin and ski, causing the ski to come off. On hard-pack or icy traverses, buckles prevented the ski from being edged completely, thus causing slips.

Skin Adhesives

Some adhesives don't work well at temperatures below 0 degrees Fahrenheit (−18 degrees Celsius) or when the skins get really wet. Ask your ski shop which glue works best. Reapply your adhesive before starting any long ski tour. It is also smart to take along some backups in case your skins just won't stick, such as violet or silver cross-country wax, duct tape, or an old pair of Nordic-width skins. Always dry your skins with the skins folded base to base, whether they are dried in the hut or outside in the sun. This prevents two problems: glue dehydration and ultra violet breakdown of the glue.

Skin Sizes

There are several brands of climbing skins that come in several different widths, from 50 to 89 mm and beyond for use with wide skis. Some skins must be custom fitted and cut with a razor blade that is provided with the skin. It's easy to do. If properly measured, the skin will cover almost the entire bottom of the ski, allowing about a half inch on either side of the skin so that complete edging of the ski can occur. Alpine or full-width skins should be used for peak ascents or touring. Half skins or kicker skins should be reserved for long rolling or flat terrain.

Using Skins During Skiing

Skins glide best when they are clean. Any old adhesive stuck to the snow side of the skin can hold snow and ice, diminishing the skin's effective-ness. Skin waxes or special "anti-glop " sprays help skins to glide more smoothly, especially in wet spring snows. Glue touch-ups may be required if the skins get dirty or wet or are used in very cold conditions. In very cold conditions, keep the skins warm and sticky between runs by putting them inside your jacket. When skiing downhill, place the skins in a waterproof nylon bag larger than the one they came in. This makes the skins easier to access and will keep your clothes drier. Be sure your skins have rubber tail clips and tighteners. These will keep the skins on securely even if the adhesive is not working. If you have new wider skins, be sure that the skin's tip hardware fits over the tip of your ski. A thumb loop added to the metal tip part makes for easier grasping in cold weather. If your skis were freshly waxed, your skins will still stick if the wax penetrated the base as it should and there is little residue-which there usually isn't.

Kicker or Half-Skins

Kicker skins were more popular among Telemark skiers as an option to full width skins (they are mentioned here for thoroughness). They are well adapted for use on low-angle ,rolling terrain where steep ascents are not encountered. Kickers or half-skins attach under the middle third of the ski (often called the kicker zone or wax pocket). The middle third of the ski receives most of the skier's weight, and therefore can deliver the most traction. However, the leading edge of some half-skins often causes much resistance to sliding. Plus, the body weight of the skier is not always in the center of the ski during climbing. As the body weight moves forward and backward, so do the center of gravity and traction – this can often cause slipping on steeper slopes.

Fig. 3.3: The proper method of drying climbing skins is to stick them bottom to bottom so that the glue is not degraded by heat and/or ultraviolet radiation. Vivesphoto.

Waxless Skis

There is no ski-base system that can really replace skins. The greatest barrier to the waxless ski idea is the inability of a ski-base system to climb up mixed snow and ice conditions. Waxless skis, although suitable for moderate slopes, do not approach skins in sheer climbing power.

Climbing Basics

If you don't like climbing, you are missing out on 50 percent of the enjoyment of backcountry skiing. It doesn't have to hurt! By using the proper equipment and techniques, you can learn to enjoy climbing and even get good at it! Technique is an important part of the art of climbing on skis.

Every climbing challenge has a solution, and trying to use muscle instead of brains is a sure way to burn out fast . Using diagonal traverses, while technically longer, can save you energy for the long haul. Sometimes going slower at higher altitudes allows you to complete a longer climb without stopping at all. You'll be skiing past the sprinters who will be stopping to rest as you head for the summit.

Transitioning

It takes time to switch ski modes from uphill to downhill mode or visa versa. This process is called "Transitioning". It takes time to remove skins or to put them on. When the weather is sunny and you have energy, it's easy. But, if you're tired and in a blizzard and miles from the hut, it is a whole new ball game. Learn to change your gear quickly and have it work the first time. Be sure your skins have a fresh layer of glue. Be sure they fit your skis exactly before you leave the house. They should not be buried in your pack, but easily accessible. Practice putting your climbing skins on fast! Some people can take off their skins without taking off their skis! For speed in bad weather, you and your skiing partners can take off each others' skins so you won't have to remove skis. This saves a lot of time and energy.

In bad weather, the longer you stop, the colder you will get. And if you are ready to go before the others, you can help those who are having trouble thereby getting the whole group going faster. Keep duct tape and repair tools handy- not buried at the bottom of your pack- in case you need to fix your skins. Power bars and water should also be easy to get to.

Safety

Before you start a longer climb (anything over 500 vertical feet [152 meters]), consider the following safety measures.

- Be sure this is a climb that everyone in your group can do in a reasonable amount of time. Give more pack weight to stronger climbers to reduce climbing time.
- Round out your turns at switch backs so as to eliminate kick turns, which can take extra time.

Ski Randonnée!

- Plan your route for maximum avalanche protection, be sure your avalanche transceiver is on. (see chap. 9).
- Plan to make turns or rest stops under natural protection such as rock outcroppings or heavy trees to protect yourself from falling snow or rocks.
- Be sure your climbing skins are on securely so they don't fall off on the way up.
- On steeper, harder climbs, be sure to eat and drink before climbing. You'll need the energy, and this way you don't have to stop your climb to eat.
- Reduce or adjust clothing before climbing to minimize stopping during climbing.

Breathing While Climbing

Correct breathing is the most overlooked technique in skiing. Unfortunate because it can make your ski touring much easier. The pace of climbing is set by your breathing pace, not the other way around. On low-angle slopes, for example, bring your right ski forward and breathe air deeply into your lungs. Feel your lungs expand. Now transfer weight onto that foot and press down and breathe out (sometimes called pressure breathing). As the slope steepens, take smaller steps and breathe in and out with each ski. As the angle lessens you may breathe in on one leg and out with the other. Develop a breathing strategy of your own and don't "try" to keep up with others. Practice this conscious breathing when you are weight lifting or hiking with a heavy pack. At rest stops, bend your body down between your ski poles with your upper body parallel to the ground so that gravity helps you increase your chest expansion.

Climbing Posture

Don't lean too far forward while climbing straight up steep slopes. This reduces weight on the middle of the ski, where the skins are doing most of their work, increasing the chances of a slip.

Don't bend over at the waist to weight your skis; bend at the knees and keep your back straight. This reduces stress on your back, especially if you are carrying a pack. Pack weight also improves the traction of your skins and can actually help you climb–but only if you keep your back straight and your weight centered! Strength and good technique are both needed during climbing.

Stopping While Climbing

Stop only at secure positions on the slope. Put your skis across the slope and stomp out a good platform to rest on – stopping with your skis facing up the mountain might cause you to slip backward! Don't stop on icy slopes or where it is very windy. In addition, stay off steeper, angled slopes if a rest stop is needed. If you are fatigued on a very steep, exposed slope, don't stop but slow down-take your time. Get to the top no matter what it'll be easier if you do. Never take your pack off on a very steep slope. It may fall down the slope, plus you'll waste much energy taking it off and on and could lose your balance.

The Mental Game

Maintain a positive attitude while climbing. Clear your mind, go at your own pace, and enjoy the day. You won't be any good to yourself or your friends if you get into a bad mood, which robs you of energy. Don't try to keep up with everyone else. Find a speed and rhythm you enjoy and stick with it. Take a deep breath and relax every muscle you are not using. Try counting your steps, and add a few extra steps between rests. You'll be surprised at how this mental game can take your mind off the task.

Backcountry Climbing Techniques

It often seems like the most basic techniques often get even experts into trouble. One can get into a jam for instance while doing a kick turn on a very exposed icy slope. We're usually not doing kick turns, we are skiing the run. But then one day that beginners technique becomes very handy. Different techniques can be used for more efficient climbing on different terrain. This section covers how to perform these techniques, and which ones work best in various situations and conditions you may encounter while climbing.

Diagonal Stride on the Flat

The diagonal stride is the basis for all ski locomotion (see fig 3.4.). The motion is very similar to ice skating or roller skating. During the leg thrust, transfer your weight from the pushing leg to the gliding leg that is already

Ski Randonnée!

Fig. 3.4: These skiers are using a diagonal stride for forward locomotion. subconscientiously the body walks diagonally-that is, the left arm and right leg advance together. Alpine skiers during an early morning peak climb in the Austrian Alps.

forward. Imagine gripping the snow with your toes. Follow with a pushoff that begins at the heel and finally rolls off the inner edge of the big toe as your leg passes to the rear. Think of rollerblading with a pack on. Always rely on your legs, not your arms, for climbing or touring to maximize your energy.

In cross-country racing, ski poling is fluid and aerobic. In backcountry skiing, it is slower and more dynamic. Plant the poles straight down at the ski's side ahead of the bindings, not out sideways. This leans and pushes the upper body forward. As you shift the weight to the forward ski, begin pole planting with the opposite arm.

Diagonal Stride on Straight Up Tracks

Depending on your energy level, you can often climb straight up low- to moderate-angle slopes using the diagonal stride. This is also a good strategy if one suspects that the slope as a whole is suspected of having avalanche potential where diagonal switch backs would expose the ski party to avalanche danger. Although a straight line is always the shortest route, it may not be the easiest. As you climb, keep your skis on the snow – lift only your heel off the ski, not your ski off the snow. If the ski party's track is too slick to climb or descend safely, put one ski or both skis in the untracked snow next to it and go up that way.

Occasionally, on very short, steep, straight-up pitches, you may lean forward and use a choked grip when on skis or on foot. Advance your ski poles in short distances, and resist reaching your hands over the height of your shoulders when climbing straight up with ski poles – this will put you off-balance. Don't unweight one ski completely until you are in a position to weight your new forward ski. Aggressively transfer your body weight from the rear ski to the forward ski. Stomp down on the front ski if necessary so that the climbing skin will grip the snow. This is often a problem in wet snows or on ice, where skins can have a hard time gripping. Use your body weight to push your arms back aggressively! Plant your ski poles close to your body so you can push straight down and back with them, instead of having them push sideways.

Herringbone

The herringbone technique allows you to make directional changes on lower angled slopes. The ski's tips are spread wider than shoulder-width apart while the tails are just touching. For straight up climbing, pick each ski up off the snow, placing it higher than the last. Then edge the inside edges of both skis by bending the knees to the inside (remember, you can't edge your skis with straight legs). Plant the poles close to your body between the bindings and the rear of the ski (see figure 3.5), and push them down and backward using a walking cane grip (with your hands on top of the handles).

Herringbone turns don't work well on steep slopes where kick turns would be easier. For the herringbone turn, start in the traversing position and stem the uphill ski first, then immediately stem the other ski. When climbing and turning uphill, weight the inside edges of both skis. Don't stop in the middle of the turn – keep turning your skis until you are in the new desired position. Use small steps to maintain balance, especially on ice. Keep your poles moving, planting them just ahead of your bindings. While climbing,

Ski Randonnée!

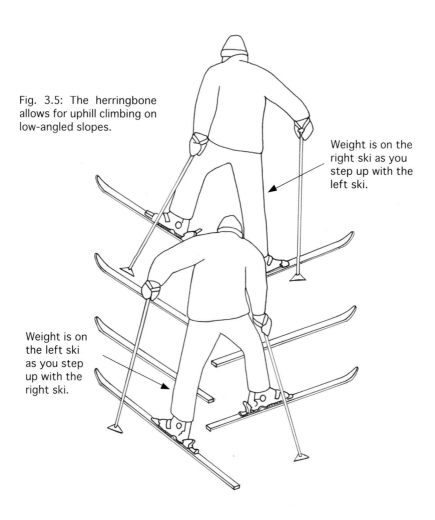

Fig. 3.5: The herringbone allows for uphill climbing on low-angled slopes.

Weight is on the right ski as you step up with the left ski.

Weight is on the left ski as you step up with the right ski.

the poles can be held normally until you reach the apex and steepest part of this climbing turn, when you can shift your ski pole grip into a walking cane position, allowing you to push down and back to complete the turn (see figure 3.6).

The normal manner of gripping your ski pole handle is to push your hand up through the handle strap and then back down so you are gripping the strap and handle within the hand (see figure 3.7). This allows you to apply arm pressure down on the strap, providing you with more climbing and touring force.

Fig. 3.6:   Walking cane grip.

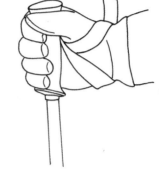

Fig. 3.7:   Normal grip.

When overcoming terrain obstacles, utilize the entire shaft of your ski pole by using a choked grip. In this technique, you grip the ski pole down the shaft from the handle. On steeper traverses or climbs this keeps the body from leaning downhill, therefore maintaining balance and reducing energy use. Wrap duct tape or electrical rubber tape at one foot intervals on the shaft of the ski pole to provide for a better grip over the whole shaft of the ski pole.

Sidestep Climbing

Often in the backcountry, one must navigate around very small obstacles such as rocks and trees. Sidestepping involves climbing up the slope sideways with both skis parallel across the fall line and edging both skis into the hill at the same time. You should be able to sidestep up slopes both forward and backward to avoid obstacles and unnecessary kick turns. Sometimes sidestepping can occur on very exposed slopes, and therefore technique is critical to avoiding a fall. Climb up in short steps while using a choked grip on the uphill ski pole half-way down the ski pole shaft, and get as close to the slope as possible. Step up with one ski and plant it firmly on the snow above the obstacle, then shift your weight over the uphill ski to be sure it won't slide out from underneath you. On very steep slopes,while supporting yourself with both ski poles, do a leg press up to your new stance while pushing down on top of the downhill ski pole (walking cane grip). While climbing, always keep three points of contact with the snow in case you slip: two poles and one ski or two skis and one pole. Reduce superfluous pole movements. The more time you have your pole tips in the air, the less time they are in the snow supporting you. Keep your back straight and your head up for balance. Skiers can lock down their heels when sidestepping for extended periods or in awkward situations for easier and more precise climbing.

Traverse Climbing With Kick Turns

The kick turn is an essential technique for beginners and experts alike during ascending or descending. Kick turns can be done facing outward during descending (downhill kick turn) or facing the slope during climbing (uphill kick turn). The uphill kick turn has the advantage since you can readily get into a self-arrest position if you slip on steep terrain, whereas a slip from the downhill kick turn position can throw you into an uncontrolled fall. Both turns are very similar except for the pole positions.

For the downhill kick turn, first kick a flat platform in the snow. Now, plant

Fig. 3.8: The Uphill Kick Turn is invaluable during steeper climbs. However, heel elevators make them more difficult to perform. In this case, it would've been easier to round out the climbing track, eliminating the kick turn completely. Vivesphoto.

a.

Fig. 3.9 (a) Downhill and (b) uphill kick turns allow you to go up or down any slope.

b.

your poles securely into the slope behind you for support in case you slip. Your upper body is facing down the slope. The skis must be parallel to each other and strictly across the fall line or else they will slip out from under you. Next, pick up your downhill ski by bending the knee and lifting at the thigh (see figure 4.9a). Don't be lazy and rotate the tail of the outside ski in the snow. It will jam into the snow, causing a fall. Pivot the ski around in the air while keeping your poles where they are, and plant the ski back in the same place, but facing the opposite direction now. Once the ski is firmly planted, pick up the other ski and bring it parallel to the first, bringing the other ski pole with it.

The uphill kick turn is similar, other than the following exceptions –

Fig. 3.10: Heel elevators reduce the distance that the heel drops during climbing effectively reducing the energy required for long climbs. They should be activated before they are needed. Vivesphoto.

you do a kick turn going uphill, above the same-sided ski pole, and in the direction of the turn. In the case of left kick turn, the left pole is planted above you, a few inches above your uphill ski, between the binding and the end of the ski. Then the uphill ski is pivoted so it lies above the ski pole (see figure 3.9). The more parallel the skis, the easier the uphill kick turn will be. Transfer weight onto the uphill ski and bring the remaining ski and ski pole around together into the new direction. Beginners will do themselves a big favor by becoming experts in both turns, as both turns are invaluable in the backcountry. Practice on low-angled slopes, increasing the steepness with experience. Uphill kick turns are essential in roped skiing.

The platform is the key to this turn. It must be perfectly level, especially on steep, exposed slopes. To increase the speed and safety of the whole group, advanced skiers should stomp out kick turn platforms for less experienced skiers. Use low-angle climbing traverses between kick turns to conserve energy. Tip your knees outward slightly to keep your skis and skins flat in relationship to the slope for better traction when traversing.

Climbing Using Heel Elevators

Heel elevators artificially reduce the angle of climb by providing a higher resting position for the foot. This reduces calf and thigh fatigue and conserves energy. As with ski crampons, you should anticipate the need for heel elevators before they are needed. Heel elevators are best used during straight-up climbing or steep traverses. They should not be used on long, low-angle traverses where they can keep you unbalanced. Round out your turns in order to eliminate the kick turn completely to minimize discomfort while using elevators.

Climbing on Foot

Sometimes it is more efficient to walk or climb on foot than on skis. Those conditions could be:

- When climbing a face, ridge, or shoulder devoid of snow;
- When climbing ice or snow that is too steep to climb effectively on skis and where crampons or boots may be more efficient.

Fig. 3.11: Climbing on foot can be very effective in climbing longer slopes during the Spring. This can increase climbing efficiency by 200%! 2,500 feet above Hendersen Mine on Day 7 of the Colorado Haute Route. Vivesphoto.

ROCK CLIMBING AND ROPE HANDLING

It's likely that you'll encounter rock climbing only on high-mountain tours. If you encounter any rock formations during your ski tour, remember that stiff ski boots hold well on big footholds, but they are not rock climbing shoes. Plan your route carefully to avoid rock climbing, which cannot be navigated using basic climbing techniques.

A good knowledge of rock climbing and rope handling techniques can be valuable to the backcountry skier heading to higher mountains. This is not to say that you will always carry climbing gear on ski tours, but knowing basic rock craft can give you an added sense of security, especially when you have to climb a short section of rock while carrying your skis to get from one slope to another or climb up a peak. It is also a valuable tool in emergencies.

The need for a rope in backcountry skiing is unusual – at least in the United States, where glacier travel typically doesn't occur in the contiguous 48 states. But rope use is not restricted to glacier travel. For larger groups, carrying a rope may be a good idea. It can be used for rescue purposes, such as pulling someone out of a creek with high banks, or making and hauling a sled. A typical rope approved for glacier travel by the UIAA (Union Internationale des Associations d'Alpisme) would be a 165-foot (50-meter), 8.5 mm Perlon rope (special touring ropes are 8.0 mm). A rope "throw bag" similar to the one used on whitewater rafts that contains 100 feet (30 meters) of 7 mm Perlon rope is an alternative that could be quickly dispatched during a crevasse rescue . Always remember – never throw a rope to someone unless you are anchored.

As the old mountaineering saying goes, "two pounds on the feet equals one pound on the back". The saying refers to the biomechanical advantage of placing the load (skis and skins) on the large muscles of the back rather than on the legs. On a recent tour, I carried skis, skins, and ski boots and hiked up very hard Spring snow in lightweight hiking boots. It made it so easy – it is the way to go. Carry your skis on your back not in your hands which should be holding ski poles for climbing support and available to make a self arrest in case of a slip.

Fig. 3.12: Carrying skis across the back is not a problem when climbing straight up a low angle or on a flat area as the photo shows. The problem arises when this skier has to traverse a steep slope. The skis will hit the skiers' heels and knock into the slope itself, causing a balance issue. Jeff Russell Photo.

French Technique

French Technique was originally developed for ice climbing using crampons. But it is also very effective without crampons, as well on moderate to steep snow. On low-angle snow slopes, climb straight up like a duck (en canard), with toes out to rest your calves. As the angle steepens, try walking sideways up the slope like a crab – this is fun and works great! You can use your ski poles or an ice axe for support.

Kicking steps with plastic ski boots is much easier than using leather boots. You don't usually need to slam your boot into the snow for it to stick; this just wastes energy. Experiment with the amount of effort needed to make the boot stay in the snow. You'll find that you are working too hard. Kick your steps straight into the snow horizontally to prevent the boot from slipping out of the snow. Keep your heels down while climbing

63

Fig. 3.13: Carrying skis "A" frame style. Tips are strapped together so that the ski tails are displaced outwards away from the feet. They are also high enough to where a steeper traverse on foot would not be affected. Jeff Russell Photo.

to avoid stressing your calf muscles. If you are traversing, use the edge of your ski boot like a saw and cut side ways into the slope. Used a choked grip on your uphill pole so that you aren't thrown off balance.

Fig. 3.14: The rewards of climbing! A mile or so beyond the top of Snowmass Ski Area (Colorado). East Snowmass Creek with Maroon Bells Wilderness in background. Vivesphoto.

your crampons sharp – dull crampons can cause a fall. Don't over tighten crampon straps when wearing leather boots; this can cut off circulation and cause cold feet. Finally, learn to pick up your feet when you climb so that the points of one crampon won't snag your opposite gaiter and cause a fall.

A good basic mountaineering ice axe made of lightweight aluminum is the most versatile. A medium-length axe (about 70 to 75 centimeters) can be used on steeper terrain and also as an anchor in softer snow (see appendix for books on crampon and ice axe use.)

Conclusion

Increasing our efficiency and our climbing ability increases our pleasure of the backcountry experience. Those who haven't learned how to climb will experience more difficulty in the backcountry, and probably won't enjoy skiing the backcountry as much as they could. Skins are far superior to wax for sheer climbing power. Learning sport breathing is the most overlooked aspect of backcountry skiing. There is a psychological game in climbing: those who are able to relax their minds and the muscles that <u>are not</u> being used will have the greatest endurance at the end of the day.

Fig. 3.15: A staggered ski pole helps in keeping the body "square" to the traverse, increasing climbing efficiency. Carter Photographics.

Descent   4

Ski Randonnée!

We often marvel at the ski pros. How do they ski that way? You would ski great, too, if you lived at a ski resort and skied every day! However, the majority of us don't live at ski resorts. We usually have to learn how to ski on weekends or ski holidays. Not as romantic as being in the mountains, is it? Randonnée skiing's biggest attraction to the resort downhill skier is that there is no need to learn an entirely new way of skiing to ski the back-country. Many parallel skiers think you have to learn Telemark technique to ski the backcouuntry. But the fact is that there are more than a million Europeans skiing the backcountry without using any Telemark techniques at all! Practice at an alpine ski area, especially with a qualified instructor, can accelerate the acquisition of new skills. The aspiring backcountry skier should already know basic techniques like snowplowing, side slipping and parallel skiing. The following chapter will emphasize several techniques in order of their use on increasingly steeper slopes. The ultimate goal should be to ski safely, effectively, and efficiently and not to fall. You don't have to be pretty. Just get down the hill!

General Descent Safety

Consider the following points before descending an unknown slope.

- Avalanche transceivers should be double checked (having already done a sound and battery check before leaving the car).

- Always wear gloves to protect hands from cuts from ice even in warm spring conditions. Button up in case you fall.

- Fatigued or timid skiers should leave climbing skins on to reduce speed.

- Always space out skiers - give each other plenty of room - especially in poor snow or reduced visibility.

Downclimbing on Foot

When you take your skis off and downclimb on boots you are exposing yourself to a fall if you slip on ice. Be sure that your route is low angled and away from cliff areas. If you're walking down a snow-packed slope, always drive your heel into the snow (often called the "plunge step") with each

Cover 4.1: There is nothing like putting in a nice pair of tracks when the snow is great and the day is beautiful. This is what Randonnée is all about! Current Creek Bench, Berthoud Pass, Colorado. Russellphoto.

Fig. 4.2: Slabby conditions where the upper crust is fragile doesn't respond to hard downweighting. An upright stance keeps the skier unweighted and balanced. Vivesphoto.

step before taking the next step. You should have your skis strapped to your pack and are using both poles together for support. As usual, avoid cornices or potential avalanche hazards. For practice, try the plunge step and self arrest with ski poles on a groomed black run with a safe run out below.

Releasing the Heels on Low Angled Slopes

Randonnée skiers may increase their speed on inclined "flats" by releasing their heels and using the diagonal stride, without using climbing skins. This greatly increases travel speed and efficiency and should not be overlooked.

Sidestepping and Sideslipping

Sideslipping can control your descent on very steep, hard-pack snow or ice. On steeper slopes, sideslipping allows you to rescue yourself from a very steep passage where a kick turn could cause a fall. During sideslipping, the upper body should face downhill (anticipation) with skis across the fall line. Downhill pole plants should occur in a vertical line below the bindings. Knees should be angulated into the hill. Feet should be weighted flat on the skis so that body weight is equally distributed and balanced over the whole ski fore and aft. Don't overedge on ice or you might lose your grip. Unweight the edges by simply rolling your ankles and knees outward. Regain your edges by cranking them into the slope, but don't plant your downhill pole too close or too deep – you could ski onto it, causing a fall.

Fig. 4.3: Sticky snow can be removed by using another ski as a scraper. Sticky snow on the Haute Route near Verbier. Vivesphoto.

Fig. 4.4: A wider stance in warm, Spring corn snow turning into an inch of slush in the later morning on a very warm day between Copper Mountain and Vail Pass, Colorado. Vivesphoto.

Falling Leaf

This maneuver, which involves sideslipping forward and backward, is used very often – though most people are not aware that it is an actual technique! The falling leaf is great for navigating tight spaces between trees

Fig. 4.5: Sideslipping often allows you to ski in control down an area where the snow isn't to your liking, allowing you to by pass and set up for a turn on better snow. Russellphoto.

or boulders and descending icy trails and steep chutes. It's also good for controlled descent on steep slopes with unknown obstacles, or when hands are being used to push back tree branches, or when steering a sled. When sideslipping forward you should feel the front of your shins against the top of your boots as you bend at the knees to weight the front half of your skis (see figure 4.3). Feel the sides of your feet edging into the hill. When sideslipping backward, feel your weight on your heels and the tails of your skis. Feel the back of the calves hit against the top of the back of the boot. Keep your knees bent! Your upper body should face downhill. When looking at terrain above or sideways, turn your head only by itself without rotating your body, because you could fall. Falling leaf is an excellent exercise for any skier who wants to learn how pressure and stance affect skiing.

Traversing

Traversing allows you to ski across a slope from one side to another. While it's easy on good, soft snow, it can be difficult when carrying a heavy pack or when the slope is icy or exposed.

FALL LINE

Looking for a ski "line" is jargon meaning looking for a line of descent. It could be down a trail, down a face, or through some trees. Your line should follow the same rules that a climbing route does: safety from avalanche and rockfall, consistent snow conditions, lack of obstacles, and so on. How deep is the snow and how does it compare with your past experiences? How long is the run? Can you handle it? If you fall, where will the fall take you? Many of the answers will depend upon where the fall line is. To determine the fall line, imagine the route a drop of water would take down the mountain. The route it travels is the true line of gravity – the fall line. Always think in terms of your fall line. Instead of fighting gravity, learn to use it. Put your skis across the line and you'll stop; point them down the line and you go. Sideslipping is a good exercise in experiencing and feeling the fall line. A double fall line is more difficult to navigate.

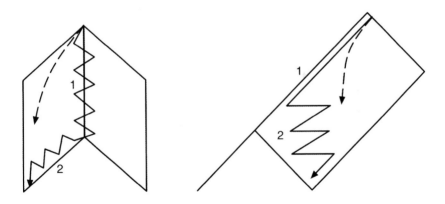

Number 1 is the primary fall line, while number 2 is the secondary fall line. Picture an open book. If you tilt the book, it looks like the illustration above. It will be easier to ski number 1 than trying to ski the resolution of the two fall lines together (dotted line). Avalanches will also follow this vector resolution. Taking one fall line at a time is easier and more fun.

Ski Randonnée!

Your skis should be across the fall line, shoulder-width apart. Knees should b e bent, with the edges angled toward the hill. A shallow, low-angle traverse allows you to cross the slope slowly; a steeper angle increases your speed. Your uphill ski should be ahead of your downhill ski for balance (most of your weight is on the downhill ski) and to prevent crossing of the skis. Keep your hands above your waist so you can see them and focus your weight on the downhill ski. On steeper slopes, your uphill hand can grip the ski pole lower on the shaft (choked grip) to keep your shoulders square to the slope and your body balanced. Fear may cause you to overedge on steep slopes. Avoid overedging as it will cause your skis to slip out from under you (see figure 4.8). Angle your traverse to go faster across suspected avalanche areas from one "island of safety" to another. On hardpack, shaped skis have a natural tendency to turn upwards. In order to maintain a constant elevation, begin by angling slightly downwards and pay special attention to your edges so that your traverse arcs back up to your starting elevation.

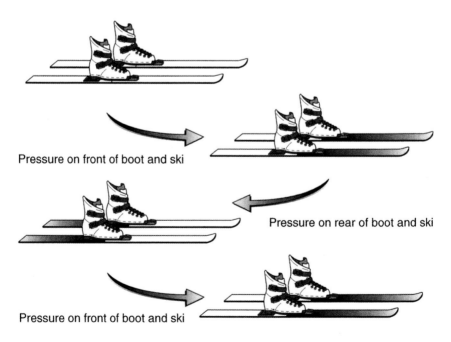

Pressure on front of boot and ski

Pressure on rear of boot and ski

Pressure on front of boot and ski

Fig. 4.6: Falling leaf sideslipping lets you ski down steep terrain while positioning yourself for your next turn.

74

Fig. 4.7: Traversing allows us to descend in preparation for a turn or to cross over to better snow. Note lower leg is angulated into the slope. High on the Continental Divide, Winter Park, Colorado. Russellphoto.

Skate or Step Turn

The skate or step turn is useful in accelerating on low-angle slopes or dodging obstacles. As if you were ice skating, simply push off one ski to the other ski, gliding in the direction you want to go (see figure 4.9). Transfer your weight aggressively while gliding on the first ski. Bend your knees a little before the transfer – this will give you more spring into the new ski. Double pole at this time to give extra forward momentum and maintain balance. Remember to pick up your skis at the thigh instead of just picking up your heels, which allows the ski tails to drag.

Wedge Turn ("Snowplow")

The lowly beginner's technique of snowplowing is even used by ski patrollers because it allows them to go slow while inspecting the snow ahead for obstacles or while pulling a sled or carrying equipment. The snowplow technique can be used to control your speed, turn, or stop completely. It is the preferred turn in glaciers or anytime undercut snow is suspected

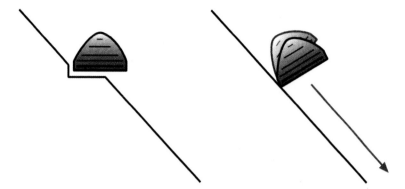

Fig. 4.8: View of ski tip on traverse: Left: ski properly edged. Right: ski overedged with resulting loss of control .

since it distributes body weight over a greater area. Skiers can use half of a snowplow on ice trails for speed control while carrying a heavy pack.

Stem Christie

The word "stem" is originally from the German word describing the pushing sideways of the skis (fig. 4-11). Begin in the traverse position and go into a snowplow turn, weighting the outside ski as you normally would. But this time make it a smaller snowplow – more of a pie wedge. As centrifugal force turns you, slide the inside, unweighted ski alongside or parallel to the outside ski, keeping it flat. Accompany this with a pole plant on the inside of the turn for balance and turn initiation. Equally weigh both skis to complete the turn. This turn is very good on a hard windslab that supports your weight. The Stem Christi can be linked together with short or long traverses.

Hockey Stop

The hockey stop is just a parallel turn coupled with an edge set hard enough to stop you (see fig. 4.14). A strong pole plant helps you to balance your upper body while up unweighting and pivoting the skis across the fall line. This is an excellent technique for stopping on icy trails. Practice the hockey stop on various terrain while skiing at a ski area to get the feel of it. It is excellent practice for skiing steeper terrain.

Wide-Stance Parallel Skiing

The Stem Christi leads naturally into wide-stance parallel skiing (see fig. 4.12).

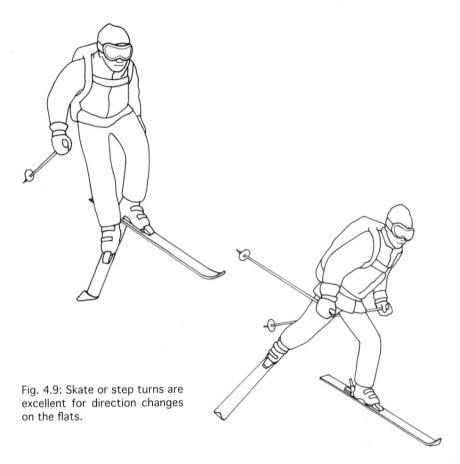

Fig. 4.9: Skate or step turns are excellent for direction changes on the flats.

Parallel skiing means both skis are parallel throughout the turn. A wider stance provides a bigger base of support. While pole planting, pivot both skis across the fall line. Angulate your knees into the hill, edging the skis. Try to pivot both skis together, but if you are unable due to snow conditions or skill level, a slight hop to unweight the skis while pole planting will allow them to release their edges and turn. The tails will swing out due to centrifugal force. Have the inside ski parallel to the outside ski while applying more bodyweight to the outside ski.

Short Swing Turns on Steeper Slopes

Short swing turns are very effective in controlling speed on steeper slopes. This the old Austrian technique of "wedeln". The word "wedeln" means to wag in German. This is what happens when the skier swings his skis back and forth in a series of closely linked, parallel turns. Try to keep your weight centered on the skis. This can be practiced on packed slopes of moderate angle and then applied to powder or hard pack. Linked hockey stops are great for control and represent wedeln with very complete turns.

Pole Planting

Pole plants help to initiate turns, and increase timing and directional control during turns. On hardpack snow, pole plants are vital to speed control and they help to define the radius of turns. On hardpack you need to just touch the snow. While in powder the inside pole plant may be more forcefully planted which will help pull the body inwards into the new turn.

Powder

Backcountry skiing is all about skiing powder! There is a definite advantage to skiing powder with your legs closer together. You will have more flotation and control over your skis. The more space that there is between the skis, the more likely you will do the splits. Maintaining a relaxed, slightly lower posture will help you keep your skis equally weighted in powder. Stay centered and slightly bent at the waist, knees, and ankles. Keep your upper body facing downhill (anticipation) when doing short turns down the fall line. Staying in the fall line and building up some speed will help you overcome the resistance that the snow offers, making turning easier. At the end of each turn you will feel the snow pile up under your skis, forming a platform. Bounce off that platform while keeping your skis equally weighted. Maintaining a rhythm to this bounce and linking it to the next "bounce" is a key to the powder skiing puzzle.

As you turn don't over-rotate at the waist. If you have a heavy pack on, it could rotate you into a fall. Watch your hand position. In deeper powder, swinging or banking the outside arm in the direction of the turn helps to amplify whole-body angulation and rotation during a powder turn which helps the feet surf two skis as one. You'll find it very helpful in heavy snows to link up several turns together. This adds to your momentum and rhythm.

Keep your head up and look down the slope to where you want to go. Your head weighs about 20 lbs and will pull your body down with it. Your body follows your head and your head follows your eyes. Keep your bodyweight centered; while keeping your skis together throughout the turn really helps to complete the turn in powder. Putting too much weight on the heels and weighting the tails of the skis can really upset your balance. Equally spaced pole plants encourage timing and tempo on powder. Equally sized turns help to control speed which allows you to concentrate on the slope ahead. You don't know what is in the snow (rocks, stumps, etc.) unless you've skied up it. So while you're having this great powder run stay vigilant.

Junk and Crud

Junk and crud are slang terms for snow that has become hardened over time, wind damaged, or saturated with water. This heavy snow grabs skis and bindings, preventing ski edging and binding release, and can result in strains, sprains, and sometimes leg fractures. Steepness can actually help when making parallel jump turns over crud because of the added momentum given the skis to drive through heavy snow. Larger-radius turns can be more effective in heavier snows because you can build up some speed

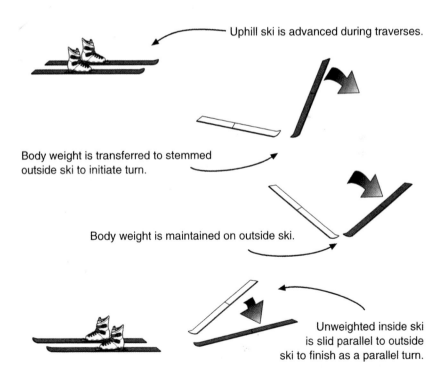

Uphill ski is advanced during traverses.

Body weight is transferred to stemmed outside ski to initiate turn.

Body weight is maintained on outside ski.

Unweighted inside ski is slid parallel to outside ski to finish as a parallel turn.

Fig. 4.10: Stem Christie Turn Progression: The stem christi is an excellent technique on crud, even on steeper slopes. The uphill ski is always in front during the traverse.

Ski Randonnée!

Fig. 4.11:   Powder skiing in British Columbia above Battle Abbey Hut. Brian Litz photo.

for the turning effort. When you are in changing snows and suddenly hit a batch of very heavy snow, absorb the sudden deceleration at the knees instead of buckling at the waist, which can throw you over your leading ski and cause a fall.

Matching Turns to Snow Conditions

Even the color of snow can give clues as to the type of ski technique you should use to reduce falls and increase performance in the backcountry. Sometimes snow will not support body weight – thin windslab, sun crust, crud, and powder are the worst offenders. Telemarkers often fall victim to these snows because so much of their weight is committed to the forward ski, which breaks the snow pack, causing a fall. Turns that distribute body weight over a greater surface area prevent the skier from breaking through the snow. Learn to feel what the snow can or cannot hold. Ski smoothly without making hard, percussive-type movements.

Descent On Ice

Parallel technique was made for all snow conditions but is a far superior

80

technique on hard snow and ice than Telemarking. Even telemarkers use parallel techniques at times. Powder and ice often occur together in patches on windblown slopes. Caution is always necessary on ice, especially when wearing a big pack. You know that your skis will want to shoot out from underneath you once you hit the ice. The trick is try to stay sensitive to the hardness of the ice. Not all ice is the same. Some ice is soft like plastic and easier to edge on, other ice is like steel and you might as well wear ice skates. The trick is to stay balanced when you ski, and to stay centered on your ski so that it is equally weighted fore and aft. On very hard snow or ice on a lower angled slope, beginners can use Stem Christie or a wider, stance parallel and make turns of equal size down the slope. If you are tired, stop often and conserve strength. Those who rush down the slope are asking for a fall and the additional fatigue from getting up from a fall. On steeper slopes one can use short swing turns or hockey stops to control speed.

Icy Patches

Icy patches can often cause you to suddenly accelerate. This is OK unless you are on the edge of a cliff above a raging river, and you weren't plan-

Fig. 4.12: Skiing powder above the Durrand Glacier Hut, British Columbia. Brian Litz photo.

ning to be an Olympic skier today, and you are wearing a heavy pack. If the ice persists, it is OK to revert back to your old reliable basic techniques such as side slipping or wedge turns. On wide open slopes, look for hard snow that has an opaque color. Avoid shiny patches that are obviously ice (unless you like ice of course).

As stated previously, avoid kick turns on steep exposed slopes and if needed descend via side slipping or falling leaf technique.

Using Terrain to Your Advantage

Use terrain features to help you initiate turns, control speed, and maintain your line of skiing. When skiing on low to moderate angled terrain with deep snows, it is often difficult to get enough speed to make a turn. Often, on a bigger slope, you can find many "rolls" or "knolls." If you ski it right, a large knoll, formed by drifted snow, can provide a sudden burst of acceleration, which will make turning in deep snow easier. Go over the top of the slope anticipating a turn at the bottom of the knoll. But be patient. Don't try to turn until you feel your skis speeding up. In late winter, such knolls can be used for jumps. Watch it during early winter when the snow pack is still thin, when a landing can be hollow and injurious for ski and skier alike.

Extreme or Freestyle Skiing

There seems to be a fascination in the ski press and cinema with very steep skiing on avalanche prone slopes. The term "freestyle" is replacing the term "extreme", but freestyle doesn't really describe the risk level involved. As I write this I am aware of the sudden death of the great skier Doug Coombs, who died while attempting to rescue a fellow skier at La Grave, France. He will be missed. He was a great example of a thoughtful, careful skier who had accomplished many first descents. To be fair, most ski fatalities don't occur while skiing steep slopes. Most fatalities happen while tree skiing at a resort. Or from skiing into avalanche terrain without the proper knowledge or equipment. Fatalities from steep skiing are just more glamorized in the media. It's good to know some steep skiing techniques, just to have them in your knowledge base. You never know when you might need them. Every backcountry skier makes a conscious decision to make skiing safe or unsafe. It is a choice that every backcountry skier must make. In the end, it is a question of life or death.

It pays to climb up the route you plan to see if it is safe. I'm not saying to

Fig. 4.13: Edge setting is an invaluable exercise in developing quick stopping and turn skills. The author skiing on summer conditions on Corona Pass, Colorado. Vivesphoto.

ascend an avalanche chute that may be ready to slide. Examine your descent route from a parallel ridge, for instance. This lets you know the angle of the slope first hand, the snow's condition, and the position of rocks and the narrowness of passages. It would have been nice to design the route down so that any major fall would occur above a nice big run out area. This luxury is not always available. Making many short turns with stops for rest and examining the route below is better than long sweeping turns or straight schusses (don't pay attention to today's ski movies – you'll notice that those skiers are skiing powder not crud or ice).

How Steep is Steep?

Looking straight on at a slope from afar often foreshortens the length

Fig. 4.14: Steeper skiing in above Winter Park, Colorado Russellphoto.

84

and angle of the slope. You need to see it from the side. You get the same effect if you take a ski lift ride up a hard run. It looks easy until you are on it! What are average angles of most ski slopes? According to Lito-Te-jada Flores in his book, "Backcountry Skiing", most beginner slopes are 10 degrees, while intermediate runs may be 20 degrees, and advanced slopes may be 30 degrees. 40 degrees is really steep and usually scary to look down (Flores, 1981). The famous Gervasutti Couloir at Chamonix that was originally skied by Anselme Baud, is estimated at 60 degrees. See Appendix I for ski grading systems and more examples of steepness. Iin the end, anything that is scary for you to look down is just plain steep.

The Jump Turn

Historically, extremists had a few famous turns of yore at their disposal, mainly developed during the 1960's: the Windshield Wiper Turn by Sylvain Saudan and the Pedal Turn of Patrick Vallencant. These are really both hybrids of the Jump Turn. This is basically a hyper version of a Short Swing Turn. But because the terrain is so steep the skis can become airborne. Think of this turn as going from one hockey stop to the next adding some side slipping in between turns, if needed, to lose elevation. The hockey stop is used to make an edge set which also provides the skier with the rebound needed to lift the skis quickly into the next turn. The skis are lifted making a 180 degree pivot and end up facing the opposite direction. Most of the lift comes from the legs while balancing with the poles. There is almost no forward speed. Weight is centered on the skis and mostly on the downhill ski as you set your edges. Clean and decisive pole plants are a must. On steeper terrain, longer poles make downhill pole placement easier and sup-port the upper body during unweighting, but they also make a bent knee stance more difficult. Utilize adjustable ski poles to find your most efficient length. Consistency helps control speed. Make each turn the same size. Use equally hard edge sets.

Preventing Falls on Steep Terrain

Only advanced skiers should attempt steep skiing. While learning, they should always practice steep skiing on slopes that provide smooth slopes below in case of a fall. Self-arrest techniques must be mastered. You should ski the steep with ski pole straps off in case a self-arrest is necessary. Remember not to attempt a kick turn on a steep slope. The odds of completing the turn without falling are very low. It is easier and safer to sideslip down the slope. Bindings should be adjusted so they cannot prerelease and come off. Additionally, ski pole baskets should be small enough so that they do not interfere with pole placements. Keep your weight away from the slope, over your skis. Leaning inwards towards the slope can cause your edges to lose their edge, causing a slip.

General Notes on Avoiding Falls

Falling in powder is not as bad as falling on hard-pack snow, especially with a pack. Before heading down, judge the angle of the slope, the type of snow, the length of the run, and the possibility of falling . Once you decrease the fear of falling and its stigma of failure, you can progress faster in learning to ski. You can minimize falling by using some of the following techniques.

- Be honest with yourself. Ask yourself one question: "If I fall, where will I end up?" Don't pick a ski line that crashes you into a boulder or takes you off a cliff if you miss a turn. Have an escape route.

- Ski defensively. On more exposed terrain, pick descent lines that provide for a long run out just in case.

- Keep your ski pole straps off during the descent.

- Wear abrasive ski clothing. Slick XC pants may be cooler during spring outings, but can add speed to your slide.

- Climb up the slope that you intend to ski and inspect it for rocks and icy patches, especially during Spring descents. If your boots can't penetrate the snow, it will be difficult to do a self-arrest later on. Pick another route with softer snow.

Preventing Runaway Skis During Falls

Always fall to one side of the skis into the snow. Beginners have a tendency to sit down on the tails of the skis when they actually mean to sit in the snow. When you sit on the tails of the skis, the skis accelerate, which can be especially hazardous on steep, icy trails.

Headfirst Falls

"Headers" are a common falls in skiing. Usually short falls, they can turn into long, sliding falls on steep, hard slopes. When falling head first, you instinctively extend your hands out in front of you to keep your face off the snow and ice; however, spring slopes have many small, icy ridges that are sharp enough to cut your hands (so always wear gloves during spring skiing). A rollover stop can help you stop more quickly on steeper slopes. This stop was first attributed to ski instructor and guide Bill Briggs of Jackson Hole, Wyoming, who was famous for his extreme ski descents. The rollover can be done forward or sideways. It is best done on steep slopes with soft snow, but can be done on hard snow as well. As

TIPS FOR BEGINNERS

It's difficult to be a beginner! You're always falling, and then thinking everyone gets mad at you for holding them up. Don't despair! Take a deep breath and remember that three techniques can help you get down almost any hill:

1. Wedge-Snowplow

2. Sideslip

3. Kick turn with linked traverses

Avoid These Mistakes

1. Ski warm. Warm up your body with some easy flat skiing and stretch your muscles.

2. Always maintain good posture – stand up straight and bend at the knees, not at the waist.

3. Don't look at your ski tips. Keep your head up!

4. Use just the muscles you need to use and relax everything else.

5. Don't forget to breathe! Without knowing it, you might hold your breath because you are nervous. Breathe fear out and breathe power in! Visualize doing beautiful turns, turn by turn by turn.

6. Attitude is everything! Laugh at your falls and don't take them personally. Believe it or not, learning how to ski is an exciting time!

you go into a headfirst fall, keep on falling, bringing your skis all the way over your head and pointing back downhill, all in one move. Get your skis across the hill on the downhill side to protect your body from impact with unseen obstacles such as trees or rocks.

Ski Pole Self-Arrest

The self-arrest is an important survival technique in backcountry skiing, even if you don't intend to ski anything steep. Weird things happen in the backcountry – you can get off route or get talked into something over your head. The most important thing to remember is to always get on your stomach immediately after a fall and arrest early and aggressively. Get your skis spread out downhill from you, across the hill to protect your body from impact with unseen objects. Grab both ski poles just above the baskets and jab both ski pole tips into the snow (see figure 4.15). Do not extend your arms! Keep your body weight over your ski pole tips instead of relying on strength alone. If at first you can't get the tips in, wait a second, then try again when you reach softer snow. Arrest early before you start picking up speed. Hopefully, you are not wearing sleek outerwear that will increase the speed of your fall. Even if your speed is increasing, don't abandon this technique; keep trying repeatedly while keeping your skis across the hill below you. Keep your head up and off the snow.

Self-Arrest With Self-Arrest Grips

Self-arrest grips make stopping easier in desperate situations. The same principles used during a ski pole self-arrest apply to the grip arrest. Always use both arrest grips together for maximum stopping power, as one grip may arrest before the other. Bring both grips together under your body to apply body weight to the arrest effort. Remember that arrest grips, regardless of design, can work only on snow that they can penetrate. It's very difficult to stop on ice, even with an ice axe! Don't expect a self-arrest grip to do any better. This is yet another reason to scout out the slope you intend to ski.

Falling in Deep Powder

Falling in very deep powder can be like being buried in an avalanche. You are buried, the snow chokes you, and you are drowning in a mass of white.

The skiers behind you can't see you, especially if the visibility is bad. Be sure to keep your distance with other skiers. Know where everyone is. Use a buddy system and watch each other. Once, while powder skiing, I fell after skiing off a boulder. I didn't know somebody was right behind me. That skier didn't see me and landed on my head. His skis practically cut off my right ear. One ski patroller said "yeech!" It was a good thing there was a conference of trauma surgeons at the resort that weekend!

Recovery From a Fall

Getting up from falls is tiring, which in turn causes more falls. Good technique

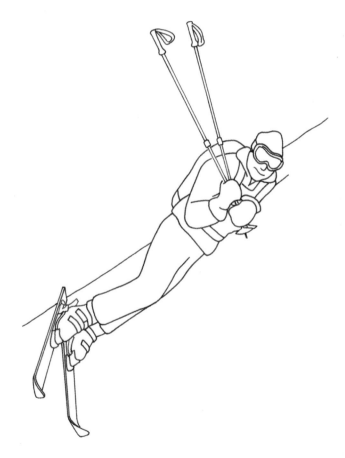

Fig. 4.15: Get your weight on top of the ski pole tips or self-arrest grips for maximum snow penetration. Illustration by Leggitt Design.

Ski Randonnée!

will save you a great deal of energy. There are several important things to remember to make it easier.

- Get your skis across the fall line. Even seemingly flat surfaces have a fall line. This eliminates slipping, falling, and more wasted energy.
- Leave your heavy pack on the snow. Get up, then put it back on.
- Always plant your poles on the uphill side to take advantage of gravity when you try to pull yourself up.
- Take some deep breaths and take your time. Plan it out and do it right the first time. Conserve energy.

To get up on hard-pack snow, put both ski poles together. Plant the ski pole tips as one unit on the uphill side, right next to your hip, as you sit on the snow. Push down on the ski pole baskets with your uphill hand, and at the same time pull down on your ski pole straps and stand up in one fluid movement (see figure 4.16).

Fig. 4.16: On hardpack snow, get up from the uphill side. Get yourself up first, then put on your pack.

Fig. 4.17: In powder, make an **X** with your ski poles to create a better lifting platform.

To get up from powder or soft snow, form an **X** with your ski poles on the uphill side right next to your hip. Crossed poles form a platform in bottomless powder. Organize your skis so they're downhill from you, across the fall line. Grip the intersection of the poles and push down on it to push yourself up into a standing position (see figure 4.17). Stand up and reorganize yourself. Place your skis across the fall line and kick out a solid stance so they don't slip out from underneath you. On steeper terrain, try putting your downhill ski on first, then your uphill ski. Now put your pack on. To save your back and for balance, always pick up heavy packs with bent knees. Take your time – your friends can wait – you will actually do things faster as a result.

Fig. 4.18: More upright position on Spring snow on Colorado Haute Route, Day Two between Copper Mtn and Vail. Vivesphoto.

Conclusion

Getting down the mountain may involve down climbing and or skiing. While getting those powder shots may be our ultimate goal – doing it safely may be a higher goal. Ironically, though, good proven, basic techniques will take us the farthest in the backcountry. Reducing the number of the falls we make increases our endurance and reduces our frustration. Climbing up the routes that we plan to ski helps us to plan our descent. Learning to ski steeper terrain encourages us to extend our borders and dares us to try new things.

Terrain 5

Ski Randonnée!

This chapter considers specific techniques that will help you ski over, around, and through problematic terrain and snow conditions. With good snow sense, you can ski places that you have avoided until now. Winter backcountry travel means more than skiing – it entails pathfinding through varying snow and terrain conditions. It real is what makes this sport so interesting and challenging and fun!

Navigating Obstacles

Unknown snow conditions must be approached with some caution. There is no ski patrol to check out what lies underneath the snow – that's up to you. We can only tell what lies beneath the snow by what shapes or clues appear above the snow. This is the art of pathfinding in natural snow conditions.

Cover 5.1: Cornices like this are best left alone. It was down climbed in a fit of stupidity. Vivesphoto.

Fig. 5.2: Trail breaking should be done with the legs not with the arms and with a fair amount of patience. Vivesphoto.

Fig. 5.3: Mine shafts such as these can be encountered in the Western mountains where mining activity occurred in the 1800's. This was found on the very well traveled route to Crested Butte from Aspen over Pearl Pass. I wonder how many people have missed it by mistake? Vivesphoto.

Buried Trees

Small buried trees that cross your line of travel can appear as long, skinny mounds of snow (see figure 5.2). They should be approached with caution on downhill sections. You can be skiing fast down a trail in powder and your ski can nosedive under a buried fallen sapling or log, trapping your ankles and causing a fall and injury. Watch for these buried logs across the ski trail and respect them. Stop and step across and proceed.

Holes and Old Mines

In the continental United States, crevasses are rare but holes left from mining activities are numerous, especially in the North American Rocky mountains (see figure 5.3). Your topographical map will show mining areas with many small X's. After a big storm, these holes are covered up with fresh powder, making it difficult to see them. They may appear only as a crease or slit in the snow.

Fig. 5.4: Hollow snow can collapse under the weight of your skis during spells of hot weather during Spring ski touring. Always be leery of areas with branches sticking out of the snow pack-its probably hollow underneath. Vivesphoto.

Dirt and Mud

Bare dirt will stop your skis so fast you will fly over your tips before you know it, so always avoid it! Carefully step or ski around sections of dirt or mud so you won't have to stop to take off your skis. For longer sections though, it is better to carry your skis around to save time and energy. Always warn fellow skiers by yelling "dirt" or "rock" when you encounter obstacles.

Brush-Covered Slopes

Beware of small twigs appearing above the snow – these indicate snow-covered brush (see figure 5.4). Brush creates air pockets under the snow that are easy to fall through, especially during periods of shallow snow conditions such as in the spring. Always give wide berth to these areas when ascending or descending.

Sun Cups

In the late spring, you can see whole slopes covered with rounded-out depressions called sun cups. These can reach a depth of up to two feet

(0.6 meters) and are very bothersome to navigate through or around (see figure 5.5). Sun cups are caused by melted water running down the slopes under the snow pack, and by radiation bouncing off big rocks underneath the snow. If sun cup ridges are close together, you may be able to sideslip down these with the tips and tails of the skis riding the ridges. It's often easier just to walk up or down these areas or to find an alternate ski route on a less sun-damaged area.

Spring Skiing

In the spring, snow melts during the day and freezes at night, turning each slope into a sheet of ice. Lightweight gloves should always be worn regardless of the heat to prevent the serious cuts that can occur to hands during falls. In the morning, stay out of shady areas. If a shady trail must be skied, beginners should leave their skins on to help reduce their speed. Later in the day, ascend slopes in the shade to take advantage of firmer snow and to reduce fatigue from the heat.

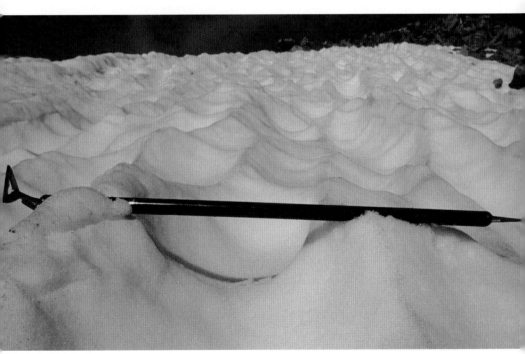

Fig. 5.5: Sun cups are very difficult to ski but are best skied at mid day when they have softened so that at least they will flatten somewhat under body weight. Vivesphoto.

Rockfall During Peak Ascents

It's always a good idea to climb up your line of descent to inspect the slope, especially for rocks. You can always see pockmarked snow where rockfall occurs daily. While climbing up, be cautious of rockfall from side walls bordering ski slopes or couloirs (see chapter 8 for a description of mountain architecture). Rock rarely falls straight down, but it curves outward – so the safest spot is really what you'd think is the worst spot, up against the wall. The center of a couloir is also no good because rock comes straight down the center from above you. If you must ascend these slopes, do so before the sun hits the upper slopes and thaws out rocks frozen in place. Helmets should be considered for such conditions.

Corniced Areas

Jumping cornices can be great fun in the spring. The avalanche danger is lower and the conditions are always great, it seems. But they should be examined be-

Fig. 5.6: Jumping cornices can be fun in the Spring, especially when they have been well scouted out for the stability of the cornice as well as the length of the run out beneath the cornice. Vivesphoto.

fore being jumped. Cornices are places where the snow is undercut due to wind or water. On ridge lines and passes, cornice edges – when seen from above – seem strong, but you cannot determine the extent of this undercut (see title page). You may see a large crack in the top of the cornice. But be aware that the hollow space beneath the cornice extends far back into the slope – further than you would expect. Stay back off the cornice unless you have been able to inspect in from below, especially if you are considering skiing off of it. In poor visibility, it is especially dangerous to try to downclimb around these obstacles. Find another route around. You are somewhat safer with older cornices during the morning hours in spring. These have survived the winter and have peeled off some of their layers. However, during spring or summer skiing, cornice collapse is a real danger after midday. Cornices can also occur along creek or river edges, and can get quite large. Always probe them for thickness with a ski pole before attempting to get water. Remember that they are hollow underneath and waiting for you!

Boulder Margins (Moats)

Rocks absorb heat, causing snow to melt out around their bases (see figure 5.7). This space is called a moat. On car-sized boulders, this moat can have a cornice surrounding the entire boulder. Before crossing a moat, reach over to the rock and get some handholds first, in case the snow collapses. Give some distance (especially in foggy conditions) to large boulders and

Fracture line of cornice

Fig. 5.7: Boulder margins can become large enough for a skier to fall into.

bottoms of cliffs, which will have corniced edges and are prone to collapse if skied on.

Powder Skiing: Trees

It's best to learn tree skiing during excellent powder conditions. Start with trees that are spaced widely apart, and then work into tighter groupings. Here are some basic precautions.

- GOGGLES – Besides preventing tearing of the eyes and improving vision, ski goggles can save your face! While I was doing research for an article on goggles, a young ski racer told me about her close call with a large aspen tree. While skiing in deep powder she missed a turn, landing her face straight into the tree. Her goggles absorbed the force of the impact and probably saved her life!

- HELMETS – Helmets are becoming more popular, especially among skiers who like to push the limits. They go together with the backpack for the backcountry "look". Newer models are getting lighter and lighter each year. While a rockclimbing helmet is meant to handle rockfall, it may not handle skiing impacts such as face-on impacts as well. You have to make the call on what hazard is greater. Helmets must be strapped on during use for maximum protection. Some features that you might appreciate include hardshell construction to prevent penetration by skis, tree branches, or rocks and allow for shedding of snow; an insulating, impact-resistant liner; a goggle strap to keep goggles centered on the shell; side openings to allow hearing during skiing; a helmet profile that allows optimum side vision; and a quick-release chin strap to keep the helmet on during impact.

- LOOSE CLOTHING – Tuck in all loose clothing before skiing. Long, pretty ski scarves or hats can get caught in branches, causing falls. Use a neck gaiter instead. Double-check your clothing before each run.

- SKI POLE STRAPS – Ski pole baskets are likely to get caught in brush and tree branches, causing falls and thumb fractures if you are using the straps. Take all straps off, including the break away releasable type.

- SPACES BETWEEN THE TREES – Your body follows your head and your head follows your eyes. So don't look at the trees, as beautiful as they are! Look at and concentrate on the spaces between the trees. Your body will follow.

Fig. 5.8: Avoid angular snow shapes in the snow. They could indicate a buried tree stump. Vivesphoto.

- TREE TYPE AND TERRAIN – All trees can have large overhanging branches. Aspen's can be the worse since one skinny branch can be sticking out and you won't be looking for it and wham – right in the face (lucky you had those goggles on!). Some forests such as lodgepole often have large fallen dead trees sometimes occupying the space between trees blocking the way (there's no trail crew in backcountry).

Tree Stumps

Also watch out for old tree stumps, fallen trees, and debris, which can allow air pockets to form that will collapse under your skis. Square, angular snow shapes should be avoided, as they are probably hiding a tree stump underneath (see figure 5.8). Trying to ski over small stumps is tricky and should be left to expert snowboarders and skiers.

Fig. 5.9: We were actually quite relieved when this stump turned out to be much more rotten than we thought! Vivesphoto.

Tree Wells

During or after a new snowfall, your skis may fall through the air spaces surrounding the tree trunk or run into it, causing injury. Look for a better line. A shallow or unconsolidated snow pack hides both air pockets and the potential of collapsing snow around smaller trees. Solar energy is absorbed by bigger trees, causing the snow to melt around the tree bottoms so that a "well" is formed (see figure 5.9). These can be small enough to grab a ski or large enough to swallow a skier! During powder storms, these wells fill up with powder so that they become invisible. You won't see the trap until you fall into it. These edges can also collapse during hot weather. Skiers and snowboarders have died from falling into them and hitting trunks. The trunks of even small trees are sturdy enough to knock you out! Try to ski equidistantly between very large trees to avoid these hazards.

Turn Under the Tree, Not Above It

Be cautious above trees, where windblown snow is often thinner than the snow below the tree, which will slow you down but still allow you to control your turns. In addition, doing a hockey stop or hard turn above a tree is not a good practice as the uphill side may be undercut (corniced), which could collapse and cause you to fall into a tree well. Why not just stop or turn below the tree?

Breaking Trail in Deep Powder

Breaking trail in deep powder can be difficult for leaders and followers alike. It will take muscle, along with patience and good technique. Use your legs to break trail in powder, not your arms! Use arms only for balance and occasionally for support. Do not keep your hands in the ski pole grips – this is very tiring. Use regular ski poles, as poles with large powder baskets load with snow and are difficult to pull out of the snow. Choke up on the ski pole halfway down the pole shaft – this relieves much shoulder fatigue and tension, especially when carrying a heavy pack. Concentrate on your breathing as you lift your skis. Keep your skis close together and drag the following ski over the front of the forward ski that has already broken the trail. Take periodic breaks and switch leaders often when skiing in a group.

Fig. 5.10: Snow around tree bottoms can melt, forming dangerous wells.

Ski Randonnée!

Bushwhacking

According to Outward Bound research, bushwhacking is the biggest cause of injury to its students. If you get lost, whether on a hut tour or just during a day of skiing off the backside, remember the following points:

- BE SURE your glasses or goggles are on. There's nothing fun about having a tree branch snap back into your face. You must protect your eyes. Always hold branches for unsuspecting others.

- SLOW DOWN. Time is energy. Go slowly and measure each step so you don't fall into a hollow or snag your skis under a fallen branch. Slow down, and you'll go faster.

- USE YOUR SKI POLES. Take your ski pole and use the upper shaft to punch dead tree branches out of your face. They snap off easily and make the passage much easier for those behind you.

- USE YOUR SKIS. Place your skis on top of brush; don't just slide your skis blindly forward, or they'll get caught in the brush.

Creeks, Rivers, and Lakes

Water courses such as creeks or river beds are natural and fun avenues for skiing during cold weather when heavy forest is difficult to navigate. But they should be avoided during late spring or when warming trends occur. Rocks absorb heat, weakening the ice. In addition, currents in the center of the creek or river thaw ice more quickly in the center than on the edges of the main flow. Snowplow and stem christi turns will disturb the ice the least. Examine your route carefully for holes and weak spots. A fall in 35-degree Fahrenheit (2-degree Celsius) water can cause hypothermia. Creeks have undercut snow banks with sometimes very huge corniced rimmed embankments. Climbing out may be almost impossible. Fording a creek or river is done only when alternate routes are not available. Never cross a creek or river that is deeper than mid-thigh. Put your boots in your pack, roll up your pant legs, and go barefoot. Find the shallowest area to cross – the faster flow often belies a shallow spot. Deeper areas are often at the creek's edge. Carry your skis on your pack and use ski poles for support while crossing. Probe for deep pockets under the water to be avoided.

Also beware of log and rock crossings. Logs and rocks can be iced over with creek spray and mist. Check the log or rock carefully for ice before stepping on it. Sometimes you see photos of people with elaborate rope crossings across a stream (referred to as Tyrolean traverses). However, it will save considerable time and effort to just go upstream and cross rather than setting up such a system. Creeks and rivers get wider the farther they get from their source, so you want to go upstream. The crossing there will be narrower, thus shorter and easier as a result. Cross streams in early morning hours when water levels are lower because of the lack of snowmelt upstream. Snow bridges are also stronger in the morning hours before the sun gets to them. If in doubt, probe snow bridges for thickness with your ski pole or proble pole. Proceed across snow bridges quickly, without stopping.

Crossing lake ice can be tricky in the Spring during warm weather. Weather.com estimates that the ice must be at least 4 inches thick to hold a person, 5 inches for a snowmobile, while 8-12 inches are necessary for a auto. Skiing over a lake should be done in late season during early morning hours on a mature ice pack during cold weather. Falling into a lake with lake ice with it's sharp edges is a difficult rescue situation that must be avoided.

Glacier Skiing

Glacier skiing would be great if it weren't for all those crevasses! There are several good books on crevasse rescue (see Bibliography). This is only an overview pointing out areas of particular concern to skiers. It hardly represents an exhaustive review of the literature. Some information from those books is included. It is assumed that the skier already knows basic climbing skills such as belaying, snow and ice protection placement, etc. Practice in rescue techniques is very important if you intend to spend any amount of time on glaciers. There is a science to setting up roped hauling systems which must be studied. Skiers with rock climbing, caving, or cayoneering experience will have used many of these techniques already.

I have been lucky in the glacier travel area to date anyway. One time in Chamonix, I was roped up with another skier. That skier fell into a hole while breaking trail in deep powder on descent during a storm in low visibility. He disappeared briefly, and I felt a tug on the rope. Fortunately, it was late winter and the crevasses were choked with snow and he didn't fall far. I was able to give him some tension and he climbed out on his own power. But that is not always the case. An instructor friend was skiing in the Bugaboos in Canada and while skiing on descent (unroped) he fell into a big crevasse and he ended up hanging free upside down still in his bindings. He had facial cuts but luckily he didn't break any bones, and thank goodness, his bindings did not release. A guide was lowered down, roped him up and he was pulled out using the helicopter as a wench.

Glaciers

Glaciers are often encountered above 2500 meters (8,000 ft.) in the Alps and are present in the Northern Rockies in the Northern continental U.S., the Cascades, Canadian Rockies, and Alaska. Glaciers can be very steep where they fall off of ledges called Icefalls. They can also create vast glacial plains, where the effects of gravity are less. Over lesser ledges, they create crevasses. There are two basic types of crevasses: Tranverse crevasses are perpendicular to the flow and Longitudinal crevasses are parallel to their flow. There can be a combination of the two. The largest crevasse, the Bergschund, is located where the glacier pulls away from the mountain at it's upper margin. Skiing above this particular crevasse can be especially hazardous in high avalanche conditions since even a small slide could sweep you into it.

Skiing on the Glacier

During skiing, there should be as little slack in the rope as possible in case there is a breakthrough. Coils of rope shoud never be carried in the hands, since this allows more slack and a greater shock on the rope if there's a fall. This will result in a big jerk on the second skier pulling him off his feet. Rope management is very important as you move up or down the glacier. Uphill kick turns come in handy on the ascent. Downhill skiing on a glacier is harder than you think. You can't just ski fast down a glacier that you are unfamiliar with. Often, crevasses can't be seen from above. Fresh snow may hide crevasse cracks. Ski perpendicular to the crevasses. That sounds easy enough until you find out there are crevasses at many different angles! Snow bridges should be crossed quickly while the second skier maintains rope tension. An ice axe belay can be used in case of marginal conditions. Skiers should always be roped in at the waist (never at the chest). When the pull from a falling skier comes, the skier's center of gravity will aid in holding the fall. The skier may be wearing the following equipment:

Fig. 5.11: Getting out of a crevasse is not easy and rescue practice plays an important role for more efficient results. Photo courtesy of Peter Cliff (see Bibliography).

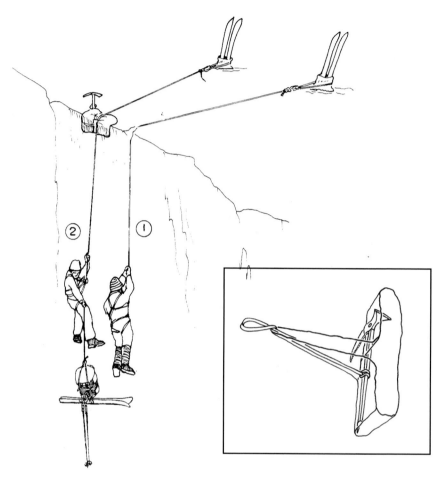

Fig. 5.12: Crevasse rescue: A second rope can greatly facilitate a rescue, especially with a skier that is injuried. Skis can used as anchor under the right conditions. See insert for ice axe anchor. Courtesy Peter Cliff.

- Harness with two prussik slings, two locking biners, figure 8
- Pack with two mechanical ascenders in top flap, ice axe pointed downwards for fast access, snow picket/ice screws depending on season.
- Team gear: second rope (50m x 7.7mm rope)

Crevasse Rescue

- DURING THE FALL: The second person experiences a big yank which puts you on your face, especially if your bindings aren't locked down. But at least you have stopped your friend who is in the crevasse probably scared out of his mind. You need to set up an anchor and tie in. You stick in your ice axe, clip into it and tie a prussik knot into the belay rope to take the weight off of you. The third skier assists you in placing an anchor(s).

- ROPED RESCUE: During a rescue there are several key concerns:

   1. COMMUNICATION between rescuers and victim

   2. ROPE PROTECTION: the rope will dig deeply into the snowy lip of the crevasse unless it is padded with a pack or with an ice axe or snow shovel handle. This will also increase raising efficiency by reduce friction in the rope system between rope and snow.

   3. MEDICAL ATTENTION TO VICTIM. In powder there is a lot of friction from the rope and in fact the rope can cut down into the powder so that the victim is now looking up into an overhang. Time for the victim to put on their warm cap and zip up because they will be there for a while, and hypothermia can be a concern since they are out of the sun and in the shade of the crevasse. Communication is a biggest problem since snow greatly muffles sound. If one thought about it, two way radios would be nice so that the victim and rescuers could communicate, but I digress.

Uninjured Skier Scenario:

The second skier should immediately set up an anchor/belay station using multiple anchors such a snow pickets or ice screws depending on the snow/ice available. Deadman anchors can be made out of ice axes, rucksacks, and skis (see illus.). Rescuers should remain roped up and clipped into an anchor(s).

Two options:

1. A THROW ROPE can be sent down to the skier if there are no injuries. The victim can remove his skis and rucksack and attach them to the throw rope. The victim can now jumar or prussik up the same throw rope since it is under tension from the weight of the skis and rucksack. Or the skier can similiarly ascend the rope he is tied into.

2. The skier can also jumar or prussik the rope he is belayed on. The skier attaches one prusik for his two feet and one for chest. Once attached the skier can untie and attach his pack and skis to the end of the rope that he was tied into. Sounds easy doesn't it?

Ski Randonnée!

Injuried Skier Scenario:

This is a much more serious situation since the skier is unable to communicate or help with hauling himself out of the crevasse. This is where a larger party is a big plus. The "throw rope" can be used by one of the rescuers to rappel down and over the lip of the crevasse to help the victim. As he descends he should keep telling the victim what he is doing since he will be dumping snow on the victim who may be in shock and getting colder. First of all, the victim may be hanging upside down in which case he must be righted, a jury rigged chest harness applied and a prussik knot adjusted above the chest so the body is upright. Basic first aid should be immediately applied using advanced first aid protocols. Once the victim's condition is stabilized, then his equipment can be removed and attached to the rappel rope below the rescuer. The rescuer should make sure the victim is as warm as is possible. The rescuer can jumar or prussik back up to the surface to help in lifting operations.

Equipment Issues

Some books on crevasse rescue say to go with prussik knots since they work better on icy ropes, while others say mechanical ascenders work better than knots. Knots are a pain, especially when your hands are numb. They jam up, stay tight, and have a mind of their own. Mechanical ascenders (Jumars) are heavier to carry and are pricy but if you are planning to make glacier skiing a habit, they are worth the investment and weight. They make everything including getting over the crevasse lip much easier, since they are much easier to move than knots. Mechanical ascenders should only be used to hold body weight and not be used in lifting systems where 2:1 or 3:1 mechanical advantage is used. Ascenders have teeth and can shred a climbing rope if used improperly. There has been recent research into the use of small diameter low stretch static ropes (7.7mm) versus the traditional dynamic ropes for glacier travel (Smith, Blaine. Sterlingrope.com., 2006). It has shown that a static rope can hold a crevasse fall in half the distance of a dynamic rope thus preventing injuries. Most injuries occur due to hitting the inside wall of the crevasse, ice blocks or "corking" (falling into a tapered crevasse) and getting wedged in as a result. The use of double stitch plate belaying devices has also been shown to be effective in holding falls.

Weather 6

Ski Randonnée!

Clear and quiet conditions are great for skiing. But if you are only a fair-weather skier, you are missing a beautiful part of backcountry skiing. Understanding mountain weather allows you to take advantage of good conditions and avoid violent ones. Always ask yourself, "If the weather does change, how will it affect me?" The best rule is this: be prudent! Make camp or turn back before you are forced to. The good backcountry skier has a habit of constantly looking above and behind for weather changes and making mental notes on the route already skied.

Mountain Weather Changes Quickly

Each mountain has its own weather pattern that is associated with its shape and surroundings, causing air currents to lift, cool, and condense into clouds – this is called orographic lifting. Mountain valleys are warmer during periods of warm weather, but during the winter they become cold sinks, holding super-chilled air at night. With the morning sun, air heats and rises up the mountain to create wind and storms on the peak tops. After sunset, air cools and once again descends into the valleys for the night.

Changes of Season and Storm Frequency

In the United States, storms occur more regularly during the middle of winter, from January up to and including March (roughly June, July, and August in southern latitudes). During winter, the sun is lower in the sky, with sunset occurring much earlier than in summer. Skiing normally occurs between about 8:00 A.M. and 3:00 P.M. during deep winter. It gets cold quickly as the sun drops in the sky. Spring brings fewer storms and longer days more suited for ski touring. For exact sunrise and sunset times and the length of days in the United States, consult the Farmer's Almanac. Try national weather Web sites on the Internet for international data.

Regional Influences

Mountains close to oceans with Maritime climates (Sierras, Alps, Cascades, and New Zealand Alps, for example) have higher humidity, and snowfalls of 3 feet (0.9 meters) are common. Mountains far inland from oceans have

Cover 6.1: Red sky at night, sailor's delight? The next day it was snowing hard. Such sayings need to be backed up with what the barometer is saying. At the Jackel Hut, 10th Mountain Hut System, Colorado. Vivesphoto.

Continental climates (for example, Rockies and Wasatch)and have less humidity and snowfalls of 6 to 10 inches (15 to 25 centimeters) are more common, with occasional snowfalls over 2 feet (0.6 meters). Humidity is a natural junk maker as it keeps the snow saturated with water, but this wetter snow stabilizes quickly with few avalanches (although it allows snow to stick to steeper slopes). Inland areas of the United States such as Colorado and Utah have dry, cold conditions perfect for dehydrated dry powder snow and powder avalanches.

How Weather Affects Skiing

You should know what weather you are heading into so that you'll be aware of the kinds of conditions you and your equipment may be up against. Often, the knowledge of a possible storm may cause you to cancel a ski trip and seek other plans. Or maybe you are a person who enjoys skiing the backcountry in changing weather conditions, in which case the possibility of a storm makes you want even more to keep your plans. Here are some considerations to take into account.

Fig. 6.2: Perfect weather! Clear blue sky, no wind. Still, calm conditions near Winter Park, Colorado. Russellphoto.

Ski Randonnée!

New Snowfall

New storms bring in new snow and powder skiing, but new snow can also impede progress by forcing you to break trail and thus increase energy expenditure and food demand. Waxing your skis with antiglop wax may be necessary in order to accommodate new wet snow may slow your travel speed. Avalanche danger may increase, forcing you to reroute. Increased cold and wind demands more clothing. During deep winter ski tours, you will need more food, more stove fuel, and more clothing. With this in mind, snow camping could be reserved for spring tours, while hut tours are more ideal for the deep of winter.

Rain

Rain is the scourge of skiers. It can follow a recent snow when a warm, low-pressure system hits coastal mountains. Rain destroys the snow pack by cutting bonding layers between snow layers, or between the whole snow pack and the ground. Skiing becomes difficult in rain because the snow is reduced to slush. Climbing skins may fall off due to moisture if they don't have a backup attachment system besides adhesive. The skiing is miserable and sloppy. Goggles fog up, making navigation difficult. It might be a good time to make camp or turn back.

Route Planning for Bad Weather

Have alternate routes planned in case of bad weather. It's good to have several high (haute) routes and low routes to choose from. Remember that the temperature normally drops 5 degrees Fahrenheit (–15 degrees Celsius) per 1,000 feet (305 meters) in elevation. Valleys may be sunny and comfortable, but you can still find blowing and snowing higher up. High routes are exposed to more weather and so they are better suited for periods of stable weather and low avalanche danger, like in the spring. Low routes are below the tree line, sheltered from the weather and avalanche activity. These two route design options let you ski the backcountry all winter long.

Getting the Complete Weather Picture!

You can get a good idea of what the weather will be doing by getting up-to-date weather forecasts, and by being observant in the field. Using an altimeter will back up your observations by detecting pressure changes in

Fig. 6.3: The diameter of a sunspot in the clouds can show how close a storm is. Incoming clouds and moisture Russellhoto.

the atmosphere. At home, there are several different sources of weather information: the internet, television, radio, ski phone reports, the local forest service, and resort ski patrol offices. Where has the storm been and where is it going? Is it coming off the ocean with wet, heavy snow and difficult skiing? Is it coming out of the Arctic, bringing light powder snow? The satellite radar image shows where the big "storm cells" are. Ask yourself: how big is the storm mass? Does it have breaks and clearing areas? A mountain travel advisory with a winter storm warning that alerts motorists of blowing wind and poor visibility will also hold true for skiers. If you know where ski resorts are located and the snow amounts they are receiving, you can deduce the direction and speed of the storm. For long-term planning, a national weather bureau will have 5-, 10-, and 30-day forecasts that are invaluable for multi day trips.

Making Field Observations

The look of the sky and the feel of moisture in the air can tell you if a storm is moving in. There are many indications that bad weather is moving in – you simply must know what to look for. For example, clockwise or anticyclonic wind and cloud movement is related to high pressure and good weather. When the clouds are moving counterclockwise, you can expect low pressure and bad weather within 24 hours. Following are some other observations you can make.

Rings Around the Sun or Moon

Rings around the sun or moon indicate moisture in the air and announce incoming bad weather. However, sometimes they just mean some harmless moisture is in the air. As the storm approaches, the halo around the orb will shrink due to increased moisture in the air. The important observation is the speed at which the halo shrinks. If there is no front, the halo will stay one size. The faster the shrinking, the higher the probability of stormy weather. While most people think a full-moon period guarantees good weather, this is not necessarily the case – it is often the opposite!

Star Visibility

The stars will twinkle brightly during periods of high pressure and good weather, especially if it's windy. If the stars seem vague or misty, then moisture is aloft. If you can't see any stars, then obviously some clouds are present. A clear night sky with a high barometer (over 30 mmHg) is a sign of good weather. A lower night barometer reading means bad weather is coming. Morning clouds down in the valley confirm the low barometer reading. These clouds can rise out of the valley, engulfing skiers.

Sound Transmission

"When sound travels far and wide, a stormy day likes betide" is an old saying based on the echoing effect thick clouds or a clear sky holding moisture have on sound. You'll notice that the sound of a jet plane is sharp and clear as it passes overhead during dry, clear weather. Because moisture dulls sound, the plane will sound hollow when moisture and clouds are aloft.

Compass and Cloud Direction

It's easy to lose your sense of direction in the mountains when you are tired. Your compass will tell you precisely where the clouds are coming from – this way you can't miss. Remember the storm system you saw on TV? Are those clouds coming from the same direction?

Temperature

Temperature can give you clues to future weather. During winter, a period of good weather with high temperatures often precedes a few days of bad weather. This is because the low pressure cells are spaced between high pressure areas. Warm weather is pushed in front of the cold front. As the cold front arrives, temperature drops and snow and wind begin. But when it clears up, it is really cold! (As the cold front passes, it is followed by very cold air for at least 24 hours after the storm.) If you are in your sleeping bag, you can tell 80 percent of the time whether it's clear outside just by the temperature. Cloud cover acts like a blanket, keeping warmth closer to the ground. With clearing, the warmth of the earth escapes to the atmosphere.

Stages of Incoming Weather

If you watch the sky carefully, you will see signs of the weather to come. Weather is not an exact science, so the following stages may not work precisely every time. But based on many years of observation, I can tell you that the odds are good that these stages will occur as presented.

Stage 1: Warm, Sunny Weather

There's nothing like good weather in the mountains! However, during changeable winter weather, a very warm, sunny day may be an indication of high pressure air being pushed by the next low pressure air mass (storm). A dropping barometer during the day and night will warn you of an incoming storm. Very warm winds called the Fohn (Europe) or Chinook (North America) often accompany these conditions, and they can hold bad weather off for days while ruining ski conditions and causing avalanches. But when the high pressure finally breaks, be prepared for storms!

Stage 2: High Cirrus Clouds

The "tails" of cirrus clouds point in the direction of an incoming disturbance. You know a low pressure system is on the way, but how big and how soon? The rule of thumb is, the bigger the tail the bigger the disturbance. The tail simply tells you that the sky is active, and the next 24 hours will reveal more specifically what's in store (see figure 6.1).

Stage 3: Lenticular Clouds and Wind

Lenticular clouds – called cap or mountain wave clouds when they rest on mountaintops – are long, lens-shaped, high cirrus clouds (see figure 6.4). They are a sign of major jet stream winds aloft, while on the ground there may be flurries even on a clear, sunny day. These flurries

Fig. 6.4: A warm, beautiful day at Snowmass Resort, Colorado. But the sky is showing a change is on the way. Horse tail clouds point westward towards incoming clouds. High cirrus is also moving in. Vivesphoto.

can exceed 60 mph, obviously making it difficult to ski. You may need to hike if you are in an exposed situation, such as close to a cliff or cornice edge, because a change of weather is either coming in or passing over within the next 24 hours. If puffy, high clouds accompany the wind, there is an increased chance of an immediate storm.

Lenticular clouds accompanied by a sudden increase in wind temperature indicate that a Chinook or Fohn wind has arrived. These southerly or westerly winds ruin ski conditions and raise avalanche danger by driving warmth into the snow pack, melting the snow.

Stage 4: Altocumulus Clouds

White, puffy altocumulus clouds are a sign of good weather in most cases, but can also accompany cumulonimbus clouds, which cause bad weather – especially when sighted in the morning hours (see discussion in Stage 5). The morning clouds in figure 6.4 appeared just four hours before the cumulonimbus clouds in figure 6.5.

118

Stage 5: Cumulonimbus Clouds

Clouds that give us the majority of our snow, rain, and hail are those marked by the term nimbo, which means "rain bearing". These clouds can move in while you are socked in (covered) by low clouds or mist in the valleys, and you won't even know it. They might just move over like they do on spring afternoons, threatening, but just passing by. But total cloud coverage is a good indicator of bad weather to come.

Rule of Thirds.

The amount of the sky that is covered by clouds is related to storm potential. A handy formula is called the Rule of Thirds: when one third of the sky is covered, there's not much to worry about. If two thirds of the sky is covered, storm clouds are moving in or passing over. If the entire sky (three thirds) is covered, the clouds have stopped moving and are solidifying into a cloud mass with precipitation – time to make camp or head back! Another way to think of it is to remember the phrase "clouds are thickening and lowering (bad weather); or thinning and lifting (good weather)".

Lightning.

Cumulonimbus clouds may also contain lightning, which skiers may encounter during spring ski touring on higher mountains. High-mountain rain or hail is a good indication of cumulonimbus clouds with lightning. If you feel your hair standing up, descend immediately but carefully. Many people get hurt while getting off a summit to avoid being hit by lightning. Just ski

Fig. 6.5: Huge Lenticular Clouds above the Owens Valley, CA. These are always a sign of high winds aloft and weather that is moving in or out. Couple this with your barometric pressure reading. Vivesphoto.

Fig. 6.6: Incoming weather high above Ashcroft, Colorado. Notice winds whipping off the peaks as clouds are darking and lowering–a good time to ski back. Vivesphoto.

or climb down carefully – but do descend! Get down to a lower altitude until the storm clouds have blown over. Take your skis off your pack, because they can act as lightning rods. If you must continue to move, hold them horizontally. Stay off ridges, summits, or high points. Avoid solitary trees or tall boulders. A party of skiers should spread 10 feet (3 meters) apart from each other, as lightning can travel horizontally. Ski on open slopes rather than down narrow chutes and couloirs, because lightning follows cracks and chutes down from the summit. Wet dirt and rocks conduct electricity better than dry dirt and snow (which are actually poor conductors), so stay away from them during the descent. If you need to stop, get away from all metal objects, including skis, ice axes, and other equipment. If you must stop, squat down on your pack or ensolite pad "third world" style with your hands off the ground to insulate yourself from electrical conduction. The rubber soles of your boots coupled with the insulated materials will protect you from ground currents.

Stage 6: Descending Ceiling and Wind

There is now a solid cloud cover above. The clouds no longer move sideways, but are now descending. Cumulonimbus clouds now touch the mountain-tops and descend the valley walls as fog and mist. Compute in your head: the valley walls are 3,000 feet (914 meters) high, and the clouds descend 1,000 feet (305 meters) every 10 minutes. Therefore, 30 minutes remain before you are stuck with poor visibility and falling snow. Now is the time to make camp or return to the trailhead before the snow picks up and covers up your tracks.

Stage 7: Increasing Winds With Ground Flurries

At this point, fog and snow are in your face – it's goggle weather! Snow will continue to increase, forming a solid wall of snow (see figure 6.6). According to the National Weather Service, a Blizzard is defined as a storm with heavy snow, reduced visibility, winds of 35 mph or higher, lasting at least three hours, with temperatures below 20 degrees Fahrenheit (–7 degrees Celsius).

6.7. Classic descending cloud ceiling taken from Wildcat Ridge above Snowmass Village, Colorado. Vivesphoto.

Ski Randonnée!

Fig. 6.8: Altimeters are invaluable for navigation and for weather forcasting, as the Table 6.1 shows. A wrist model may be preferred for navigation purposes. Vivesphoto.

Using an Altimeter for Weather Forecasting

A weather change is always accompanied by a measurable change in barometric pressure. A barometer works by actually measuring the weight of the air mass above it in increments of inches, millimeters, or millibars of mercury (Hg). Altimeters are both altimeters and barometers, but are usually referred to as altimeters. Altimeters are more popular in Europe than in the United States because there is more featureless Alpine landmass above tree line with fewer marked trails. However, more American adventurers are discovering them. Altimeters are scorned by many because they are thought to be too complex to use, too fragile, or just too expensive. Wristband altimeters are easier to use, since they are readily accessible for both navigating and weather forecasting.

Calibrating Your Altimeter

The key to altimeter use is repeated recalibration, which is easy to do. Just recalibrate your altimeter whenever you're at a major landmark of known altitude such as a lake, river, creek, town, pass, or summit. Unlike the United States, in Europe (and other countries) altitude is displayed on trailhead signs, huts, and ski lift terminals, making altimeter calibration even easier.

In the field, keep a note of your altitude when you reach camp in case you forget. For consistency, reset your altimeter in the morning to the altitude it was the night before, even if there's a change in the barometer.

Simplifying Your Readings

The general rule of thumb for barometers is that if the pressure is falling, the weather will worsen. If the barometer is rising, the weather will get better (see table 7.1). (A falling barometer is usually accompanied by northern or easterly winds, and a rising barometer is usually accompanied by southern or westerly winds.) How much of a change is important? The following degrees of change should be noted:

1. No change is a change of .01 inches Hg or less over 3 hours (.04 inches over 12 hours).

2. Slow change is a change of .01 to .05 inches over 3 hours (.04 to .20 inches over 12 hours).

3. Rapid change is a change of more than .05 inches over 3 hours (more than .20 inches over 12 hours).

Elevation Changes Overnight

What if the elevation reading on your altimeter has changed overnight even though you haven't gotten out of your sleeping bag? If the elevation has gone up 150 feet (46 meters), it means that there is less air pressure pushing on the altimeter, so it thinks it is 150 feet higher than it actually is – this means bad weather. Conversely, if the altimeter reads 150 feet lower, it means high pressure and good conditions. The general rule is that above 7,000 feet (2,133 meters), an increase of 150 feet overnight means the chances of a storm are high. Below 7,000 feet, a change of 100 feet (30 meters) overnight is significant.

Altimeter Tips

- Keep your altimeter in the same place (on your wrist, for instance) at all times so that storage conditions are held constant. This will give you more consistent readings over time. Keep it away from hot areas such as the top of your pack, which could get warm from the sun.

- Make a foam case for handheld altimeters so that your investment is protected from falls during skiing or hiking.

Ski Randonnée!

- Carefully read the information booklet that came with your altimeter – make a photocopy of it for use in the field.

- Practice using your altimeter at home. What is the elevation of your home and the market you go to most? Match up your barometric reading with your local television weather forecast. The more you use it, the easier it will be to use.

Skiing in White Out Conditions

No one plans to get caught in a blizzard, but it happens to expedition skiers and day tourers alike. For experienced powder skiers doing a day tour, these a great conditions for skiing. But for a larger group en route to a hut it may be a different matter. An intense blizzard can cause fatigue, cold, and disorientation, making it difficult to return to your starting point. Skiing in poor-visibility conditions is difficult and potentially dangerous. Here are some ways to deal with it:

- Ski slowly downhill. Use snowplowing, sideslipping, and kick turns to make a slow, controlled descent. The less falling the faster the group travels as a whole.

- Goggles should be on.

- Button up your clothing to anticipate any unexpected falls.

- The best skier should go first to be the pathfinder.

TRUST YOUR INSTRUMENTS

While climbing Mt. Blanc, a ski group I was with stayed at the Grand Mulet Hut (10,009 feet [3,051 meters]) while skiing up the standard route. The evening was clear and beautiful. That night, my barometer kept dropping with concurrent increase in my altitude readout. The next morning, we awoke at 3 A.M. for the climb. It was clear, but that's not what my altimeter was telling me – according to it, there was a storm coming in. With daylight, I could see that the whole Chamonix Valley was covered in clouds. My barometer was steady but low. I had seen these clouds before and knew they meant trouble. By the time we got our skis on we were covered in clouds! The moral of the story: believe your instruments!

124

Fig. 6.9: Climbing up The Commando Run between Vail Ski Area and Vail Pass in terrible weather conditions late in the day (Colorado Super Tour). We were able to reach the town of Vail by nightfall. Vivesphoto.

- Everyone should ski within visual contact.

  ALWAYS wait for stragglers. A lost skier may stay lost.

- Use trees for visual cues. Stay in scattered trees for depth of field cues. Follow the edge of a grove of trees for terrain contour information in flat light.

- Stay in the track of the skiers in front of you. Watch how they handle the terrain and be ready for it. Ski cautiously and defensively.

- To minimize chilling, don't stop on the top of a windy pass during storm conditions. Ski right over the top without stopping unnecessarily.

- Read your map carefully and stay away from corniced areas that might be hidden by white out conditions.

Table 6.1

BAROMETRIC READINGS AND WEATHER OBSERVATIONS

Wind Direction	Barometer	Type of Weather
SW to NW	30.10 to 30.20 and steady	Fair with slight temperature changes for one to two days.
SW to NW	30.10 to 30.20 and rising rapidly	Fair followed by rain or snow within two days.
SW to NW	30.20 and above and stationary	Continued fair, no decided temperature change.
SW to NW	30.20 and above and falling slowly	Slowly rising temperature and fair for the next two days.
S to SE	30.10 to 30.20 and falling slowly	Rain or snow within 24 hours.
S to SE	30.10 to 30.20 and falling rapidly	Wind increasing in force, with rain or snow in 12 to 24 hours.
SE to NE	30.10 to 30.20 and falling slowly	Snow or rain in 12 to 18 hours.
SE to NE	30.10 to 30.20 and falling rapidly	Increasing wind and rain or snow in 12 hours.
E to NE	30.10 and above and falling slowly	In winter, rain or snow within 24 hours. In summer, with light winds, rain may not fall for several days.
E to NE	30.10 and above and falling rapidly	In winter, rain or snow with increasing wind often sets in. In summer, rain probable within 12 to 24 hours.
SE to NE	30.00 or below and falling slowly	Rain or snow will continue for one to two days.
SE to NE	30.00 or below and falling rapidly	Rain or snow, with high winds, followed within 36 hours by clearing, and in winter by a colder wave.
S to SW	30.00 or below and rising slowly	Clearing within a few hours and fair for several days.
S to E	29.80 or below and falling rapidly	Severe storm imminent, followed within 24 hours by clearing, and in winter by a colder wave.
E to N	29.80 or below and falling rapidly	Severe NE gale and heavy precipitation. In winter, heavy snow followed by a cold wave.
Going to W	29.80 or below and rising rapidly	Clearing and colder.

Reprinted, by permission, from Peet Brothers, Inc. 1308 Doris Avenue, Ocean, NJ, 07712

Fig. 6.10: Clouds lifting and thinning above the Chamonix Valley. Barometric pressure was also increasing. The next day was perfectly clear. Vivesphoto.

Making Camp in Bad Weather

Always make camp before you have to. When making camp in a storm, it's important to be patient with others because the wind, noise, cold, and fatigue can make for a confusing situation (see chapter 11 for more information on making camp). Do things methodically and quickly. Here are some tips to remember:

1. Be sure everyone has all their cold-weather gear on.

2. Pull the tent body out and throw all gear inside, then zip the doors to prevent ballooning. Get cold individuals into the tent body before it's erected. This gets them out of the weather right away, reducing anxiety in a strange situation. The bodies also anchor the tent, making it easier to put up in high winds.

127

Fig. 6.11: Fog and reduced visibility on the Haute Route. You could still ski but with caution. Vivesphoto.

3. All skis should be stuck straight up in the snow for tent anchors so they aren't buried in the fresh snow.

4. Stake down the tent and double-check loose guy lines. Check to see that all gear is either in the tent or tied down outside.

Conclusion

For centuries, the old mountain guide has awakened early in the morning and walked out to see the sky and feel the air. What was he looking for? What is going on in his mind? Can he know how the morning snow will be? How it will change by the afternoon? By seeing how weather works in the mountains, we can learn how to work with it. By missing so-called bad weather, we are missing the drama and intensity of the mountains. The very stuff we ski on is caused by this phenomenon called weather. With a good understanding of weather we can learn how our clothing, food, and ski equipment can help us make the best use of both good and bad conditions.

Navigation 7

Ski Randonnée!

The ability to navigate is probably the most important skill in the backcountry. In this chapter, you will learn how to use a compass and altimeter and learn to design ski routes that make the best of terrain, weather, and avalanche safety. Navigation takes into account many factors, including ski ability, physical condition, and terrain difficulty. It is not just map and compass work. While global positioning satellites (GPS) and cellular telephones are helpful, you still need to develop a three dimensional view of the terrain in your mind. To do this you need to know how to read a map and develop a sense of direction.

Getting Information About Your Route

A guidebook should always be accompanied by a map of the travel area and its surroundings. The best scale of map to use is the 7.5 – minute USGS (United States Geological Survey) map because it has more detail and is easier to read. But rather than buying paper maps, the trend is moving towards using computer software such as TOPO™ to print up custom 7.5 minute maps. 15 minute maps such as the Trail Illustrated™ series are more readily available commercially, and are often waterproof and tearproof (National Geographic Maps).

Maps and Developing 3 – D Vision

You need to develop an internal 3 – dimensional map of the area you are going into. Exhaust all sources of information about the area. Hike the area in the summer. Get postcards of the peaks. Read mountan bike, hiking, and ski guides to the area. Read all the guidebooks. Photocopy route information from the guide book to save weight. Ask the local outdoor shop personnel if they find the guidebook accurate and usable. Talk to people who have been to the area you are going to. Get all the topographical and forest service maps of the area.

Types of Maps

USGS topographic (topo) maps were originally commissioned by the United

Cover 7.1:   No we're not skiing Everest – at least not this week anyway. The classic Everest topographical map produced by the National Geographical Society using aerotriangulation using vertical photography from a West German metric camera aboard the U.S. Space Craft Columbia, December, 1983.

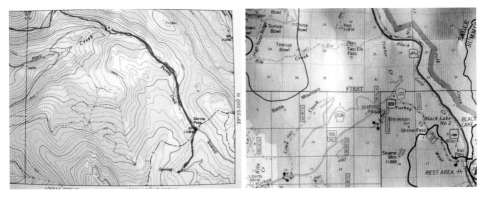

Fig. 7.2-7.3: You wouldn't know that the Shrine Mountain Inn (Vail Pass, Colorado) was on this topographical map – unless you had a forest service map of the same area. Also notice how Turkey Creek is marked as a GPS route with waypoints 6 and 7. The USFS map also shows access roads towards the backside of Vail Ski Area. GPS waypoint 6 coincides on both maps.

States Congress as a means of promoting commerce, transportation, and the exploration of natural resources. These maps are very precise, with over 90 percent of the features being correctly plotted to within 100 feet (30 meters) of the exact location. You can order topographical (topo) maps from outdoor stores. The maps are drawn from plane and satellite photographic data. They usually come in two different scales or levels of detail: 7.5 minute maps have the greatest detail since contour lines are 40 feet apart and 1 inch equals 24,000 feet. 15 minute maps

Fig. 7.4.-7.5: You can't depend on ski area maps for accuracy. See that the brochure from a ski area (Keystone Ski Area in this case) is not an accurate depiction of reality. Even the restaurant is not clearly marked. Notice on the map that the goal wasn't to climb Keystone Peak, but to reach the Gondola ridge at GPS waypoints 10 and 11. Notice that the route followed the treeline across the large but low angled open bowl below my note "Yes".

Ski Randonnée!

are coarser, with 80 foot intervals and 1 inch equals 48,000 ft. The popular Trails Illustrated Maps are slightly coarser, still being 15 min. plus maps, and 1 inch equals 66,66,667 ft. European skiers, typically rely on 15 – minute maps, and that trend is spreading in the states as well. You cannot mix two maps of different scales – it doesn't work.

Why Topographical Maps?

They're useful because they show terrain relief and altitude by using contour lines. And because they are drawn to within engineering tolerances, they are excellent for determining slope angle when one uses a slope measuring devices such as the Topo – Graf (Lifelink, Jackson Hole, Wyoming). In photo 8.8 you can see that it has two scales which correspond to two different types of map.

Why Forest Service Maps?

If you are going into an area that has no guide book, also look into gettting Forest Service or National Park maps – whether domestic or foreign. These are useful because they show backcountry logging or industrial roads and snowmobile routes, which make for natural ski routes. These maps are updated more often than topographical maps, but they don't have contour lines. They still can help to give you the big picture of a given area. Map sources are listed in the appendix.

Computerized Map Software

As mentioned in the introduction, map software such as TOPO often sell topographical maps by the state. These are fantastic maps that you can interact with. You can plot your ski tour course along with GPS waypoints. It's like drawing a route blue print. These waypoints can then be entered into your field GPS device and a route plotted as GOTO entries. GPS devises with GOTO functions then guide you with an arrow to those waypoints on your route. These two technologies work great together and take the guess work out of route navigation – once you master them! Some can even calculate slope angle on your route automatically! Rescue groups and ski groups like these computerized maps because they can print up several copies of the same map in case of a rescue. The only problem with these smaller maps is that you may ski off the map into an unknown area. Maps of your ski route and the surrounding area should always be taken.

GPS Navigation Systems

Global positioning satellite (GPS) receivers use the signals of 27 satellites to provide the coordinates of your location as a measure of latitude and longitude, which is the most widely used coordinate system. GPS receivers are so popular that many map makers include GPS readings for hut and landmark locations right on the map. The United States military once allowed only a degraded satellite signal for civilian use due to national security reasons. This policy of Selective Availability (S/A) was unpopular with many who felt that it was necessary only during wartime, and it has since been done away with. This allows for a very precise signal to within a few feet of your actual position. At least four satellites are needed for GPS to work. For best results, you should have as few skyward obstructions as possible. When skiing above tree line there is no problem but below tree line, a dense forest or being in a narrow ravine could limit reception.

Fig. 7.6: There are many GPS devices on the market. The key element is that they have topographical maps of your area preloaded in them or they allow for loading of the maps from your computer.

Ski Randonnée!

Going to the edge of a frozen lake or river would be ideal. An understanding of latitude and longitude is a must when using GPS. Most maps have longitude and latitude markings, since you will need to superimpose your GPS reading onto your map. You will have to do this unless you printed off maps with your GPS waypoints already printed on the map – this is the only way to go (see figure 7.6). And most importantly – don't forget extra batteries! Set your GPS to turn off automatically after one minute of no use (a feature commonly offered on most GPS devices).

Reading Your Map

A map is no good unless you know how to read it. Topographical maps hold a lot of information. The more you study your maps before the trip, the easier it will be to navigate once you are in the field. The more you memorize the route, the more comfortable you will be. Besides, it's always fun to take out your maps before a trip to see where you are going!

Mileage Scale

Mechanical mileage counters that have adjustable calibration for different scales of maps make it easier to count mileage. Or you can use string by simply cutting a piece that is the exact length of one mile (1.6 kilometers) on the map. Be careful not to measure the whole scale! Start in the middle, at zero (see figure 7.7). String bends and can follow your route more easily than a ruler. Both methods are helpful but will give you an underestimate, because you can't take into account every move you will make that will add mileage.

Map Date

The older the map, the greater the chance that the current terrain differs from it. Look for a blue notice stating: "Photo – Revised 1984" (or other date); this means that the map area was photographed by plane and the map was updated. 1984 – that was over 20 years ago. Check out a forest service map for sure, since they are revised every few years.

Describing Location

Describing location precisely is a valuable skill. Using common names such as "Herman Lake" or "Dix Hut" won't always be helpful – you may need to describe location to someone with absolutely no familiar-

134

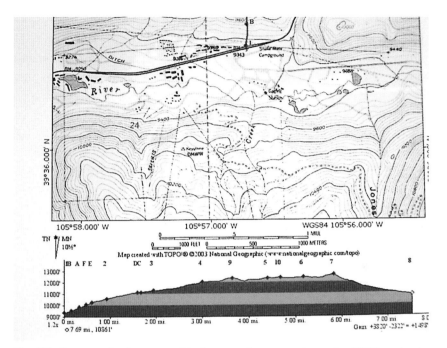

Fig. 7.7: Computerized topographical map software such as the TOPO series by National Geographic Maps allow us to merge our home computer and our "onboard" GPS. The bottom blue scale shows distance, slope angle, and our GPS waypoints along the top of the scale. Thus, we build a virtual route we can follow in the field.

ity with the area; there may be more than one Herman Lake on the same map. Providing precise location information to a rescue party can save time and confusion (in case there are two Herman Lakes). This is where a GPS device comes in. Two major reference grids are in common use: latitude – longitude coordinates and UTM coordinates. In our discussion latitude – longitude will be stressed because UTM was developed for military use and is more confusing than anything if you are not familiar with it.

Understanding Latitude and Longitude

Like a circle, the earth can be broken into 360 degrees. Each degree has 60 minutes, and each minute has 60 seconds, just like a clock. (You just need to know that there are seconds, but you won't really use them for measurements.). As mentioned, there are 15 minute and 7.5 minute maps. A 15 minute map is a bigger piece of the earth pie than a 7.5 minute map.

Your position is described as the point at which latitude and longitude coordinates intersect with each other. Every map is bordered on its top and bottom by longitude markings and on each vertical edge by latitude markings. Zero longitude is at Greenwich, England. Zero latitude is at the equator. You can remember the difference between latitude and longitude by remembering this saying: "Latitude becomes Lat, which is Fat, and so is the Earth."

Latitude and longitude coordinates are printed on each corner of your map. In the simulated map in figure 7.8 you can see the markings: 106.00 to 105.52.30 (degrees, minutes, seconds) are the longitude or vertical lines on your map, and 39.37.30 and 39.45.00 are the latitude or horizontal lines. Notice the difference in these markings is 7.5 minutes – the size of this map. You can always tell latitude markings, because they are the same at opposite top or bottom corners of the map.

Find your position with natural landmarks around you. Now find them on the map. Using the latitude and longitude coordinates on the map, draw perpendicular lines that intersect at your location. Notice latitude and lon-

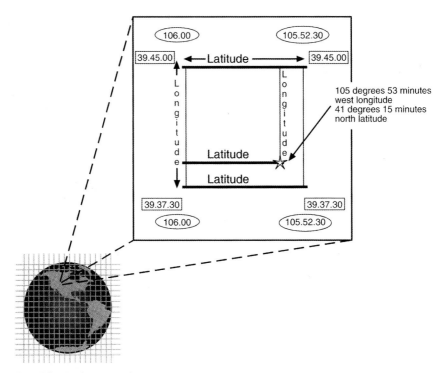

Fig. 7.8: Finding your location with latitude and longitude. Longitude coordinates are circled, and latitude coordinates are boxed (map not drawn to scale).

gitude figures on the map's edges. In this case, you would say, "We're at 105 degrees 53 minutes west longitude (since you are west of Greenwich, England) and 41 degrees 15 minutes north latitude (since you are north of the equator)." Seconds are not normally used in describing location.

Matching Map to Terrain

One of the hardest skills to learn is matching map features to the actual terrain you are looking at. It is an important skill because all your route finding relies on it. See how the map in figure 7.12 goes with the terrain in figure 7.11. This is a good study . See the close contour lines in the map and how it relates to the steep section to the left of center in the photo.
It takes time to learn and develop an eye for it.

Map Color

Green map shading means that it's covered with trees, brush, or meadows. Trees can protect you from high winds during the winter and protect you from the sun during the spring, providing you with better conditions. The map alone can't tell you what the vegetation is like. It could also mean fallen timber or underbrush – always look for existing hiking trails for alternate routes. Green usually means protection from avalanches, whereas white depicts areas without trees or vegetation, where there may be an increased potential for avalanches. For safe skiing, place your ski route "in the green" as much as possible. Old avalanche chutes are more obvious below tree lines than they are above tree lines, where steep funnel shapes depict chutes and couloirs. Reroute around these areas during high avalanche hazard.

Avalanche Hazard: Contour Lines and Slope Angle

Topo maps are covered with contour lines showing elevation. On a 7.5 minute map the elevation difference between lines is 40 feet (12 meters), and 15 minute maps show contours with 80 foot (24 meter) intervals. The steeper the slope, the closer the lines. The Topo Graf Scale (Life -Link, Inc.) can be used to accurately measure slope angles right on the map before you even leave the house! Check out your route for possible avalanche danger zones. See if you can reroute around them. It is safer to travel on low-angle slopes (lines farther apart) since most avalanches occur on slopes between 30 and 45 degrees. From a fatigue standpoint, as the saying goes, always follow the path of least resistance!

Mountain Features as They Relate to Skiing

PASS (1)

Passes are low points in a valley wall that allow skiers to hook up one valley to the next. Always double check the pass location on your map – it is easy to confuse low points on a ridge with passes.

BOWL (2)

A rounded headwall of a glacial valley where glacial action has molded the mountain into a concave area. They are great for skiing but prone to avalanches. Cirques (smaller bowls) may have higher walls (headwalls) that are often too steep to climb.

POINT (3)

The end of a ridge or a stand-alone pinnacle. Often a mistake will bring you to this impasse. Points can be good viewpoints. Often navigated on foot.

RIDGE (4)

An often skiable broad or narrow rampart usually connecting one or more points. "Knife edges" are much narrower, unskiable ridges.

ARETE (5)

Bare rock technical climbing routes that may provide access to skiing routes alongside them. Similar to ridges, aretes run vertically rather than horizontally and are like ribs of the mountain itself. Aretes are typically avoided by skiers.

CHUTE (6)

Wider and shorter than a couloir, comes off a ridge. They might not follow the fall line, or they might split into even narrower branches. Chutes are prone to rockfall, and are safest to climb during early morning hours.

COULOIR (7)

Meaning "hallway" in French, couloirs are natural access routes to summits and are usually wide enough to ski and climb. Rockfall is a constant problem, so travel them in the early morning hours.

SUMMIT (8)

This true peak top may be preceded by many false summits. Pointed summits are difficult places in which to put skis on, especially in high winds.

COL (9)

Also called a saddle, this is a low point between two peaks. Check your map before using a col as a pass - the terrain may be too steep to ski on the other side.

FACE (10)

A broad, open area running vertically that often originates at a summit or ridge. Faces provide excellent skiing during stable snow conditions.

Fig. 7.9: Common mountain features and how they relate to skiing.

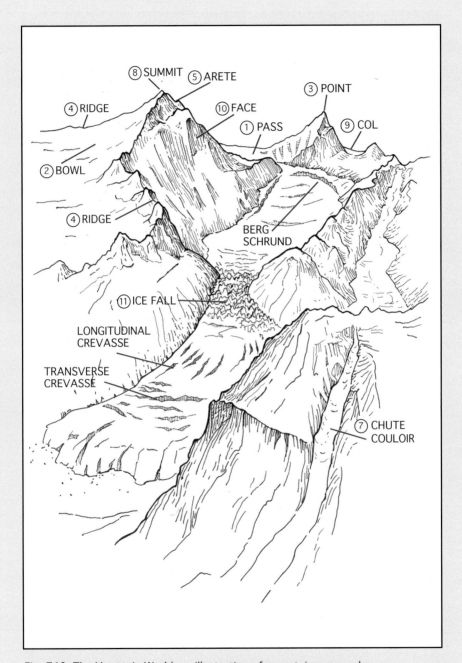

Fig. 7.10: The Mountain World: an illustration of mountain geography.

Ski Randonnée!

Fig. 7.11-7.12 Does the map match the photo? Notice that this is a photo of the area between waypoints 10 and 7. Day 4 Colorado Haute Route between Keystone and Loveland Ski Area. Vivesphoto.

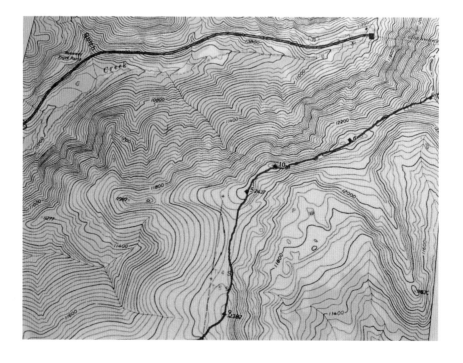

CARING FOR YOUR MAPS

Fold your maps into thirds lengthwise, and then into thirds again with the map side facing out. Put them into a large freezer bag or map case so you can read the map without taking it out of the bag. The less you handle maps with wet hands, the longer they will last. The less you write on a map the better (unless they are computer generated of course). Use a fine lead pencil and be as neat as possible so details aren't covered. Erasures weaken map paper, causing tears. If you have several maps of the same route, number and name the each map on its back with a pencil for fast field reference. Don't use a black marker pen as it will bleed through the map, making it difficult to read. A yellow highlighter can be used if needed.

Navigating With a Compass

How many of us get lost trying to find a street address? The same thing can happen in the backcountry, but with more serious consequences. Don't forget that fatigue and altitude can play tricks even on those who rarely get lost. Carrying maps and a compass can help you find your location and stay on course.

BUYING A GOOD COMPASS

A compass is an important piece of navigational equipment. A good compass will have the following features:

- Lanyard (1) – A compass must be attached to something to avoid loss. Wear the compass around your neck or tied to a pocket or pack zipper pull.

- Straightedge (2) – A straightedge is important for drawing triangulation vectors, bearing lines, and magnetic north lines.

- Sight (3) – A sight increases the accuracy of measuring. With the mirror, you can read the exact bearings of a landmark.

- Liquid – filled (4) – A liquid-filled (usually with oil) dial compartment dampens pointer movement and reduces the time needed for the pointer to find a bearing.

- Enclinometer (5) – The back pointer is used to measure slope angle and avalanche potential.

- Adjustable magnetic declination (6) – This built-in split movable ring lets you preadjust magnetic declination to save you from having to do the measurements in your head. This can make the difference between finding a hut and not finding it at the end of the day.

- Aiming mirror (7) – This mirror allows the compass reading to be read off the dial as you sight the compass at the target. It can also be used as a signaling mirror in an emergency.

Magnetic Declination

Magnetic declination refers to the magnetic pull the earth exerts on metals (including the metal of your compass needle). For precise readings, keep the compass away from radios, avalanche beacons, and wristwatches that have magnetic fields. Each area of the world is affected differently by this force. It will be slightly greater if you are on the west coast of North America than if you are on the east coast. You can navigate using magnetic bearings or "true" bearings, as long as you use one method or the other consistently.

At the bottom of your map you will see an angle drawn with a star on the vertical axis showing true north, and an angled line showing magnetic north. The declination is the difference between the magnetic pull of the magnetic North Pole and true north bearing (vertical edge of the map, i.e. grid north, see figure 7.11). Notice the date. Remember that the declination changes by approximately 1.60 minutes west each year. For example, if it's 2006, and your map is dated 1995, you need to adjust for 10 years. Look at that angle diagram at the map bottom with a magnetic north date that says 12 deg. E. Calculate: 2006 -1995 = 11 years x 1.60 minutes = 17.7 deg. 17.7 deg minus 12 deg gives you 5.7 degrees W. The actual value from the National Geophysical Data Center Web site is 6.35 deg. W. Internet sources or map retailers can usually tell you the declination in other parts of the world. Is 1 degree a big deal? While you would rarely navigate by instruments alone, repeated errors of 1 degree over 1 mile (1.6 kilometers) could throw your course off 984 feet (3 football fields!). This could be a big problem in a heavy forest or foggy weather near cliffy areas. For updated specific declinations for US locations, look up this Web site: http://www. ngdc.noaa.gov/seg/geomag/jsp/struts/calc declination.

For the compass without adjustable declination, you'll need to adjust the map. Notice the magnetic declination symbol at the bottom of the map. The vertical line with the star points to true north and is parallel to the side of the map. The magnetic declination (MN) line goes off at an angle (you will have to update this angle as well). GN pertains to UTM grid north, which is not used in our calculations. Simply draw a continuation of

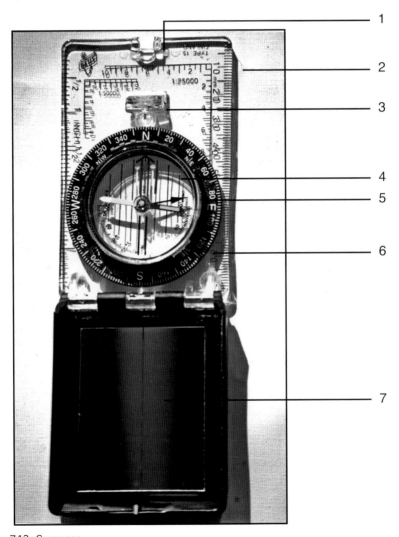

Fig. 7.13: Compass

Ski Randonnée!

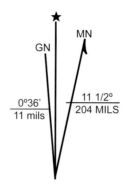

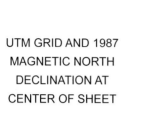

UTM GRID AND 1987
MAGNETIC NORTH
DECLINATION AT
CENTER OF SHEET

Fig. 7.14: The map's declination symbol should be compared to the date of the map's most recent revision.

this line right across the map. Now draw parallel lines to this line. Point to north on your compass – this is actually magnetic north. Align the lines on your map to the north you have found. Now your map is oriented to true north, indirectly but precisely.

Orienting Map to Terrain

You have adjusted your declination, now be sure to line up the N with the sighting mark on the compass frame. This makes your compass frame straightedge parallel to north – a very important detail! Now place your compass frame exactly on the vertical edge of the map with the N pointing to the top of the map. Lay out your map on your backpack and move compass and map together so both point to true north. Cross-check important landmarks on the map against the same landmarks in front of you. Don't be surprised if they don't look the same; you'll need practice to develop an eye for matching map to terrain.

Using Landmarks for Navigation

Once you have your map and compass oriented to true north, you can read a bearing to your first landmark, whether it's a peak or a valley. A bearing is a numerical degree description of direction. Saying "75 degrees" is more precise than saying "easterly." Keeping the red needle on the N, turn the compass frame until the gun sight is aiming at your next landmark. In figure 7.13, the first landmark is at 75 degrees, the second one is at 120 deg. Every time you recheck your course, you must correctly orient your map and compass to true north before anything, or you will get lost. Recheck

144

your bearing more often if the terrain is unusually rough, or if the weather is closing off your view of the landmark. Even if the landmark disappears, you can follow your original compass bearings, keeping in mind obstacles en route.

Finding Yourself

Getting lost is not the end of the world, but it can be disconcerting. You can find yourself more easily if you have good visibility and some landmarks such as peak tops. In heavily forested areas such as the eastern United States and Canada, a GPS receiver can be helpful. In any case, getting to higher ground or to an open area will help you see more landmarks and receive satellite signals.

Find Yourself With Reverse Bearings

Remember the reverse bearing of the direction you are heading in case you need to backtrack and find that your ski tracks are buried. Let us say you are traveling at 75 degrees northeast. Traveling up a valley would make

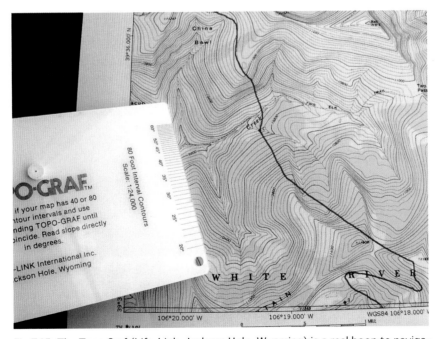

Fig.7.15: The Topo Graf (Life-Link, Jackson Hole, Wyoming) is a real boon to navigation for backcountry skiers. It can easily and accurately measure slope angles which are then related to avalanche hazard.

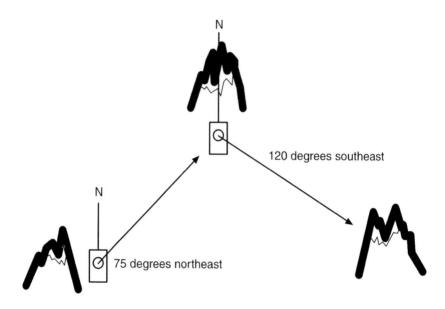

Fig. 7.16: Multiple landmarks can be linked together with compass bearings.

reversing direction easy. But what about a large, featureless plain? The reverse degree (in this case 255 degrees) would help you return to your starting point.

Find Yourself With Triangulation

Triangulation can be used to locate yourself if you have good visibility and distinct landmarks. Always start by orienting your map and compass to true north. Find two landmark peaks (this can work with two lakes or passes also). The two landmarks should form close to a 90 degree angle with each other, with you as the apex of the angle. With your compass oriented to true north, read the reverse bearing from landmark A (see figure 7.17). On the map, draw a long, straight line down the middle of the compass housing from landmark A across the map. With your compass still oriented to true north, take a bearing using the compass sight off landmark B. Using the reverse bearing from landmark B, draw a line down the middle of the compass housing from landmark B across the map (see illustration). You are located where the two lines cross. Using landmarks at 45 - 90 angles

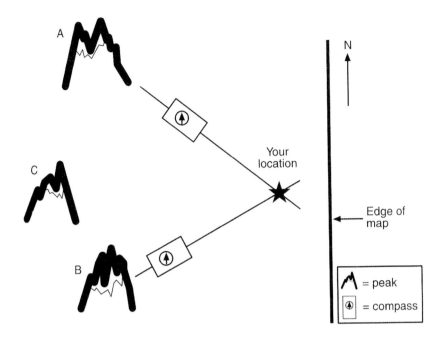

Fig. 7.17: Use triangulation to determine your location.

work better; (landmarks A and B) will give better precision than two that are closer together, such as B and C.

Find Yourself With Zero Horizon

There are two ways to travel in a straight line during very poor visibility. With the first method, you can leapfrog skiers. Have one skier go out 50 yards (46 meters) or as far as visibility permits. Move the skier until he lines up with your desired compass setting. Ski to that skier and repeat. With the second method, you can do the same thing sighting off trees. If you can't see at all and conditions are worsening, stop and make camp.

Find Yourself With an Altimeter: Contour Navigation

In addition to helping you evaluate weather conditions (see chapter 6), altimeters are the ultimate navigation tool during bad weather because they can measure your altitude. Since each contour line represents a different altitude, when you know your altitude you can find yourself on the

Fig. 7.18: Old ski tracks can give clues to the proper return route, but should be followed suspiciously. Vivesphoto.

corresponding contour line on the map. Viewing local terrain features will further verify your position. With that information, you can find your location on a contour line on your map, which is often enough to establish your location. It is a good exercise to circle the altitudes closest to your route to see how the route fluctuates in altitude. By studying your maps, you may find ways to minimize the total number of vertical feet needed for climbing and maximize your downhill skiing. Longer and faster days can occur when there are more downhills en route.

The altimeter and a compass can be used very effectively together. First, find your altitude and corresponding contour line. Next, use your compass to take a bearing off a known landmark (refer back to the triangulation section for help). Where this bearing crosses your contour line marks your position. Finally, an altimeter reading can be used to verify a location previously <u>found</u> by triangulation.

Designing the Ski Route

Plotting out a ski route takes into account many factors that are often forgotten by novices and experts alike. Matching the skills and physical abilities of several people to a particular ski trip will increase speed and safety and make it more enjoyable.

Travel Speed

The time needed to break trail in powder is surprising – 1 mile per hour in the backcountry is typical for a group of three to four because of the interaction of many factors, including: difficulty of route, physical condition and fatigue, equipment condition, weather, snow conditions, avalanche terrain avoidance, falling, navigation problems, food and bathroom stops, climbing time, and the distance to cover. You can never go wrong by having everyone start one hour earlier than planned. An alpine start before daybreak can really pay dividends when you expect a tough day ahead.

Experience, skill, and strength will pay big dividends – even a .5 mph increase makes a big difference. That's 6 hours for 9 miles (14 kilometers) instead of 9 hours! A 10 mile (16 kilometer) day on either telemark or AT equipment on variable terrain is very good. You can add an additional hour for each 1,000 feet (304 meters) of climbing and cut 50 percent off the time for downhill sections. For instance, a 3 mile (5 kilometer) uphill may take 3 hours. But going back down will take 1.5 hours (depending on the weather), a 50 percent reduction in time. Naismith's formula allows 1 hour for each 3 miles traveled and 1 additional hour for every 2,000 feet (609 meters) climbed; the Alpine estimate allows 1 hour for every 800 feet (244 meters) climbed. Both estimates apply best to summer hiking rather than winter ski touring.

Route Difficulty: Subjective Dangers

You're trying to get from point A to point B. One alternative is 1.5 miles (2 kilometers) shorter than your second choice. The first choice is steeper going up and down. The second is flatter but longer. Consider this – are you in shape? Is everyone in your group in shape enough to do all the climbing? How about falls? Consider the time it will take to get up from a fall for one person. Multiply that by the number of people with you. You will save a lot of time by taking the longer route that everyone can do without falling. The shorter route is not always the fastest way. Pick a ski tour where

Fig. 7.19: Beware of signs giving you travel time, since there might be a different story in bad winter weather. Euro sign. Vivesphoto.

in shape? Is everyone in your group in shape enough to do all the climbing? How about falls? Consider the time it takes to recover from falls for one person and multiply that by the number of people with you. Is there a chance of injury by falling, cold or fatigue? These are Subjective Dangers that can be avoided by going the longer boring way. Pick the route where everyone's equipment is equal to the task. Are everyone's climbing skins working propertly. Fix it before you start. Redistribute pack weight so no one is overburdened slowing the group down.

Natural Ski Routes: Objective Dangers

Pick a route that is easily plotted and followed. Use marked hiking, ski hut, and snowmobile trails. Summer trails may be marked with trailblazes (see figure 7.16). Always look behind you as you go because the blaze might be on the other side of the tree. Above the tree line, look for cairns (rock piles) that mark summer hiking routes. You can travel faster when you don't have to stop every 10 minutes to check your map. Follow natural travel avenues such as valleys or main waterways. Avoid getting too close to dropoffs or dead-end canyons that could be encountered mistakenly during bad weather. Pick a route that affords a continuous flow of skiing unchallenged by Objective Dangers, such as large creek crossings and avalanche hazards. The more time you spend figuring out your route, the less time you have to ski.

Escape Potential

A part of your self-rescue plan should be to look for ways of getting off your route if problems arise. It could be something serious such as an injury, or it could be something minor like a change of heart and a desire to end the ski tour. At what point will it be faster to finish the route instead of backtracking? How far is the nearest road? How far is the nearest town or ski area? You should know all aspects of the route!

Games Ski Tourers Play

Skiers play games with terrain to design ski tours. We can use natural terrain characteristics to make our tour easier to ski and navigate. Each of the following ski route designs has different features, such as different amounts of climbing and downhill skiing or the use of other transportation modes (cars or ski lifts, for example). In addition, some ski routes are more difficult to travel during bad weather than others, and some routes will be more enjoyable at different times in the ski season than others. Whatever the design, the idea is to have fun and adventure!

Fig. 7.20: Skiers on the John Muir Trail near Mt. Whitney, Sierra Nevadas, California. Vivesphoto.

Ski Randonnée!

- BASELINE SKIING – The most basic of ski route designs employs what is called a baseline. You can use a road or an imaginary line between two landmarks as a baseline. You can then draw a perpendicular line in the direction you want to go – for instance, you want to go east. Many summer trailheads are located on roads perpendicular to a trail. Skiing out, the compass reads 90 degrees (east), so on the return trip you will come back on the backbearing 270 degrees (west). Your ski route should also have navigational backups. In this example, a primary backup could be a stream that parallels the route. The stream runs right into the road or imaginary line, and will bring you back to the starting point with or without a compass. Stay on the same side of the stream, returning on your own ski tracks. You now have three navigational backups:

  1. The perpendicular backbearing compass bearing (270 degrees)
  2. The stream
  3. Your ski tracks

- LOOP SKIING – You can feel pretty safe about skiing out for the day or for a few hours, as long as the weather is good. A loop tour is done in much the same way, but instead of coming back on your tracks you make a big loop that ends at your baseline.

- VALLEY HOPPING – You can connect several valleys together via passes going the same direction. Valleys can provide you with relatively easy skiing and good weather, water, and camping. They are easier to ski than windy ridges. But in bad weather, valleys may hold deep snow that might not be avoidable. Trees can also provide easier navigation and shelter during poor weather.

- HIGH (HAUTE) ROUTE – High (haute) routes usually follow high altitude plains, passes, and ridges. Spring is the best time for these routes. They should be avoided during deep winter and periods of bad weather, unless skiers are experienced in bad weather navigation and avalanche avoidance. High routes are exposed to wind and cold and require that you carry appropriate storm gear and extra stove fuel for melting snow for water, since you will rarely find running water up high. High routes can be skied later in the season and offer the opportunity for more interesting technical skiing such as peak skis and chute skiing. There are very few natural obstacles such as streams, forests, or brush – it is wide-open skiing!

- PEAK SKI – For maximum vertical feet of skiable terrain, you can't beat skiing a peak. These are best done during the spring, when snow and weather conditions are moderate. Always climb up your ski route to examine the snow for rocks or ice (unless there is high avy danger). If the snow is too hard to climb on foot, it might be too difficult to ski even if you wait for it to soften up. For the hardcore skier-climber, it may not be a problem. But for the weekend skier, another descent route may be safer and more fun. You can do an Alpine traverse of the peak from one side to another. This involves precise planning, a much longer day, and an Alpine start (4 a.m.) so that you get back to the trailhead before dark.

- BASE CAMP – Skiing into one spot and making camp for several days while skiing the area around you is a good way to travel. Since you don't have to carry a heavy pack every day, you can concentrate on skiing a given area in-depth. It's fun to return during the day to have lunch or take a nap at a camp that is already set up. It's great for large groups with inexperienced people, since they can go back to camp if they are cold. Base camp skiing is especially fun during the spring.

- SNOWMOBILING – If you use snowmobiles to access the backcountry, is it still backcountry skiing? Or if you use helicopters or snowcats, is it backcountry skiing? Sure the snow is untracked but you are using mechanized access. You could say the same thing about ski lifts. The controversy is far and wide. But I say what the heck – if that's what you like to do and you aren't bothering anyone, have a great time ! Snowmobilers and skiers shouldn't be at war because they can help each other. I have often used a snowmobile track to ski into and out of otherwise difficult ski conditions. And backcountry skiers have often rescued snowmobilers in avalanches. Skiers who snowmobile should know better than to ruin prestine runs with unnecessary snowmobil-ing. You know, just treat each other with some respect. It's not that hard. It isn't the snowmobile itself that is obnoxious – it is the person driving it that needs to be considerate of people who are on skis.

- CIRCUMNAVIGATION – One of the problems with skiing around a mountain is that you are required to ski against the grain of the peak's drainages. You must ski across gulches and ravines and will undoubtedly have to traverse some possible avalanche paths. Planning should include the pos-sibility of some snow climbing and snow camping over several days.

Ski Randonnée!

- SKI LIFT – Some ski areas will allow you to use their lift and then ski out of boundaries via backcountry access gates. These out of bound areas are increasingSome resorts even have cross-country ski trails starting on the top of their mountains. You are wasting time and energy skiing up a mountain that has a lift on it. Plus, many resorts won't let you ski up against skier traffic due to safety considerations.
- CAR SHUTTLE – While not wilderness skiing per se, using a car to access terrain can be fun. Drop one car off at the end of the proposed run. Take the other car to your starting point. This is great for a day tour where you want to get as much skiing done as possible.

Towards A Ski Route Grading System

Several schemes of grading a ski route whether it be a tour or ski descent have been offered by several authors and organizations such as the Toponeige Ski Rating System by Volodia Shahshahani, a well known ski alpinist in Europe and the "D-System and D-Scale" by Louis Dawson and Andrew McLean both well reknown American ski mountaineers. Both systems have their merits. The Toponeige system has been in use in Europe for some years while the D-System is still in its birth but will soon appear in guidebooks written by Dawson. The TopoNeige System and the D-System are both presented in Appendix I. It is extremely difficult to give universal measures to any route. How does weather or fatigue affect the rating? They can only act as guides and as a means of comparing one route to another. In the future, their use will become more widespread as they become more refined, used and understood.

Conclusion

The most important navigational skill in the backcountry is the ability to match the map to the terrain around you. You need to do your homework at home before going on your ski tour. Maps contain the most accurate slope angle information, which is often overlooked during a planning session. Once in the field, bad weather can move in, but a thorough knowledge of the terrain and a trust in your instruments (compass and altimeter) will get you to your destination. GPS systems are more understandable when you have a good foundation in map navigation as a start.

Fig. 7.21: The Gervasutti Couloir first skied by Sylvain Saudan in 1968, Chamonix, France. The mother of all couloirs. Vivesphoto.

Avalanches 8

There is an argument to be made that there is an over reliance on stability testing. You can spend all day digging snow pits to measure snow stability. Once dug, novices often have a hard time knowing what they are seeing. To be exact you need to dig multiple pits, since one pit dug in the wrong place will only tell you about that location and not conditions at large. Do you want to spend all day digging or do you want to go skiing? We traveled 170 miles in winter across the Colorado Rockies (twice) without digging any pits. We just gave everything a High rating and used defensive terrain selection to route around hazardous areas.

Ski tourers, unlike resort skiers, must often venture up slopes before they go down them. This automatically puts them under a potential hazard rather than skiing down on top of it. Small avalanches also set off bigger slides. If you get into a sizeable avalanche, you will get hurt. You may not get killed, but a life changing injury like torn ligaments and broken bones can threaten your continuing the sport or being able to hold down a job. Skiers always have a choice. They can wait for more stable conditions. They can ski around a suspect slope – it's that easy. One should remember the old climber's maxim: follow the route of least resistance.

To Go or Not to Go

The ultimate question in the skier's mind is to go or not to go. It is a question that is often answered emotionally rather than objectively. Keep it simple. Answer some basic questions:

1. Is it steep enough to slide? Measure slope angle.
2. Are the snow layers bonded weakly or strongly together?

   Obtain field observations and snow pit data.
3. How far are you from help?

There must be a positive answer to all three questions or forget it.
Turn back and go ski something else.

What Is an Avalanche?

Every snow pack has a certain inherent strength, or lack thereof, due to the bonding of snow. When this snow pack is stressed and snow bonds break there, is an avalanche.

Cover 8.1: BIG FRACTURE – Gee, I'm glad I missed that one! At the fracture line, Denny Hogan Photo, Courtesy of Colorado Avalanche Information Center.

Table 8.1
FIVE-STEP AVALANCHE DANGER SCALE

Danger level / Color	Avalanche probability / Trigger size	Degree / Distribution of slides	Recommended travel precautions
LOW (green)	Natural avalanches unlikely, human-triggered slides unlikely	Generally stable snow, isolated areas of instability	Travel is generally safe, normal caution is advised.
MODERATE (yellow)	Natural avalanches unlikely, human-triggered slides possible	Unstable slabs possible on steeper terrain	Use caution in steeper terrain on certain aspects.
MODERATE to HIGH (orange)	Natural avalanches possible, human-triggered slides probable	Unstable slabs probable on steeper terrain	Be cautious on steeper terrain.
HIGH (red) ed. ward	Natural and human-triggered avalanches likely	Unstable slabs likely on a variety of aspects and slopes	Travel on avalanche terrain is not recommend- Safest travel is on wind- ridges or lower-angle slopes without steeper slopes above.
EXTREME (black)	Widespread natural or human-triggered slides certain	Extremely unstable slabs certain on most aspects and slope angles. Large, destructive avalanches possible.	Travel on avalanche terrain should be avoided. Travel should be confined to low-angle slopes that are well away from avalanche path runouts.

Courtesy of Dale Atkins, CAIC (Colorado Avalanche Information Center).

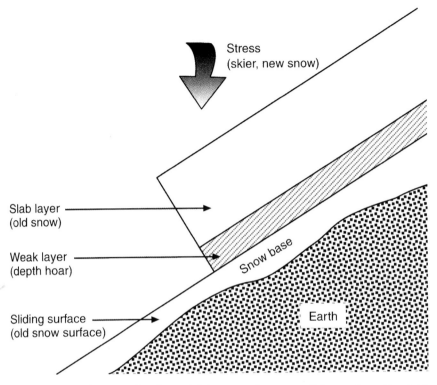

Fig. 8.1: Recipe for an avalanche: a slab layer, weak snow, a sliding surface, the right angle (over 35 deg.) and a stress (you).

Recipe for an avalanche:

1. A slab.

2. An existing weak snow layer .

3. A sliding surface

4. Inclined slope (gravity).

5. A stress. (New snow weight, sudden temp change, you).

Avalanche Education

There is an abundance of books on avalanches and avalanche rescue (see bibliography). Many mountaineering and ski clubs give avalanche workshops. A field class is often an invaluable learning situation where you can actually get out and learn from the experts. The American Avalanche Research

Ski Randonnée!

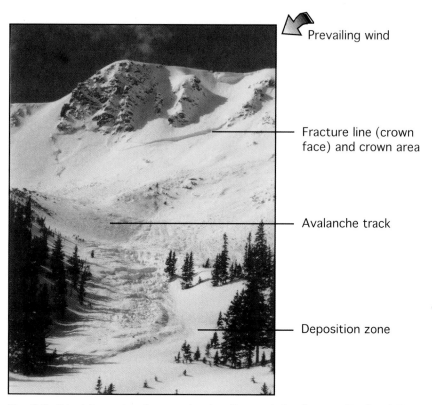

Prevailing wind

Fracture line (crown face) and crown area

Avalanche track

Deposition zone

Fig. 8.2: Principle parts of an avalanche. Secound Creek, near Berthoud Pass, Colorado.

and Education Association (www.avtraining.com) and it's associated state affiliates give excellent field classes each winter. These are often referred to as Level One, and Level Two Courses include indoor lectures and hands on field sessions.

Seasonal Factors

January and February (July and August in southern latitudes) have the greatest number of snowfalls, and thus the highest likelihood of unstable slopes. More than 75 percent of avalanches occur between December and March (June and September in southern latitudes). March through June are the best months to ski tour and ski steep slopes, because increased snow-pack depths bring strength and stability to snow slopes.

Get An Avalanche Forecast

Weather can be a stabilizing or destabilizing influence on the existing snow pack. Avalanche and weather forecasts are available for most mountainous areas of the world via telephone, radio, and now the Internet daily. Things can change overnight! Get a new forecast each morning. The avalanche danger ratings in table 8.1 are only meant to serve as general observations. <u>Low</u> hazard doesn't mean <u>no</u> hazard. A low rating should ease your mind somewhat, but it shouldn't close your eyes.

Avalanche Types

Avalanches come in several types, depending on the weather's effect on the snow. Slab Avalanches are the most dangerous type. Wind redistributes snow into slabs of snow that are strong enough to rest on, but not bond with, which creates a weak snow layer (see figure 8.1). For example, early-season snows can be followed by days of dry and cool conditions that turn the snow into a weak, sugarlike snow (Depth Hoar multi faceted (faced) snow crystals). This old, weak snow pack is later covered by heavy snows accompanied by wind – a perfect avalanche situation.

These slabs can be many inches or feet thick and are very common in open areas, mostly above tree line, whenever and wherever wind deposits snow. Slabs usually occur on leeward sides of ridges (protected sides) and can be the size of a football field with tremendous weight and destructive power (see figure 9.2). Soft Slabs can occur right after a windy storm, while Hard Slabs are older slabs that have grown larger with time, wind, and sun. Wet Slab avalanches are common in all snow climates as well as maritime climates. These can occur when there is free water in the snow pack due to warm winds or rain. Dry Slabs can occur during or right after a storm. Dry Sluffs usually occur during or right after a storm and help stabilize a slope by triggering many small slides rather than letting a big one build up. Wet Sluffs can occur anytime after a storm. The modifiers wet and dry depend on the moisture content of the snow. Point Release avalanches occur when a small amount of cohesiveless snow starts to slide, picking up more snow. A good example is when a snow-laden tree or cornice drops a load of snow on a slope, and a slide occurs that looks like an upside-down ice cream cone.

Ski Randonnée!

Factors Affecting Avalanche Formation

Several factors work together to create ripe conditions for avalanche formation. As you will see, avalanche hazard can even increase during clear weather!

Amount of New Snow

Snowstorms come in many varieties of moisture, wind, and duration. One inch (3 centimeters) per hour is enough snow to cause avalanches. Eighty percent of avalanches occur during a storm when enough snowfall is present. What is sufficient? A storm total of 4 inches (about a hand width) of fresh snow with enough wind can increase the danger dramatically. Twelve inches (30 centimeters) of new snow over 12 hours is not the same as 12 inches over four hours. The longer time gives the snow time to bond to the snow-pack surface, whereas shorter time doesn't allow for bonding.

Wind

Wind can blow more snow unto starting zones than a storm. Winds can keep the snow suspended in the air long enough to push the starting zone further down the mountain, increasing the hazard. Pay attention to wind forecasts in clear but windy conditions. Direction, speed, and duration are the most important components of wind, and should be noted on a continual basis.

Awareness of Your Environment

In addition to snowpit information, you need to become very aware of the skiing environment. Was there a storm last night? How much snow fell? While driving to your ski location, did you see natural slides on the side of the road? This may indicate wide spread instability. Do you see snow plumes off the ridges indicating high winds and therefore loading of open slopes up higher? On the ski in, how much new snow is there? Are your ski pole plants on firm snow, or are they breaking down through multiple hollow spaces interspersed with sun or wind crust? Is the snowmaking noise? When skiing over a meadow, does the whole meadow settle with a "whompf" ? All these signs are data for your avalanche computer: you.

Temperature During the Storm

It is preferable that a storm start off with warmer temperatures than with

Courtesy of Snowmass Ski Patrol, Snowmass, Colorado

Fig. 8.3: Even sparse trees can hold enough snow enough snow to start an avlanche. Hanging Valley, Snowmass Resort, Colorado.

colder temperatures. Warmer temperatures mean heavier snow that bonds better to old snow, improving the chances of bonding of new storm snow, resulting in lower avalanche hazard. A storm coming in cold and leaving warm will prevent the snow pack from supporting the weight of new, denser snow. If there is wind during the storm, the sliding potential skyrockets!

Poststorm Conditions

The colder it stays after a storm, the longer it takes for the snow pack to stabilize. Cold weather keeps the snowflake from bonding. What is better is a nice, slow warm-up over 48 hours where bonding can occur. At times, it can actually get much colder after a storm so that the earth is warmer than the air. This temperature gradient transports water vapor upwards recrystallizing snow, causing a debonding action between flakes and a growth of snow crystals into multi faceted depth hoar snow. The "flakes" are getting bigger while the bonds or "necks" between flakes shrink into a very weak snowy exoskeleton. That increases avalanche potential on snow that was safer when it fell! Watch for very cold weather (below 20 degrees Fahrenheit or –7 degrees Celsius). This happens mostly in shallow snow packs during early season. Thicker late season snowpacks have more even temperatures throughout the snow pack, making them more immune to temperature gradiants. Cloudy weather supports a equitemperature snowpack, while clear cold weather supports a temperature gradiant snowpack.

Conditions Between Storms

Look for the amount of sunshine and wind occurring between storms The more wind, the more windslab development. Deep snow layers undergo evaporation and recrystallization during periods of bright, sunny weather, and become Faceted Grains crystals that are weak and unstable (previously called Depth Hoar). If there has been a lack of snow for a few weeks, the snow pack will have a smooth, icy surface. Four to six inches (10 to 15 centimeters) of new snow will have nothing to anchor to, making for prime avalanche conditions.

Slope Ecology

The slope's appearance in the summer affects its ability to generate avalanches in the winter. While grassy slopes are obviously slick, rocky and

Fig. 8.4. Wind transporting snow from the windy windward side to the leeward side of the mountain, where it dumps it onto a slope, This becomes a potential fracture zone since the additional snow has "loaded" the slope, waiting for that last little stress (you) to fracture like it has in Fig. 8.2. Vivesphoto.

bushy slopes generate air pockets that allow for deep, weak snow layers – these cause avalanches. Ask local forest rangers or skiers about the slopes on your route.

Above and Below Tree Line

Avalanches can start above tree line or below it. Dense trees mean safety, but widely spaced trees do not (see figure 8.3). Trees can hold clues to signs of past avalanche activity and future events. Look at the forested slopes around you for signs like vertical chutes and clearings that run down a hillside, or tree damage on the uphill sides of bigger trees. Clumps of snow in the tree branches and avalanche debris on the snow are signs of very recent avalanche activity.

Aspect of Slope

Aspect is the direction the slope faces. Northern slopes face north, for instance. During deep winter, every aspect of a mountain is a possible avalanche slope. Three conditions influence avalanche potential on a given aspect: sun, wind, and temperature. Always immediately recognize the

Fig. 8.5. The classic Five Finger Chutes at Aspen, Colorado. Obvious avalanche terrain where a skier was killed during an avalanche workshop. Vivesphoto.

aspect of each slope you encounter. If you are confused (it could happen), use a compass! The use of the terms "cold" and "heat" in most avalanche texts can be confusing. These are relative terms. Remember, snow does not exist above 32 degrees Fahrenheit (0 degrees Celsius). Any descriptions of temperature refer to temperatures below 32 degrees Fahrenheit. Both heat and cold are needed for the bonding of snow. Ironically, the same sun that melts snowflakes apart melts snowflakes together when coupled with cold temperatures. This is the melt-freeze cycle. The snow pack is weaker when it's thawing (daytime) than when it's freezing (nighttime). With sunrise, the air temperature penetrates the snow pack, melting frozen bonds within the snow pack. Climbing slopes early in the day is preferable to late-day climbing, due to increasing hazard with increasing daytime temperatures. With sunset and falling air temperatures, the snow pack starts to solidify again. This occurs after the afternoon avalanche cycle, which is amplified during the spring with the warmer season.

South and West faces are not necessarily more stable than North faces during the dead of winter in the cold Alpine environment, due to the low temperatures prevalent at high altitude. South and West faces can be solid in the early morning but hazardous in the afternoon, especially after 2:00pm when the temperature has had time to get into the snowpack.

The sun hits the east faces first, so climb eastern aspects before the warm-up. Don't wait for the sun to get to them, when they will be more likely to slide. Spring time is the best time for backcountry touring, since avalanches are less likely when the snow pack is older and more stable. Above treeline, plan your route to go from east to west if at all possible. The morning sun heats the eastern snow pack some, but not a lot, so you can climb on skis or on foot faster. For the descent, go down a west-facing slope that has warmed up and softened enough for skiing, but not enough to cause slides. Start down before 10:00 A.M. so you are off the west exposures by noon. This increases safety during the whole winter (depending on temperature) and spring. During warmer spring conditions, snow can be so wet that it may pinwheel, or cartwheel down south-facing slopes – an indication of snowpack warming and increasing instability. Try to ski on less sun-exposed slopes (north-facing or other slopes in shade).

During winter there are more storms and more new powder snow, regardless of aspect. With prolonged cold temperatures, the powder is slow to bond and stabilize. This means that all aspects are prime for avalanche. It might be better to wait for more stable weather and less hazardous avalanche

Fig. 8.6: Snowflake card. Are weak snow crystals present? Are they over 1mm in size? Brian Litz photo.

conditions. In the field, sudden storms mandate that you assume high hazard and use wise route finding to reduce danger. Remember – there is always a safer route to be found.

Slope-Angle Measurement

Avalanches commonly occur on slopes measuring between 30 and 45 degrees, but each snow is different. Wet, slushy snow with low strength and cohesion can slide at a very low angle of 5 degrees. On the upper end of the scale, powder snow usually can't stick to slopes greater than 50 degrees except on the wetter slopes of Alaska. There is less slab formation at higher angles (since most of the snow sluffs off), but a rare slide can occur at angles up to 60 degrees. Old, age-hardened summer "neve" snow that is similar in consistency to styrofoam is very stable at all angles.

There are four different ways to measure a slope. To get a good general sense of the terrain is to use a topographical map. The second and more specific method is to use an inclinometer and to measure the slope in person. The remaining methods are included as very rough estimators at best. Short of using engineering tools, these will be approximate measurements that are useful and will help you build a slope-angle consciousness. These

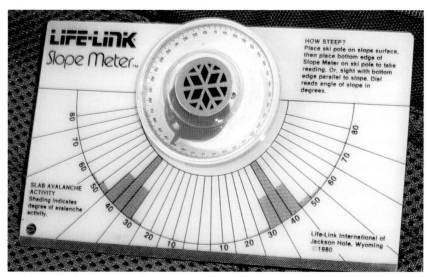

Fig. 8.7: On-site slope angle measurements can be best measured by using a Slope Inclinometer such as the Life Link Slope Meter.

methods will appear in order of accuracy.

- Topographical maps – Using a 7.5 min. topographical map with a map-angle conversion scale such as the Topo-Graf (Life-Link, Inc.) is good for general route finding, since these maps are made to such exacting standards. It's more accurate than just looking at a map with the unaided eye, and it can tell you in advance about the angle of the slope that is on your route. The map-angle conversion scale measures the distance between contour lines, converting that distance into slope angle. Generally, the closer the lines are together, the steeper the slope.

- Inclinometer – On site, angles should be measured with a professionally-made inclinometer (Slope Meter, Life-Link, Inc.). Find a nearby slope that resembles the slope you are studying. Inclinometers can be laid down on the snow on a shovel blade. Some compasses have built-in inclinometers as well.

- Fingers – Another method is to frame the slope from a distance between your thumb and forefinger held at a 90-degree angle, as if to frame the slope in a photo. This gives only a very gross estimate measurement.

- Trees – Trees always grow exactly vertically unless disturbed. Deduce slope angle from determining the angle between a small tree and the slope.

Snow Pit Testing: Common Factors in Snowpack Failure

For the non scientist, the interpreting of snow pit data can be confusing. Snowpit tests such as the Shovel Shear or Rutschblock simply can't tell you everything about the snow (ditto for the Stuffblock and Tap Test). Dependency on any one test can produce what are called "false stable" judgements where the snowpack is thought to be safe only to slide when skied. In a study of 145 fracture profiles by McCammon and Schweiizer (2002) in the Alps and North America, 9 documented false stable tests where found. This is a uncommon condition but it does illustrate the need for a wholistic view of snow stability. Besides, you won't want to be in one of those nine slides. These tests had Rutschblock scores of 6 or 7. The average fracture depth was .7 meter (27 inches), meaning that the Rutschblock test had not effectively loaded the weak layer. What is of interest is that 100% of the failed snowpacks had 4 out of 5 of the following characteristics:

1. Snow crystals associated with a weak snowpack such as multi-faceted depth hoar, surface hoar, crusts, etc. were present.
2. 65% of the weak snow crystals were over 1mm or greater.
3. 75% of the weak snow layers were 10 cm thick or less.
4. Abrupt hardness changes between layers were present.
5. In 96% of fractures the weak layer was 1 meter or less below the surface.

Snowpit Testing:

You'll need to dig a snowpit to perform the remaining three tests. The accuracy of a snowpit depends on how closely it resembles the slope to be skied. It should be on at least a 30-degree angle in an undististurbed area away from trees, rock outcrops, and other obstacles. Dig a square hole in the snow, about four feet square. How deep? It depends on how much information you need. If you have a good idea of what is happening in the snowpack, you can just dig a few feet. If you want a complete history, 6 feet should give a good recording. Square off the walls of the pit and make them as smooth and clean as possible. Probe the pit floor with your ski pole to determine whether weak layers exist under your feet. If so, dig another foot (.3 meters) deeper. The following tests should be done at three different sites for an average of readings. Digging deep snow pits takes time (hours) whereas a hasty pit that can show you surface instability can take 20 minutes.

Test for Abrupt Changes in Snow Hardness / Test for Weak Snow Layers' Depth and Thickness

Resistance to penetration measures the density and strength of the snowpack layer. The sharper the object needed for penetration, the stronger (and safer) the snow pack. Brush smooth the uphill side of the pit wall with your hat. Use your hands and fingers to penetrate the snow pack to test the hardness and strength of the layers in front of you (see table 8.2). Generally speaking, any layer that is soft enough to accept a pointed index finger easily should be considered weak. Look for hollow gaps between layers or sugar snow falling out from between layers as you dig your pit. The more hard layers, the better. More weak layers mean a weaker snow pack. A thin plastic card (a credit card works) can be run down the face of the pit. When you hit something, it might be a suncrust layer or a wind layer.

Test for Appearance and Size of Weak Snow Flake Types

Snow flake shapes in new snow should always be observed. The classic dendrite flake with six branches is seen during cold snow conditions. Light powder snow blows away in your hand and generally stresses the snowpack less than warm, heavy snow. Graupel snow crystals are snowflakes coated in ice – they are often formed in big storms where snow crystals collide with water droplets. Depth Hoar or multi faceted crystals form a weak layer more likely to slide than interlocking crystals. A snowflake card is helpful to determine new snow type and size. (See fig. 8.6).

Shovel Shear Test: Test for Depth of Weak Layers and Shear Quality

The Shovel Shear Test is not a stability test but a good method for locating weak layers that need to be studied. With a snow saw, cut out a block-shaped piece of snow at the top of your pit about a shovel-width square. Cut behind the column as well. Stick the blade of the shovel in the snow on the uphill side and pull the shovel straight toward you (see figure 8.8). After the first piece comes out, cut down again with your saw and repeat the process. The shear test should be done three times for an average of readings. Did the snowblock fall out as you stuck your shovel in? A good sign of instability.

The more effort you need to pull the snow out, the stronger the snowpack (see table 8.3). The Shear Test is best at finding multiple layers close to the surface. Another clue is the appearance of the bottom of the block that was pried out. Is the bottom of the block shear clean or is it lumpy? The cleaner the shear the higher the avalanche potential, since there was more energy released when those snow bonds were pried apart.

The Rutschblock Test: Testing for Deep Snow Stability

You did your Shovel ShearTest, now dig out your pit so it's as wide as your skis are long along the uphill wall. Dig parallel trenches parallel to the fall line going up from your pit (see figure 8.8). To isolate a block that is also as wide as your skis are long. Take the rear of your ski and slice down as far as possible behind your block as well. A lightweight metal snow saw makes this much easier, since skis are gettting so short. Be sure to cut down below the suspected layer that you located with your Shovel Shear Test. Put your skis on and carefully climb up until you are standing on the slope right above your block, but not on it yet. Now, gently step onto it. The block can fail immediately, sliding on a weak layer, or fail according to any of the levels presented in table 8.4. The more you can jump on the block, the stronger the snow. If in doubt, a skier can perform more than one Rutschblock test since it can be done quickly to get a representative testing of the snow pack, as one test site may not represent the ski slope exactly.

Testing should occur within a zone of suspected weak snow, just as the slope angles off. The top of the slope where it suddenly steepens is called the transition point, where gravity is most active in the snowpack. A strong belay stance is mandatory. If the slope fails, you will be holding not only the skier but all the snow falling on top of him! Stomp and jump on the snow, test and retest until you are convinced of its safety. If your skis don't penetrate the hard snow on a leeward slope, don't assume it's safe! It could be a hard slab waiting to release.

Find Safer Routes to Travel

It's much easier to ski around a suspected avalanche path than to try to second guess nature. Why not just ski around it and get on with the tour? The following tips will cover several terrain conditions and how to navigate around them. Backcountry skiing is, above all, the adaptation to the precincts of nature.

Table 8.2

SNOW HARDNESS TABLE

Snow texture	Penetration test	Possible snow type	Snow strength
Very soft	Fist	Powder, depth hoar	Less cohesive, weaker
Soft	Four fingers	Pack powder	
Medium	One finger	Soft slab	
Hard	Pencil	Hard slab	
Very hard	Knife	Hard slab, age-hardened snow	More cohesive, stronger

Are there abrupt hardness changes in the snowpack layers? Is that weak layer less than one meter from the surface?
©1993. Adapted with permission of the publisher from The Avalanche Handbook by David McClung and Peter Schaerer. The Mountaineers, Seattle, WA.

Skiing as a Group

In dubious conditions, skiers should never ski above, below, or to the side of other skiers. Only one person should cross a suspected avalanche path at any one time. Never take rest breaks in these areas.

Sometimes, crossing huge areas one at a time is not practical due to the time it takes. In this case, ski at least half a football field apart. Always be aware of escape routes and "islands of safety" such as large trees or rock outcrops that may protect you from a slide. When you cross a chute or slope with evidence of sliding, move quickly while using these islands for protection. Angle your path downward to use gravity to speed your passage through heavy snow. Watch out for large avalanche debris that might cause a fall.

Look for Windrippled Snow

A good sign of slope stability is the presence of snow ripples, or Sastrugi as they are called in Europe (see figure 8.11). This is a sign of ongoing snow compaction by the wind over a long period of time, and a strong snow pack is less likely to slide. However, rarer snow ripples sometimes do hide a hard windslab underneath them, which is dangerous. Usually, windripples over four inches high indicate safe (but possibly more difficult) skiing. If there is

Fig. 8.8: Doing a Shovel Shear Test. Digging a snowpit with a long handled shovel is easier, since you have more leverage and can move more snow faster. And the longer handle is great for digging your deep longitudinal trenches for the Rutschblock Test. A Hasty Pit on the left and a deep pit snow study on the right.
Carter Photographics left, Colorado Avalanche Information Center, right.

doubt, probe or ski test the slope – if it sounds hollow when you jump on it, there is probably a hard windslab underneath.

Beware of Old Ski Tracks and Established Avalanche Paths

Old ski tracks don't mean safe ski tracks. There have been many cases where skiers have skied a slope one day without avalanche activity just to get caught in a slide the next day (even on the same day)! Wind may have loaded the slope overnight. Recent avalanche activity is telling you that there is a slide cycle is taking place. Re-evaluate the snow pack each day for avalanche potential. Areas with past sliding histories should also be avoided during questionable conditions.

Use Short, Linked Turns

Smooth, short, linked turns will allow you to ski down the side of a suspected avalanche slope rather than all over it. This will disturb it less snow

Table 8.3	
SHOVEL SHEAR TEST RESULTS	
Very easy	Snow column fails during cutting or insertion of shovel
Easy	Snow column fails with very low shovel pressure
Moderate	Snow column fails under moderate pressure
Hard	Snow column fails under firm, sustained pressure

than wide turns. Wide turns will keep you traversing the danger zone too often. The less time you spend on the slope, the better; the less snow you disturb, the better.

Ski Testing: On Steeper Terrain

Before descending a questionable slope, check the slope for avalanche potential. Do this by just doing a very shallow traverse along the top of the slope, jumping on the snow as you go. If it does slide, you'll be above it instead of being trapped in it. Shooting cracks that shoot out in front of your skis are a sure sign of instability. Skiers on very steep terrain may want to use a roped ski test to determine avalanche potential on steeper terrain. Testing should occur right where the slopes dives off, the transition point, where gravity is most active on the snowpack. A strong belay stance is mandatory since if the slope fails, you will holding the skier and all the snow that is top of him. Stomp and jump on the snowpack until you are convinced of its safety. Slabs often feel and sound hollow and should be avoided.

Ski Straight Up or Climb Up on Foot

If you have to climb up a slope during low visibility and can't see the top, you can disturb less snow in hazardous conditions than if you ski climb straight up along the edge of a potential slide area. This will limit snowpack disturbance and doesn't affect the rest of the slope. You can often find a bare rocky shoulder to climb on foot that is parallel to the slope that you want to get up.

Table 8.4

RUTSCHBLOCK TEST RESULTS

Results of test	Hazard/Score*	
Block fails as you dig it or walk above it	Extreme	7
Block fails as you step onto it	Extreme	6
Block fails with sudden deep knee motion	Extreme	5
Block fails with one jump	Moderate	4
Block fails with two jumps	Moderate	3
Block fails with repeated jumping	Low	2
Block does not fail	Low	1

*See table 8.1 for description of hazards.

Courtesy of Dale Atkins, CAIC (Colorado Avalanche Information Center).

Ski Testing: Bracket Your Run in Deep Powder

A large face should be suspected of being unstable during deep-powder conditions. Even hard-snow conditions (hard slabs) are inviting, but very dangerous. Bracket skiing allows for ski testing the slope while protecting other skiers from slides (see figure 8.11). The strongest skier (S1) should ski the outer edge of the run, while other skiers (S2 and S3) stay within the area tested. Each skier should ski to a safe spot (island of safety) before the others proceed. If a slide does occur, all skiers should get as far in the trees as possible, find a tree, and hang on! Better yet, forget the wide open slope and just ski the trees if conditions warrant. Tree areas often protect powder snow from the wind which compacts the snow, making it harder to ski.

Take Ridge Routes to Access Chutes

Snowy ridges and shoulders are excellent travel routes safe from avalanches. Being alternately sun-drenched and wind-packed throughout the winter, they provide solid snow (though some may be bare dirt) that makes climbing easy. On descent, be aware of ice since your boots don't have edges-in these cases leave your skis on and side slip down. Avoid very steep snow covered ridges which are not good routes, since they are often icy and can have cliff bands. Keep clear of any cornices, as fractures can occur far back from the edge of the cornice itself.

Courtesy of Denny Hogan, CAIC, Silverton , Colorado

Fig. 8.9: The Rutschblock Test uses body weight to test deep snowpack strength. This snowpack failed. Photo courtesy of CAIC, Silverton.

Avoid Cliffs and Crevassed Areas

Traversing above cliff areas should be done with great care at all times. Small avalanches can push you off a cliff into a creek or river gorge. If at all possible, reroute around such obstacles when mapping a ski route. Always go one person at a time. If need be, set up a fixed rope so that skiers can clip into the rope during the traverse, or belay skiers one at a time. Glacial movement is usually too slow to cause a slide. On steeper terrain, the hazard is that a slide could carry you into a crevasse if you are above it.

If you are skiing off a cliff on purpose, you need to know that if the slope slides it can carry you into what?

Skiing U- and V-Shaped Valleys

When skiing inside a U-shaped valley, stay to the far side of the valley away from the corniced ridge that is overhanging the opposite wall. The leeward side (side facing away from the wind) of the valley holds the snowy deposition that could avalanche. The windward side (side facing the wind) can be quite wind-scoured and relatively safe. Look for sastrugi (wind ripples) on windward faces signifying wind-packed snow.

Stay out of V-shaped valleys, canyons, and couloirs during questionable conditions on big mountains. They are natural skier eaters. If unavoidable, stay as high up as possible on the windward wall of the valley, using natural protection as you go.

An Avalanche Self Rescue Plan

The biggest problem in avalanche rescue is the speed of efforts relative to the short survival time of avalanche burial. A two or three person team must stay together and find that buried victim. Do not go for a rescue – there is no time! Fast extrication and the maintenance of an air pocket around the face have both been shown to increase survival, as most deaths occur mainly due to asphyxiation(excess carbon dioxide). Skiers must be able to self-rescue quickly! Practice in finding buried beacons must be mandatory for backcountry skiers.

Ask yourself three questions before heading out:

1. Do I know what to do if I or my group gets caught in an avalanche?

2. Do I have the knowledge to get the job done effectively and safely??

3. Do I have the tools to get the job done?

Avalanche Safety Equipment:

Avalanche Shovels

The choice between plastic and metal is controversial and has received attention lately. Avalanche debris is made up of very compacted snow, ice, dirt, and rock. Newer metal shovels made of 6061 aluminum are actually lighter than plastic. Any shovel can break if used carelessly. Prying rocks and digging toilets are not what they are made for. The main thing is to have a shovel! Take care of it and inspect it for stress fractures after heavy use. Get a lightweight shovel as you will be carrying it always – with little use hopefully.

Avalanche Cords

Avalanche cords are only mentioned as a historical point. Avalanche cords were once the only safety devise in use before beacons. An avalanche cord is a 100-foot (30-meter) cord that trails behind the skier. It's colored bright red for visibility and marked with arrows pointing to the wearer. Tests have shown they work only 40 percent of the time. In fact, some have been found wrapped around the necks of buried victims. Do not use these cords – buy a transceiver!

Avalanche Probe Ski Poles vs. Probe Poles

Probe poles are essential during a search for a buried skier with or without a transceiver. They can be used in finding skiers with transceivers that have a weak siginal. Or, probe a potential burial site when an article of clothing is found. Some ski poles can be married together to form a ski probe. But it is usually a real pain to take the ski pole apart and make them work. You are under enough stress in an avalanche accident. Today's avalanche probe poles are extremely light and are worth the cost.

Avalanche Transceivers (Avalanche Beacons)

A non skier friend once asked me if avalanche beacons told you when the avalanche was coming. If only it were true. Non mon ami, they do not. They are radio rescue beacons that seek each other via radio waves. Everyone starts on transmit but when one or more get buried, everyone switches to receive. An avalanche transceiver beeps loudly (analog type) or flashes and points in the case of a digital beacon when you are approaching a victim's device, and more quietly when you going away from the victim. Swiss research has shown that one avalanche transceiver can search as fast as 490 people with probe poles! Like everything else with backcountry equipment, advances in technology have turned avalanche beacons into electronic marvels.

The latest trend now is to use digital technology, allowing for more precise victim location. There are two types of beacons available using two different electronic processors: analog and digital. The big buzz now is with the newer digital beacons such as the Tracker DTS or Pieps DSP beacons that have both visual LED's (light emitting diodes) and a loud audio beeping that speeds up as you get closer to the buried victim. (see diagram). Some beacons shift from analog signals far from the victim to digital signals closer to the victim in order to save energy, speed searching, and increase the precision of the signal acquistion, and therefore increase search speed. The Tracker DTS, Pieps DSP, and Barryvox have special search modes that will accomodate multiple victims. The Tracker has won over many skiers due to its ease of use, especially for the inexperienced. While the Ortovox M2 and F1 are widely used worldwide according to a recent Couloir magazine review, the Tracker is becoming more popular among ski professionals due to it's multiple burial search system.

How far can your avalanche transceiver search? Manufacturers such as Ortovox recommend not exceeding 40 percent of maximum values. The influential German Alpine Club suggests using a worse case (problems due to weak batteries, poor transmission orientation, frequency

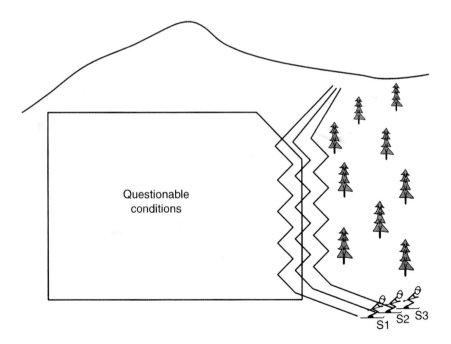

Fig. 8.12: Bracketing your run on wide open slopes provides some safety during questionable conditions. Ski the conservative line first to "test" the slope.

drift, etc.) effective range of 10 meters or a 20 meter search strip width (personal communication, Bruce Edgerly, BCA, 2006). Should people still use the old transceivers? Until you buy a new one, yes. An old transceiver is better than no transceiver. But one transceiver won't work by itself-you need two to work. Dual-frequency transceivers are no longer made. Recent research has also shown that cell phones should not be "ON" since their signal interferes with the beacon's signal making it more difficult to read.

There are several brands available (figure 8.17 shows only three). Most use AA or AAA batteries, and can last up to 300 hours in transmitting mode and 40 hours in receiving mode. The Tracker offers one hour in search mode and 200 in transmit mode. You should replace your batteries regularly with fresh batteries. Save your old ones for your headlamps. Most have three-year warranties and cost between $200 and $400. Modern digital beacons come with external speakers and/or LED readouts that show signal strength and direction of victim. External speakers allow hands to be free from keeping an earplug in. And in noisy, high winds, the LED really comes into use. Remember one thing: wearing an avalanche transceiver doesn't mean you can ski avalanche slopes without getting hurt. It simply means that your body will be found.

Fig. 8.13: This avalanche occurred the day before we crossed. It's a good thing we were late! Above Aspen, Colorado on the Colorado Super Tour. Vivesphoto.

Test All Beacons Before Skiing

Everyone in a large ski party should be equipped with a beacon of the same frequency. In larger groups, you can make one person a "tester" with their beacon on transmit while everyone else remains on "receive". Each person walks/skis past the tester. A loud audio noise from each beacon will occur, confirming proper function.

Practice is Important

Practice has been shown to be the critical factor in search success. This is often overlooked and not thought to be needed. You need to develop an "eye" and "ear" for the signals (visual and audio) coming from your transceiver – this can save a life! It can be more difficult in high wind and steady snow fall to concentrate on your beacon, especially during the near panic of a true avalanche disaster.

Optimum Working Conditions

For optimum working conditions, follow these rules:
1. The transmitter must be attached to the victim's body and not the pack, which might be thrown off during a slide.
2. The beacon should ALWAYS BE WORN INSIDE clothing to protect the batteries for maximum battery life in case of burial. I often see them worn outside! They are life saving devices! They are not for playing music! It should not be worn over the sternum, where it may cause injury during a crash.
3. Everyone's transmitter must be turned on.
4. The batteries of all transceivers must be working. Always use fresh batteries.
5. The search must be done with volume controls turned up and not down for maximum reception. Digital beacons have automatic volume controls and will not need to be adjusted.
6. All searchers must have their beacons turned on and switched to "receive."

Ski Randonnée!

Avalanche Safety:

Before Crossing a Suspected Avalanche Path

These steps should be followed before skiing onto a slope of doubtful stability:

1. Plan your route for minimum exposure to danger by using natural protection.

2. Plan an escape route – spot a tree or a large rock you can grab onto if an avalanche starts. Keep your eye on these islands of safety.

3. Use the buddy system. Make sure your friend is watching your crossing so he can watch you if the slope slides.

4. Remove ski pole runaway straps so you can easily discard the poles if you are caught in a slide. Leave packs on.

5. Button up clothing. Put your hat on.

6. Check again to be sure every beacon is on "transmit!"

7. Proceed without hesitation, one skier at a time, allowing only one skier to be in the danger zone at any given time. Ski more slowly if it means not falling. Falls do set off slides!

If You Are Caught in an Avalanche

1. Yell loudly and then close your mouth to keep snow out.

2. Follow your escape route if possible.

3. If you are knocked down, dump your equipment. Get rid of poles and skis! Your pack protects your spine and holds your shovel and probe to be needed shortly.

4. Fight for your life! Use swimming motions to stay on top of the slide or go to the closest side of the slide.

5. Cover your face with your hands if burial is imminent so you can push the snow away from your face quickly before things stop moving to make an air pocket to breathe in. Your arms are no good to you if pinned to your sides.

6. Keep snow pocket walls scraped and free of ice. Your hot breath will cause the pocket to glaze over and the ice will seal it airtight.

Fig. 8.14: Avalanche beacons increase the chances of a body being found (the condition of body is not guarenteed). They are not Ipods and should be carried within the clothing and not exposed to the elements. Vivesphoto.

7. Save your breath! Snow is a good transmitter of sound but outside noise may mask your yells.

8. Calm down and breathe slowly to use less oxygen.

If Other Skiers Are Caught in an Avalanche

1. Watch where the victim is going. Mark the last seen spot. Have your partner look above for further slide activity.

2. Turn transceiver to "receive." Do a quick search.

3. Search below the place you last saw the skier. Look for discarded equipment. Probe those areas.

4. Let less-buried victims dig themselves out. Spend precious moments digging out completely buried victims. Dig victims out carefully so you don't hit their faces with the sharp blade of your shovel. Keep digging until you find the victim or until you determine that the victim is completely unreachable due to obstructions.

The First Ten Minutes

The first 10 minutes of burial are the most critical. After that time, survival potential goes down dramatically. All efforts must be made to coordinate surviving skiers into a search team, regardless of weather conditions. An avalanche will most likely carry a skier into the deposition zone where the slide comes to rest. Occasionally, it can deposit the skier in catch-alls such as road cuts, bends, or trees. The victim could also be thrown free of the avalanche flow by gravity. In rare cases, victims can escape and walk off in shock, not knowing what they are doing.

Different Search Patterns

It saves time and energy if you are able to begin the search at the starting zone or highest point where skiers were last seen. This helps to eliminate having to climb back up the slide path to search an area. There are basically three different types of search patterns that are used depending if a digital or analog rescue beacon is used. Bracketing is often done away with since a digital beacon can go straight to the victim.

1. Search Patterns : Electronic magnetic waves are best received when the antennas are parallel to each other (see Fig. 8.16). Electromagnetic waves are best received when the antennas are parallel to each other. This is why the rescue beacon should occasionally be slowly rotated in all

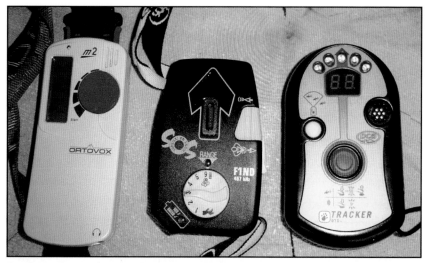

Fig. 8.15: Types of avalanche beacons for the backcountry, from left: Ortovox, SOS (Survival on Snow), and Tracker. Vivesphoto.

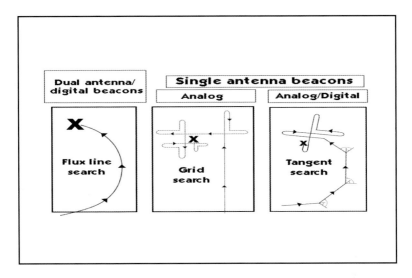

Fig. 8.16: Digital beacons are faster than analog beacons in that they can deduce distance and location much faster than analog beacons. A certain amount of circular, fine tuned, patient searching is still required. Diagram courtesy of Backcountry Access.

directions at the initiation of searching to find the strongest signal. The strongest orientation should be maintained for the rest of the search. This becomes more critical the farther you are from the victim.

2. Fine Search Pattern. Once a signal is found, the rescuer follows the strongest electromagnetic signal (flux or induction line) towards the victim. Zero in on a weak signal by increasing beacon volume (digital beacons due this automatically) to make it more sensitive. Slow your movements immediately upon picking up a signal.

3. Pinpoint Search Pattern. At the point of strongest reception, you may be feet away so take your transceiver and run it right on the snow's surface to find the precise spot of burial. Once you have a stronger signal, "bracket" your scanning but now reducing beacon volume (digital beacons do this automatically) (see figure 8.16). Wind can make listening to beacon signals very difficult. Visual LED's are a big plus under these conditions. Use a probe to examine deep below the a hot spot for a potential victim or buried clues.

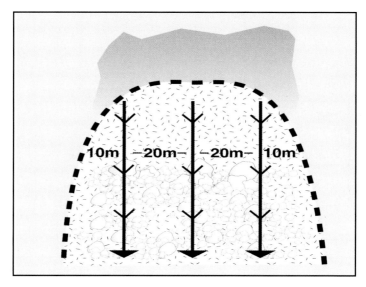

Fig. 8.17: Multiple Searchers: This diagram shows multiple searchers and distance between them. Courtesy of Backcountry Access.

Probe Search

The probe search may be your only choice when searching for victims without beacons. Searches should form a tight line and make probes every 30 inches (76 centimeters). Probing should proceed in a methodical and disciplined manner. The victim could be in any body position, from standing straight up to a fetal position. Large accident scenes will have elaborate search-and-rescue management. In the typical small ski group, everyone searches and digs.

Search for Multiple Victim with Three Circle Method

You have found the first victim but the second signal is not clear. Make a three meter radius around the primary burial site while slowly rotating the beacon. If there is still no signal, make a second circle now by taking three steps back and expanding the circle. Some digital beacons like the Tracker have a special mode (SP) that allows the beacon to pick up signals beside the closest primary signal. If the beacon is rotated slowly more than 40 deg. (instead of the searcher rotating slowly), the second victim's signal can be acquired. Once a secondary signal is picked up, always revert back to SE or search mode when you are getting closer to the second victim.

Avalanche First Aid

Turn the victim's beacon off in case other victims need to be found. Use first aid ABCs – Airway, Breathing, Circulation, Shock:

- AIRWAY – Clear the mouth and nose of snow and dirt.

- BREATHING – Check for a pulse. Begin rescue breathing even while others are digging. If the victim starts to choke on debris, you may have to do the Heimlich maneuver by getting into the snow with the victim.

- CIRCULATION – Bleeding should be stopped using direct pressure.

- SHOCK – Calling the victim's name immediately may save him from going into continued deep shock.

Keep the victim's head and neck from moving until the extent of injury is determined. Once stabilized, insulate the victim with extra clothing to protect against deepening shock and impending hypothermia and frostbite. Check for bone fractures. Lung injury from a broken bone is always a possibility. Keep legs elevated. Use CPR only if there is no pulse.

Fig. 8.18: An avalanche warning sign on top of Berthoud Pass, Colorado.

Fig.8.20: Avalanche probe line. Vivesphoto.

Expedition 9

Ski Randonnée!

The essence of backcountry skiing is the ability to be totally self-sufficient in the winter wilderness. This is where all of your skills come into play. If you can camp in the winter, you can camp anywhere. The quiet, the solitude, and the beauty are unequaled in all but a few sports. Winter camping can be some of the most fun you can have if you know what you are doing. Every year there are warmer sleeping bags, stronger tents, and more efficient stoves. But you still have to know how to use them!

Camping Gear

Good winter camping and backpacking gear will provide years of warmth and comfort during your winter excursions. In this section, we'll look at what equipment is needed and how to select it.

Backpacks

If the pack fits and carries enough, buy it! Backpacks can range in price from $200 to $300, and there are many quality brands to choose from (North Face, R.E.I., and Mountain Smith are a few). Do buy your pack and other gear close to home in case you need advice or you need to return it. Don't buy gear on the road – you could get stuck! Always look for a good name and a lifetime warranty as a start. A pack of 3,000 cubic inches is good for overnight hut or camping trips, while one of 6,000 cubic inches is better for multiday expeditions. A smaller daypack of about 2,000 cubic inches should be big enough to carry a pair of ski boots, making it usable for spring ski tours where approaches on foot may be needed. A pack that is too small requires you to hang items from it, which can grab trees and throw you off-balance. A bigger pack gives you carrying options for the future. Fit your pack so that adjustment straps are only half tight. This allows for extra adjusting room later for additional clothing, or if you gain weight!

Frameless packs are best used for skiing because they hug the body, minimize load shifting, and are less likely to snag on trees. Elaborate suspension systems allow the skier to custom-fit the backpack to the body. Side compression straps that prevent load movement are great for carrying skis. Women should investigate newer packs that offer narrower shoulder

Cover 9.1: Buddist temple in Kathmandu, Nepal taken during exercise research expedition to Everest Base Camp. Vivesphoto.

Fig. 9.2: It looks heavy but it's mostly sleeping bag. Vivesphoto.

straps with hard-soft sandwich foams that cushion while maintaining strap shape, and that disperse weight more evenly over the collarbones with greater comfort.

Packs never seem to have enough pockets for sunblock, maps, cameras, headlamps, and other assorted gear. A water bottle (weight: 2.2 pounds per quart of water) doesn't have to be carried in the top flap. For skiing, carry it within the pack to maintain a lower center of gravity. Heavy bottles packed on top increase the tendency for the pack to push the skier over. At the sides, bottles get in the way of poling movements, and they can freeze in cold weather. Newer packs with water bladders carried within are a better idea. A top flap that can be detached for use as a waist bag is great for short trips out of base camp. An exterior avalanche shovel slot keeps your shovel handy and increases interior space. Otherwise, shovel handles can

191

be carried behind side compression straps while the blade can be carried within the pack up against the back. Some sleeping bag compartments with a zipper at the bottom of the pack also act like a compression sack – a big plus for handling larger winter bags. Additionally, a thick-padded hip belt and a sternum strap – both with fast-release buckles – keep the pack firmly attached to the body during skiing. A lumbar pad on the lower back protects the back from sharp items in the pack and minimizes pack shifting.

Fitting the Pack

Many shops provide sandbags for weight so that adjustments can be made professionally. There are usually two aluminum stays or frame pieces in the pack, which can be molded to the back's contours.

Several straps are used to adjust for the ride of the pack on the back. Upper straps pull the pack higher on the back, while the lower straps shorten the arm loops, lifting the pack up off the hips. Weight on the hip joints can get uncomfortable. Alternate the weight between your hips and shoulders during the day to reduce pressure pain at these points. Large pull loops on all adjusting straps make tightening and loosening with heavy gloves or mittens easier. Before skiing down, tighten exterior compression straps to eliminate load shift. The pack should be almost too tight on your back so it feels like it's part of it. With practice, the pack can actually help your skiing by amplifying turning efforts.

Pack Weight

We would all like lighter packs. But how much weight is too much? A general rule is that a pack's weight shouldn't exceed 25 percent of body weight. For my 170 pounds, that's a comfortable 42.5 pounds. A woman weighing 110 pounds shouldn't have a pack weighing over 27.5 pounds. This is just a general rule based on years of observation, but there will be exceptions. In a group, heavier weight should be given to the fittest and strongest people because they can probably handle the weight more easily. With comfortable pack weights, people ski longer and stronger and have more fun.

People used to think that they could save weight by sawing their tooth-brushes in half. This is cute, but a toothbrush is not the problem. In the winter, you need more clothing, food, and fuel. Table 9.1 shows several weighty items of interest with some possible substitutes. When packing, match the center of gravity of the pack with that of the body. Heavy items

Top flap: camera, map, compass, trail food

Inside flap: headlamp, notebook, pen

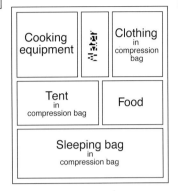

Cooking equipment

Clothing
in compression bag

Tent
in compression bag

Food

Sleeping bag
in compression bag

Figure 9.3: A properly loaded ski pack means less load shifting and easier skiing. Vivesphoto.

193

Table 9.1

CUTTING WEIGHT DURING WINTER CAMPING

Water	One quart of water weighs 2.5 lb. Take one bottle but add snow consistently to supplement your reserve.
Camera	Use a small travel camera or a throwaway camera – they take better pictures than you'd think.
Food	Use dehydrated foods made for camping. Stay away from canned foods and foods packed in glass; always transfer these and any boxed goods (with cooking information) into plastic baggies, and poke pinholes into dehydrated food bags to reduce air volume and bulk. Remember that cheese and peanut butter are luxuries.
Reading	Xerox all route descriptions instead of taking the whole book. If you need to read, get a used paperback and cut it in half to reduce bulk.
Water pump	Use purification tablets.
Tools	A small pair of pliers is lighter than a composite tool (Leatherman, etc.), and you already have a knife.
Clothing	Polypropylene underwear is lighter than wool.
Sleeping pad	Use Ensolite instead of a Thermorest.
Bulky clothing	Use compression bags.

(water, fuel bottles) can be placed in the main body, not the top flap. The sleeping bag can go on the bottom, while middle-weight items can be packed in the middle of the pack (see figure 9.3). Use several compression bags to minimize volume! By compressing bulky clothes and sleeping bags into a tighter load, you reduce outward centrifugal load shifting during skiing (which can throw you off-balance), and your pack will feel lighter.

Separate gear by category into separate waterproof nylon stuff sacks of different colors, which are easier to find in the darkness of your pack and safer from water and stove fuel leakage. Use heavyweight freezer storage bags to hold smaller items like a compass, maps, toiletries, and such. These bags are nice because you can see what's inside them, and they're reusable and recyclable. For packing out trash, use several smaller bags instead of larger garbage bags since they can be packed tighter and damage from any breaks will be isolated.

Fig. 9.4: Variety of packs to fit all sizes. Vivesphoto.

Sleds

Sleds can be good for hauling food and equipment as long you don't have to do much traversing, where you'll need someone in the rear to tether the sled so it doesn't slide downhill. It can be excellent for carrying kids and gear to a hut for the family who wants to ski together. Store-bought sleds can range in price from $150 to $400 – because of their cost, many stores rent them. Homemade sleds can be constructed using a child's toy sled, but usually the plastic is not durable enough for backcountry use.

Tents

Most modern tents are double-walled, modified dome tents with independent free-standing frames. The modern dome tent design shown in figure 9.5 was originally modeled after the aerodynamic Mongolian yurt. The shape is spacious and extremely stable in high winds. The tent fly protects the tent body from snow, wind, and flying debris. A fly should fit taut around the tent body and extend to the ground, holding in heat and keeping out wind. A flapping tent fly makes sleep impossible, which can make for a very

Fig. 9.5: North Face VE-25 dome tent. Notice how the ski bottoms face inward so the tent guy lines won't be cut by ski edges. Vivesphoto.

tiring next day. The fly should have multiple tie-ins for guy line installation. Single-wall Gore-Tex™ tents are warmer and lighter, but they're also less spacious. Both inner and outer tent fabrics should be kept uniformly taut so as not to stress any one seam. Add nylon loops to tent edge stake-down points if you want to use wider skis for anchors.

A ceiling vent is a good feature, allowing for the evaporation of moisture from snow and sweat. Additional ventilation is possible by leaving door zippers open a few inches. Get a tent with a large vestibule where you can cook and stow gear (outer boots and packs). Using an interior floor cover such as a space blanket can protect the floor from boots and fuel. Exterior ground "footprint" tarps are needed only in rocky or muddy conditions. Tents come in sizes that can hold two to eight people, and can range in price from $200 to $1,000.

It's better to get a bigger tent to accommodate winter equipment – two people will fit more comfortably in a three-person tent. Clean your tent using the same washing methods as your sleeping bags.

Tent Color

Some tents are so dark you can't see inside them! In the 1970s, Murray Pletz, a designer for JanSport, was the first to recognize the positive psychological properties of the bright colors now used in most expedition tents. Bright colors lift the spirits and have been shown to aid recuperation and rest. Bright tents provide internal illumination, saving precious battery and candle reserves. Finally, bright yellow tents stand out from the ground or air, which is important for finding your tent in whiteout conditions. Unfortunately, many tentmakers ignore these concepts. Some tentmakers even make white tents!

Tent Poles

Lightweight aircraft aluminum poles are the strongest and lightest available. Pole sets are usually shock corded so they snap together. Replace damaged shock cord yourself using 4 mm shock cord. If metal or fiberglass poles don't slide easily together, lubricate them with a little silicon spray. Be sure that all the tent poles are there before each trip! Tent poles either fit into tent pole sleeves or are clipped onto the tent. Both designs are equally rigid in high winds, but clip-ons allow faster setup and takedown in windy conditions. With sleeve designs, poles can actually freeze to the pole sleeve in harsh conditions. Always push poles through tent pole sleeves to prevent poles from disconnecting. Attach the tent pole bag to your pack so it can't get lost.

Pyramids

Pyramid tents are another tent option – they have no floors, which makes them lighter to carry. This also makes them safer for using liquid-fueled stoves because there's no floor to catch fire and you have a higher roof. Because heat rises to the tent's peak, they are best used for warmer spring touring. They also take additional time to set up because their structure relies on one center pole and multiple snow anchors along each edge. Snow blocks used to anchor the edges should be sloped to help snow slide right off (see figure 9.6).

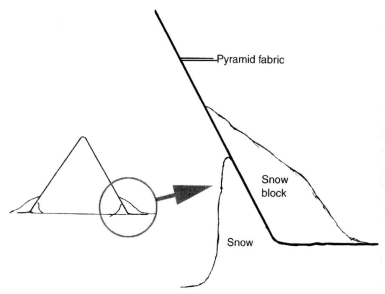

Fig. 9.6: Snow blocks used to anchor pyramid tents should be sloped to allow snow to slide off.

Tent Rigging

No tent is strong if it is not placed and secured properly. External guy lines using 8 feet (2.5 meters) of 4 mm Perlon accessory cord should be installed at all recommended locations. Always use black or brightly colored cord, as white cord will blend into the snow and trip you up. Tying punge cord around tent pole intersections can also increase tent rigidity. Remember that round cordage resists knot freezing, and that flat-type lacing is much harder to handle with mittens. Use guy line tighteners that can be adjusted easily. Always install large 16-inch (41- centimeter) by 4 mm Perlon zipper pulls. This makes entering and exiting the tent much easier, especially late at night when you are half asleep!

There are several types of anchors you can use while snow camping. If you are making base camp and using your skis daily, which eliminates using them an anchors, lightweight snow stakes or deadman anchors work well. At night use skis, shovels, ski poles, or ice axes, for example. Never take avalanche ski poles apart in an effort to use each piece as an anchor, because they will freeze in place, making removal difficult. Bury ski poles whole horizontally with the guy line looped around the center of the pole.

Deadman anchors rely on their shape and the depth you bury them for strength. Several one-gallon nylon stuff sacks can be filled with snow and buried (like a "deadman") to make great tent anchors. Add a small, metal S hook to the drawstring so you are able to attach guy lines easier. Or bury a log or a big piece of ice as a deadman instead of a ski pole. Get creative!

When breaking camp, close zip tent doors in windy conditions to prevent ballooning. Release tent poles at corners to flatten the tent before doing anything else, making it easier to handle in windy conditions. Throw out the factory storage sacks that came with your tent, and stuff your tent into two compression sacks instead (one for the tent body and one for the tent fly). One person can carry the tent poles and tent fly while another carries the tent body. Use same-colored compression sacks and pole bags so they are not confused with other tents if you have more than one tent.

Sleeping Bags

Put your money into your sleeping system. Your sleeping bag is where your mental and physical energies recuperate for the next day. If you don't sleep well, you don't ski well.

Warmth

While you can get away with a 20-degree Fahrenheit (–7 degrees Celsius) bag for hut touring, a –40-degree Fahrenheit (–40 degrees Celsius. This is the only temperature where F deg and C deg are the same) bag is recommended for snow camping. There is no industry-wide standard for rating sleeping bag temperature ranges. One company's –20 bag can be different from another –20 bag. To complicate matters, some people sleep colder than others. If you're the type of person who uses an electric blanket at home, buy a –20 bag! It might be heavier, but you'll be warmer and happier in the long run. Get a long bag so that you can warm and dry your inner ski boots at the bottom of the sleeping bag while you sleep (put them in a stuff sack first to keep your bag dry). Winter bags must have a good hood and draft tube running the length of the bag to keep out drafts. Get a bag with double zippers so you can vent your feet if you get too warm. Winter bags have a narrower cut to minimize internal convection currents, resulting in increased warmth. At the store, try the bag and see if zippers are free pulling and not snagging on excess material, and get a product with a lifetime warranty and a good return policy.

A clean bag is a warm bag. Always store your down or synthetic bag in a cotton storage sack so that the bag can dry thoroughly. Follow manufacturer's cleaning instructions. Tumble-drying a sleeping bag with a tennis shoe is an old idea that can ruin the loft of the down.

Sleeping Bag Materials

Nylon, often in combination with a Gore-Tex-type membrane, is used as an outer shell in all winter-rated sleeping bags. Softer inner liners have been developed that mimic silk and make sleeping more comfortable. Different insulating materials should be chosen according to the temperature range and compressibility characteristics desired.

- GOOSE DOWN – Down weighs less than Polarguard, is more compress-ible and warmer by weight, and some say it lasts longer. Down feathers come in different quality levels and fill densities (see chapter 1). Down is a better investment if it comes built in a Gore-Tex DryLoft shell that protects the down from snow, water, and spilled drinks.

- POLARGUARD – Goose down loses all its insulating properties when wet. This is not a problem in drier continental climates, but it can be in humid maritime climates. Polarguard is a better choice and is often used by Arctic explorers. Polarguard is a continuous filament from the bottom to the top of the bag. It is cheaper, easier to clean, insulates when wet, and lasts forever. New variations on Polarguard such as HV (High Void) and 3D are lighter and more compressible.

Sleeping Pad

The sleeping pad increases comfort and is an important part of the sleeping bag equation. Insulated pads that self-inflate are great, but heavier than a plain Ensolite foam pad. Blowing air into the mattress introduces moisture, so it's important to air out the pad by leaving it laid out at home with the valve open. Carry your pad in a stuff sack to protect it from sharp objects. Use ice axe tip covers to protect your pad from damage if carried on the outside. Noninflatables like Ensolite and Ridge Rest are lightweight and insulate against the cold quite well.

Inner and Outer Bags

Sleeping in layers extends the temperature range of your sleeping bag. Since

Fig. 9.7: With care, a cartridge stove can easily be used in a tent. Notice the amount of light that this tent has! Dark tents make you use more fuel and batteries. Bill is wearing a "Breathe Right"™ strip over his nose for easier breathing during climbing. Vivesphoto.

–20 bags are expensive, try to add a pile fleece liner with a full-length zipper inside a summer down or Polarguard bag. Don't forget to use a compression bag to reduce volume. An outer shell like a Gore-Tex™ bivouac sack adds several degrees to your bag and functions as a high-performance emergency shelter. Vapor barrier inner bags prevent the loss of body heat and moisture, keeping the sleeping bag dry to minimize further body dehydration while retaining body heat. Though good in theory, the popular market has not endorsed this idea.

Change Your Clothing

Avoid wearing your ski clothes to bed. Your body is covered with a thin layer of sweat, no matter how dry you feel. For maximum warmth, always put on dry underwear. One strategy when snow camping or hut skiing is to rotate two sets of underwear and socks at bedtime (expedition- or medium-weight, depending on the season). The next morning, don't change. The underwear just changes roles. Sleep with a polar fleece balaclava for increased warmth matched up with a polar fleece pillow cover stuffed with clothes.

Cooking Inside the Tent

Pressurized cartridge stoves have become very popular over the years with alpine climbers. Liquid fuel stoves are normally reserved for a base camp situation. Stove manufacturers recommend that you don't cook in your tent with a cannister stove. But it's not like you can stand outside in a blizzard and cook! Having said that, let me also say that I have cooked inside my tent for 30 years without incident. Alpine climbers cook inside their tents all the time. Tent fires or carbon monoxide poisoning incidents are extremely rare, and are a result of total negligence. During winter camping, indoor cooking – either in the tent or tent vestibule – is a necessity. High winds and blizzard conditions make it mandatory that you know how to cook inside. Stoves allow you stay warmer in an efficient manner. You can quickly have the inside of your tent up to 80 degrees within minutes of getting inside. People are also concerned about Carbon Monoxide poisoning. Consider that you are burning a fuel in its gaseous state which burns much more completely than a fuel in its liquid state, which does not burn cleanly. It is very unclear in reported tent deaths as to what type of stove was being used in the first place. I have often been inside a tent for 12 hours with a cartridge gas stove (Bleuet) on for heat while waiting out a storm without any kind of nausea or tiredness.

Cooking inside the tent requires patience and coordination. Always ventilate your tent with a one or two inch opening at each door. You can use a piece of Ensolite pad to insulate the stove against the snow and maximize fuel efficiency. To reduce the chance of stove flare-ups, open up the valve once to let off excess pressure before lighting. Then light your match or lighter before you open the stove valve to light it. Always light the stove at the lowest setting with a pot on the stove. In case of flare-up, the flame will go outward instead of upward and won't burn the roof. Flare-ups last only a second so don't panic – just turn the stove off and try again.

There are two basic types of stoves: those using pressurized cartridges and those using liquid fuel. I hate liquid fuel stoves -see the attched story. Each should be maintained according to the manufacturer's specifications for safe, efficient performance. Always practice using them at home first.

- LIQUID FUEL STOVES – Liquid fuel stoves are usually hotter than cartridge stoves but require a lot more care, as you need to pump and prime them. This sometimes results in getting fuel on your hands and tent, so they are best used in the tent's vestibule. Fuel bottles have been known to leak fuel while inside packs, soaking clothes and sleeping bags. Regardless of the drawbacks, many prefer these stoves, which can often use different fuels such as white gas or kerosene. These stoves are great for groups for whom larger meals must be prepared. In this situation, a cooking tent may be invaluable to isolate cooking and fire danger to one area.

- CARTRIDGE STOVES – Many mistakenly think that these stoves are not cold-weather or high-altitude stoves. That is nonsense, since they've been the stove of choice for Himalayan climbers for decades. The higher they go, the more powerful they get. Cartridge stoves (Bleuet and Primus are two brands) don't require pumping or priming – you just turn them on (see figure 9.7). Newer fuel mixtures of butane and propane don't need prewarming in a sleeping bag but it doesn't hurt to prewarm them, and it increases their efficiency. Start new cartridges in the vestibule to be sure that all connections are tight. If something does happen, you can throw the whole thing out the door. Some models hang from the roof of the tent, providing more living room but requiring additional finesse in handling. Newer fuel cartridges are self-sealing, preventing leakage. The only drawbacks are that cartridges are more expensive than liquid fuel, and the tanks do take up pack room and must be packed out after use. Unfortunately, cartridges are not as environmentally friendly as liquid fuel stoves since the cartridge ends up in a land fill. Industry efforts to recycle them have not been successful.

Utensils

For snow camping, two people can use a one-quart pot kit for cooking and eating, while a two-quart pot can come in handy for melting snow. Plain aluminum pots are lighter than stainless steel, but Teflon coatings do make clean-up easier. Stove, utensils, kitchen cloth, and lighter can all nest together into one cooking pot, which can fit into one stuff sack. Don't use metal cups, which burn fingers and spill easily. Insulated commuter-style drinking mugs reduce the need to reheat liquids, saving stove fuel, and a no-spill lid prevents messes. Inside a tent every move is amplified, another reason to have a water resistant sleeping bag. Lexan spoons, knives, and forks are lightweight and keep your Swiss army knife cleaner. To conserve fuel, measure what water you need before boiling a whole pot.

Headlamps

The big buzz in headlamps is LED (light emitting diodes).These bulbs do not heat up and can last up almost forever (100,000 hours). They produce a bright light up to 40 feet for working, climbing or cooking. They are good for Proximity Lighting. But-they are not good for finding landmarks at night. For Long Range Lighting you need a Halogen bulb that goes 300 feet. One night with a torn ACL on the backside of Vail I did find a hut around midnight that was marked with one tiny blue reflector. And I must praise my Petzl zoom halogen lamp for finding that tiny speck of color in the darkness. Talk about luck! Thank God the weather was clear. You think a LED could do that ? Maybe-maybe not. They now make a headlamp with both LED's and a Halogen combination lamp - a great compromise.

In summary, a good headlamp with both a narrow and wide beam is a must for night travel, rescue signaling, or just plain cooking. It must be able to operate in low temperatures. A lamp using standard AA batteries (especially rechargeable batteries) should have a battery pack that is worn inside the clothing for use in very cold conditions. But how many people do that? If the battery pack is worn on the head, use lithium batteries to prevent cold degradation in extreme conditions. Rechargeable batteries don't last long in the cold. Always test your batteries before leaving the house, and always bring backup batteries and bulbs (both high and low intensity) for emergency use. Lithium batteries are very reliable in extreme cold and have unlimited shelf life. One idea is to use a small lightweight LED headlamp for reading while saving the big headlight for important stuff like pathfinding. A small hanging tent light can be valuable while preparing meals. Use the same size batteries for all electrical appliances for maximum interchange-ability. Place a piece of duct tape over on-off switches to prevent accidental activation while in a pack.

Placing Your Camp

Always establish camp before you have to. Don't wait for darkness to make camp! The ideal campsite would be right at the tree line. This way, you

Fig. 9.8: Headlamp selection. Vivesphoto.

could have a great spot to make camp while taking advantage of the tree-less bowls above for skiing. This ultimate campsite would of course be on a level spot, next to a creek in a sheltered wooded area, with no overhanging branches laden with snow that might come down in the night. This ideal campsite would also be at the eastern edge of the forest so that when the sun came up, your tent would get the first rays of the sun. But often, we cannot find such an ideal location.

Camping Below Tree Line

Of course, in a storm, camping below tree line is always preferred. Get into a thick grove of trees to protect the tent from violent winds. A small opening within a thick grove of trees is ideal. Don't camp underneath trees that hold large snow deposits. These can get big enough to destroy a tent. Look out for dead trees hanging within live ones ("deadfall") that can fall suddenly in a windstorm. Don't camp below rock walls as there's always danger from falling snow or rock.

Ski Randonnée!

Camping Above Tree Line

Although the views are great above tree line, camping can be more complicated. In leeward areas, snow is carried over from the windward side increasing avalanche hazard. Wind is your enemy. On the windward side your camp may be buffeted by high winds. Wind is worse than snow because it works on a tent by loosening guy lines, weakening your tent, and keeping you awake. Snow is the better choice since it can partially bury a winter tent, acting to insulate it. Look for evidence of past or present avalanche activity on the slopes above you. Always ask, "What will happen if it does slide?"

Setting Up Camp

You're stopped for the night and the temperature is dropping fast. You've exercised hard, so put on extra clothing to stay warm. Practice putting up your tent at home before you go camping. Try to put it up quickly with your gloves on. It's not easy, but it can be done. Handling tent wands with tight glove liners is easier.

There are several steps in setting up your camp at the end of a long ski day. Once you have found a level spot, repeatedly ski pack and boot pack the area into a sleeping platform. The entrance should be facing opposite the prevailing wind. Pack out a four-foot (1.2-meter) square area in front of the door, so that when you go outside to relieve yourself you won't fall waist deep in snow. Dust as much snow off your clothing as possible before entering the tent. This keeps the floor and your sleeping bags drier. A space blanket on the tent floor protects the floor from wear and tear. Sleeping pads and bags go down next. Put your extra gear against the walls of the tent to keep cold tent walls from touching your sleeping bag, thus keeping it drier. Have your feet pointing toward the entrance so you can get out more easily.

Before coming in, pack your cooking pots with snow for water. Take your boots off outside the tent and put on camp booties to prevent snow from entering the tent. Get into your sleeping bag and change into a dry set of underwear. Drink some cold water, followed by a warm drink (hot chocolate or soup) – this begins carbo loading for the next day. Your body is most receptive to carbs at this time. With practice, you can be warm inside your tent within 30 minutes after stopping!

After dinner, you may want to study your maps or do some reading. Use

DIGGING A SNOWPIT

If you are caught above tree line, you can dig a shallow pit to place your tent in and with the displaced snow build a circular mound of snow around the pit to block driving wind. The harder the wind, the deeper the pit. Most open snowfields are cleaned of loose snow by the constant winds, so your snowpit won't get buried with too much blowing "spindrift" snow unless it is snowing very heavily. But I'd rather dig out the snow occasionally

Wind

during the night than deal with the wind. Burying tent edges with snow prevents the tent from being lifted off the ground in high wind as well.

a headlamp, since candles and oil lanterns use large amounts of oxygen, drip wax or fuel, get in the way, and generally make a mess. Carry extra batteries and forgo the romantic ambience. If you need a candle, keep your tent ventilated and use plumber's candles, which burn cleaner and longer. As you read, melt more snow to fill up your water bottles for the next morning and for drinking during the night. Hot water bottles placed inside your sleeping bag can increase your warmth immediately and will prevent their freezing overnight – plus, the extra warmth feels great! Place your boot liners inside your bag as well so they are warm for the morning ski. Place cooking pots and stoves where you won't bang into them if you roll over while sleeping. Remember – a neat tent is a happy tent!

Before turning in, walk outside one more time. Check guy lines to see that they are tight so you won't have to get up later to do it. If it's snowing, check to see that snow is not overloading the tent roof unevenly. Give your inflatable mattress a few more breaths since the cold has probably condensed the air inside. Keep your headlamp and toilet paper right at your head so as not to disturb campmates if you need to get up.

Cleaning Up at Camp

A small hand towel works well for drying dishes after being used as a hot pad during meals. It fits into your pot and pan, keeping the contents from banging around. If you use dehydrated foods that can be prepared and eaten in their packages, there is not much dishwashing. Scrape excess food remnants with a knife or fork and bury the biodegradable scraps in the snow, away from your tent, so as not to attract animals. Add a bit more water and swish out the remaining food. Alcohol wipes work great to cut grease. Wipe clean with your towel.

A clean body is a warmer body. Minute body hairs keep the body warmer if the hair has loft (dead air space) itself – but if you are dirty, the dirt will occupy the dead air space, thus keeping you colder. You can do the whole job with a full-size face towel, a small plastic bottle of biodegradable peppermint soap, and about two cups of hot water (alcohol wipes also work here). A travel-size bottle of deodorant is nice to have as well.

Of course the big question is: How do you go to the bathroom out there? During the day it's not a problem. But at night you'll be happy to have installed large zipper pulls on your tent doors and clothing. That way you can do things while half asleep! Once outside, get at least 25 feet (8 meters) away from the tent and away from all water sources. Dig a deep hole, even if it is only snow, for human waste so that it will decompose more quickly, and always carry toilet paper out with you. Paper kitchen towels can be used as toilet paper. Cut them into quarters for easier use, store them in an airtight bag, and always bring them home with you for disposal. Always wash your hands or use alcohol wipes or gel afterward. In horrible weather conditions when it is dangerous to go outside, men can use a plastic quart-size wide-mouth bottle as an emergency bathroom backup. In the morning, the bottle can be sterilized with boiling water. Extreme women alpinists know about urination reservoirs that are made specifically for this purpose.

Travel Contamination

Giardia, a parasitic protozoan, is responsible for most waterborne illnesses. Resistant to cold, it can be found in snow if animal waste is nearby (marmots, sheep, etc.) but not in freshly fallen snow. It is also in flowing streams where it is constantly suspended in the water. However, it does sink in quiet waters like a lake. It can cause gastrointestinal cramping and illness which can be quite unpleasant which may require hospitalization. According to the Wilderness Medical Society (1992) water should be boiled for two to three minutes to kill the bacteria. Anymore time is a waste of fuel. Also iodine, and other purifcation tablets can be effective. Ultraviolet light is also be used in some devices to kill the parasite. Always clean hands with alcohol wipes while in the tent or hut after toilet duties especially while overseas. In foreigh countries only eat cooked food and boiled water only (tea and coffee are usually safe since the water has been boiled).

Expedition Planning

Day tours and half-day ski tours are fun in themselves and can provide excellent training for longer multiday ski tours. With groups, it's important to have organizational meetings to discuss food, equipment, and route. Each person has their own level of comfort and their own ideas of goals for a trip. For example, talk about whether you want to set daily mileage goals and move camp day to day, or if you would prefer just to make a base camp from which you can ski the surrounding area. A planning calendar is helpful for scheduling daily mileage and menus. The chapters in this book can help you identify areas that need work. Whether you are going snow camping or hut skiing in Colorado, Europe, or Alaska, you need to plan out what you want to do in light of what you can do based on your own and your fellow skiers' abilities. It's always better to start conservatively with an easy multiday hut tour before trying winter camping, for instance. Do a shorter distance, do an easier climb. Take more food than needed, take more clothes than needed. Build on a series of progressive experiences.

Sometimes it's helpful to make a trip-planning outline:

1. Where do we want to go?
2. How much time do we have?
3. Who wants to go?
4. Are they experienced in this type of skiing?

5. Do they have all the equipment needed?
   (See the equipment list at the end of the book.)
6. Are they strong enough?
7. What will the weather be like?
8. What will the avalanche conditions be like?
9. How far is it?
10. How steep is it?
11. How hard is it?

More Alpine expeditions are using democratic leadership in which everyone has a say in decisions. Those with more experience should lead discussions on routing and timing of skiing. Expeditions usually mean more people, more waiting, and more time. Everyone should start out with the same quality of equipment regardless of experience level, so that breakdowns are minimized. Having everyone eat and drink is particularly important to keep body and mind together. With more people there are always more disagreements, but most conflicts can be resolved with patience and listening. To build team efficiency and to reduce confusion during multiday ski tours, have the same people do the same jobs. This builds specialization and saves time and tempers when making camp at the end of the day.

Hut and Yurt Skiing

Hut skiing can be a great way to enjoy backcountry skiing (see figure 9.5). Almost every mountain state and Canadian province has ski huts. Yurts, originally developed by Mongolian nomadic tribes, are also becoming popular in North America as backcountry dwellings. In Canada and Europe, huts are owned by Alpine clubs. By joining these clubs, you can get maps and reservation information. Most huts in the United States are not staffed, while the ones in Europe usually are, offering room and board. Always call local guide services to get exact dates when services are available. In North America, bed and breakfast inns can be found in most mountain towns and usually offer inexpensive lodging.

Being in a hut with a lot of strangers is similar to communal living. You need to respect each other's rights. Cell phone users should be courteous and get out of earshot if they must make a call. Being helpful in getting firewood, washing dishes, and keeping the place neat is always a plus, too. Huts are a

Figure 9.9: Typical hut accomodations on the Tenth Mountain Hut System, Colorado (Jackal Hut shown). Vivesphoto.

great place to make friends with others who share your passion for skiing, but with a large group of people it can get unavoidably noisy. Earplugs are a real lifesaver! Upon departure, be sure everything is swept neat and clean and that all power sources are turned off. Leave some firewood in the wood box and fill up the melting pot with snow for the next visitors.

Spring/Summer Skiing

Backcountry skiing doesn't stop when the lifts close – it just goes into high gear! Skiing through June is not uncommon in the American Rocky Mountains, and year-round skiing is always available in northwest North America (see figure 9.6). Of course, for those with the means, skiing in South America, Australia, and New Zealand is possible. Hard neve snow with ice in the morning is generally the norm, so freshly tuned skis are a must. If the snow doesn't freeze the night before, avoid skiing because it won't support body weight.

Conservation

Backcountry travelers often damage the very nature that they love. Exposed tundra is easily damaged with heavy ski boots. Snow protects delicate nature from damage, but it also covers a multitude of sins. Biodegradability is relative. Burying toilet paper, eggshells, or orange peels in the snow won't make them disappear. Pack everything out, especially toilet paper. Toilet paper should be placed in plastic bags to pack out or it can be burned as an alternative, as ashes are biodegradable. Human waste will biodegrade, but it should be deposited at least 200 feet (61 meters) from water sources. Use a stove in high-use areas to conserve tree cover.

Solo Skiing

I won't tell you not to solo ski. That would be a waste of time. I do quite a bit of it myself. I love the quiet and solitude, and it gives me time to think. But I have skied a long time. I know my limitations. I just go skiing – no heroics. I wear an avalanche beacon even when alone. You have to at least think about your would be rescuers and speed their rescue of you. I also tell people where I am going and for how long. I don't take risks with avalanche terrain. I have spent long periods of time soloing.One month I skied about a hundred miles of a high mountain route in the Sierra Nevadas of California. It was Spring , and one day I reached a large creek that was at flood stage and was raging. I stripped down to my bare feet even though it was snowing. I waded in. One foot deep, two feet, three feet, thigh deep. I had ten feet to go. Should I attempt it? Was possible drowning worth it? No, of course not. I had to turn back. It was an objective decision. I'm glad I saved myself. You have to stay objective like a machine and choose survival and the chance to ski another day.

Couples

Couples often think that they can teach each other skiing. This can be a big mistake. Usually it's the guy who wants the girl to ski like Seth Morrison and she can't – so he gets all upset. Then she gets upset and so on. The nice thing about Randonnée skiing is that you can practice together at a ski resort and get some miles in just paralleling. Don't try to teach other, buy each other lessons with an instructor or backcounty guide. There's just

Fig. 9.10: Vignettes Hut, Haute Route. Vivesphoto.

213

TRAIL SKIING ETIQUETTE

Backcountry skiers are not immune from manners when they are around other skiers, and would do well to observe the following courtesies:

- Ski under control at all times.
- Keep a lookout for skiers coming down the trail. They have the right of way.
- When overtaking a skier below, you must avoid the skier. Yell to the skier, warning them of your approach.
- Do not stop on a trail where you are not visible from above. If stopping, get off the trail so people don't have to ski around you.
- When entering a downhill resort trail, yield to other skiers.
- Observe and obey all posted signs.
- Keep your dog at home – dogs aren't allowed on many trails. If you bring your dog, make sure you can keep it under voice control.
- Do not ski under the influence of alcohol or drugs.
- Do not leave an accident site unless you have given your name to rescue personnel.

too much emotional stuff going on and it's not worth it. Additionally, get your girl some great equipment – get her the best – you will be glad you did. Have fun – that is the main thing! An wise old mountain guide once told me, "Son, when momma ain't happy, ain't no buddy happy!" Truer words were never spoken.

Hiring a Guide or Instructor

You actually save time and money by learning about backcountry skiing from a guide instead of going hit-or-miss on your own. Giving a gift certificate for instruction is a good way for couples to provide instruction for each other. Most guides in Europe and Canada are generally certified through the Union Internationale des Association Guides de Montagne (UIAGM). In the United States, the American Mountain Guide Association (AMGA) has its own parallel certification process. American mountains are in many ways more demanding since they lack elaborate hut systems and helicopter rescue services. The American guide may therefore be more experienced in snow camping and unsupported wilderness multiday tours than European guides who ski hut to hut. You don't have to be certified to have a good, helpful nature, and be safe and knowledgeable about backcountry skiing. Many excellent guides are not certified. Reputation is key. Find out about guides by contacting local climbing and ski shops. Phone the guide, and ask whether you may speak to some past clients. Get a price list and try it!

Skiing With Children

Always underestimate the abilities of children to cope with cold and fatigue. Take the shorter trip, use the easier route. I think kids under 10 should stay home unless they are unusually motivated and good resort skiers. It is often better to wait another year than have a bad experience which might turn them off forever. Smaller Telemark boots will be easier to find than Randonnée boots but that may be changing with the popularity of Randonnée skiing. Telemark boots can often fit into a Silveretta Randonnée bindings. Or you can use a Telemark binding as well if a Randonnée binding set up is not available. Let kids try out used short and light Alpine-width skis you can find at a secondhand store for $5 a pair. Old Alpine skins can be split in half to form two skins for easy touring. Or you can use some cross-country wax (see chapter 4). Teach kids the beginner techniques listed in the ski technique chapter (see chapter 5). Chemical heat packs and a thermos of hot chocolate can provide instant warmth and comfort. Although sleds can provide tired children a free ride, the children can get colder because they aren't exercising. Be sure children have plenty of carbs and hot liquids to keep them going. Kids should always learn basic winter survival skills and how to use a whistle. Make sure they are using sunblock and have good sunglasses – a sunglass retainer strap will help keep them in place.

Randonnee Racing

Randonnee Racing has been a big sport in Europe for many years and it is making serious inroads here in North America. Several equipment manufacturers, most notably, Life-Link™, and Black Diamond™, have given much support to a race series of events in North America culminating in a championship finale.

There are usually two categories per race – a recreational and a racing division. The pros climb 5-6,000 ft. over a 7-10 mile course while the rec

Ski Randonnée!

skiers climb 3,000 ft over a 4-7 mile course. Events cost about $35 to $50 to enter. Very light gear is used, typically Dynafit titanium bindings. AT boots with velcro closures instead of buckles and hollow air channel type skis.

The course is usually marked with color coded flagging. There will be check points along the course. Avalanche terrain may be encountered and if there is increased avalanche danger, the race course may be altered for safety. These races are somewhat like car rally racing where the excitement is more with the participants than with the spectators. The knowledgeable would definitely appreciate these races, and the effort that these racers put out is amazing.

Overseas Travel

The internet has been a boon for skiers heading abroad for skiing. Whether you are doing a major climb and ski or just heading to a resort area, you can get all sorts of information about the place you are headed. Almost every area of the world has a Web site that talks about it. Using the Google search engine can bring you more information than you needed about any given area in the world.

When you travel abroad, you are not just a skier but a traveler. Having done some foreign travel I can offer some suggestions: you will need a passport – it carries much more diplomatic weight than a visa. Know the phone number of your home countries embassy in that country. You will need vaccinations for that particular country especially if it is a third world country. The U.S. Center for Disease Control Web site has this information. Also know if the country is closed to foreigners like Americans. The U.S. State Department Web site will tell you if the country is stable enough to visit. Try to learn a few basic phrases of the language of the country. You'll be surprized what "please", "thank you", and "pardon me" can do – even if you don't know anything else.

Always carry travelers cheques and hide emergency money in travelers cheques in several different place amongst your luggage so if one piece is stolen you can have back up money. Make copies of your credit cards front and back and your medical card and your passport number. Travelers insurance is a must. If your gear is stolen (it happens all the time) you will need to be able to replace it. Or if you are injured and need helicopter evacuation you will need to show proof of insurance.

In foreign countries they want to see a credit card or cash or else you

PHOTOGRAPHY TIPS

Photos of your skiing adventures preserve great memories. Here are some ideas to make digital and film photography easier.

- Oversized buttons and controls are bonuses for a winter camera. Wear glove liners when you go shopping for one.

- Always use a polarizing lens for 35mm film cameras. Get the right kind of film –100 to 200 speed film allows for good color saturation and forgives some overexposure.

- For all cameras, get the sun behind the photographer. This really makes a big difference! Take photos in the early morning and later afternoon when the light is softer.

- Always take more than one shot if it's important, especially if you are shooting with a digital camera.
- Always carry extra film and batteries. Cold eats up both.
- In subfreezing conditions, keep camera and film inside clothing.
- Get people to wear colorful clothing to show up against the snow.

don't get help. In France, for instance, you can't get a ski ticket unless you have helicopter evacuation insurance (it's cheap). Don't trust the airline's plastic bags to hold your gear together. Use a ski bag and strong duffle bags with multiple name tags outside and inside. For protection short of having a gun which is highly illegal in most countries, you can take a can of Bear Spray. If it can stop a grizzly it should stop a human.

It's a good thing to outline where you are going on a day to day basis. Get a large calendar and pencil in where you want to be and what you will be doing. It also lets relatives know where you are so they don't worry as much. You look more together when you can show a trip timetable with multiple objectives (or no objectives). It gives structure to the trip and makes it more organized and easier to manage. Bon Voyage!

Conclusion

When you learn to camp in the winter, you are learning a very basic mountain skill: self-sufficiency. Learning to camp in the winter provides the hut skier with an understanding of snow living that is put to good use if the skier is forced to bivouac en route to a hut. This knowledge makes the hut skier more comfortable in the winter environment. Snow camping is an art. Choosing the proper stove and learning to use stoves correctly is an important part of snow camping that should be practiced.

> *"Master of his energies, rich in everything, a man may choose the life he considers worthy. So will the alpinist choose and tackling obstacles, make his way in absolute freedom. If adventure is disappearing from around us, we still carry it within us"*
> *- Maurice Herzog*
> *Annapurna, 1950*

Survival   10

Ski Randonnée!

No one is immune from making mistakes in the backcountry. And winter does not have patience with the careless. While beginners may suffer from ignorance and naiveté, "experts" can fall victim to their own complacency and laziness. Mountain emergencies usually occur in bad weather, often hours or days from help. What happens before and after such occurrences is the skier's responsibility. It's up to you to be as prepared as possible for any kind of mountain situation, be it in the face of bad weather, an avalanche, injuries, cold, or fatigue.

Preventing the Survival Situation

Dangers in mountain travel are usually divided into subjective dangers and objective dangers. Subjective dangers include physiological or psychological problems such as frostbite, hypothermia, and fatigue. Objective dangers involve environmental factors such as weather and avalanche hazards. Poor judgment is the number-one cause of backcountry accidents. It starts in the ski shop, when poor-quality equipment is purchased or rented. Everyone should have enough equipment to survive on their own. For some reason, some people go out underequipped to save weight – but this doesn't save lives. Poor judgment can continue with choosing a ski route that is far too difficult, or underestimating the length or difficulty of tours and the amount of physical energy needed to complete them. Another bad idea is making a habit of skiing alone. Turning back is unfortunately seen as defeat instead of a sign of intelligence. While generally there is safety in numbers, there is no safety when the people you travel with are unsafe. Much like pilots file a flight plan, why not file a ski plan? Tell a friend where you are going – if no one is home, leave the information on a telephone answering machine. Include date of departure and location of the tour, with a second location you might go to in case you change your mind. State whether you have food, pack, or avalanche equipment. Leave a note on your dashboard. Car keys should be hidden on the car, and everyone in the group should know where they are. No matter how much you prepare, you can't remember everything every time. Many people think they are too experienced to use a list. Their attitude changes after some time in the backcountry. Survival potential depends upon each piece of equipment that we carry. In the

Cover 10.1: Specialized medical-mountain gendarme rescue helicopter (Eurocopter, Model EC-145) on rescue location high above Chamonix Valley. Photo by Philippe Poulet from his awesome book, "Secours Extreme" (Extreme Rescue).

equipment list at the end of the book, equipment is organized for hut skiing, snow camping, and day tours. Day tours are where many people get into trouble. A few hours can turn into a few days when we least expect it.

Prepare to Survive Alone

Skiers make a mistake when they depend on others for help. The team has the tent. The team has the food. But what happens if the team disappears? Now you have nothing. Decide what equipment on your body and what information in your head will increase your survival. The ski team is stronger when each person is self-sufficient. Redundancy in equipment increases your ability to handle an emergency. Everyone in the group should have an avalanche shovel for building snowcaves; everyone should carry their own sleeping bags – you do them no favor by carrying their bags for them; each skier should carry a supply of emergency food, like athletic bars, and divide community food amongst all. Two people can benefit from one tent if one takes the body and another takes the rain fly.

Make a Survival Vest

You have been in a big avalanche and are the sole survivor. Your pack was ripped off your back and your skis are gone, buried in the slide. You are ten miles out. It's snowing hard. Now what? If you are stranded alone without a sleeping bag or tent, your odds of survival are better if the clothing you have on contains prepositioned equipment. Military pilots wear a survival vest that contains prepositioned survival equipment. Your jacket can become a "survival vest" with contents that should never be removed unless you are in a survival situation. A small knife is handy but not critical. A zipper pull compass can give you direction. Two butane lighters can give you fire. Add a small whistle and a mirror for signaling. These items will not be in your way during regular skiing – but you'll appreciate that they're there if you find yourself in a situation where you need them.

Carry a Daypack

Everyone should have a good daypack in which to carry a set of equipment that can help one survive during heavy winter conditions. A fanny pack might be okay for day skiing out from a hut or basecamp, but it can't replace a daypack for the amount of protection (clothing, survival gear) the daypack can carry. Therefore, a daypack should be carried for every ski tour, no matter how short. Two-hour tours have a bad habit of turning into longer tours. See the items marked as day tour backpack contents in the equipment list.

Weapons

Antarctic ski expeditions such as Steger and Messner have carried firearms to ward off polar bears. Outside the Poles or true wilderness areas such as northern Canada, animal attacks are very rare. Bears injure 20 to 100 people annually in the United States, but this occurs mostly during the summer at highly visited national parks. Experts advise that if you are attacked you should resist maximally, as playing dead is totally ineffective. Pepper spray is now the weapon of choice according to most animal experts. You should contact forest ranger stations for animal advisories, especially during the spring. Research has shown that women are not more prone to bear attacks during menstrual periods.

Tools

You don't need a Rambo knife to survive if you know how to use the knife you have. A Swiss army with a sawblade is excellent. This saw-blade cuts through a 3-inch (8-centimeter) pine branch like butter – very important for building shelters or gathering fire fuel. It weighs only 3.5 ounces. All of the other blades and accessories make this type of knife attractive for routine chores. Lacking a knife, you can climb up a tree and use your heavy ski boots to break off dry, dead wood at the base of trees for use as firewood.

A snow shovel is standard equipment for building survival shelters even during low avalanche hazard. If you don't have a snow shovel, use a cooking pot or the end of the ski. I've even used a big flat rock. You can even stomp a hole in the snow with your boots and get into it if you have to. Gloved hands are the last resort, since they will get wet and invite frostbite.

Setting Survival Priorities

You are lost and/or separated from your group en route to a hut. The future is unknown. Night is falling rapidly and things must be done quickly before the real cold hits you. The following steps should occur in this order:

Fig. 12.1: Prepositioned equipment (photo missing): Just having a few small tools can make all the difference: two butane lighters, a whistle. Knife, compass, strobe are optional. Vivesphoto.

1. Dig in – find shelter
2. Find water
3. Regroup psychologically

4. Make a fire
5. Signal: alert and locate
6. Prepare for rescue

Step 1: Find Shelter

To get out of the snow, get into it! As a building material, snow is sound-proof, blocks wind, and holds in heat. A story from the Will Steger Antarctic expedition illustrates this. Skier Keizo Funatsu got lost in a blizzard while caring for his dogs. Disoriented in the whiteout, he had no choice but to lie down and let the snow cover him. Like his dogs, he was soon covered with snow, and he lived to see the next morning. Though an extreme example, it gives testimony to the sheltering properties of snow.

Considerations for Emergency Shelters

Snow depth determines the type of shelter that should be built. Use your ski poles to probe the snow to determine the type of shelter to build. During shallow snow conditions where some bare ground may be showing, a lean-to shelter can be made. With a thick snow pack, snow caves and tree wells are preferred over trenches and igloos. Igloos take too much time

223

and energy to build, and trenches are a last resort because they become cold sinks that collect frigid air. If above ground, build your shelter on the edge of dense forest to avoid trees bombing your shelter with windblown snow. Build it facing south to take advantage of any available sunlight and warmth. Avoid deep canyons and valleys, as cold always flows to the lowest part of the terrain. Place your shelter up the side of a valley whenever possible. Always collect pine boughs to use for insulating your body from the snow, and get into the HELP position (talked about in the next paragraph) once inside your shelter. Don't use your skis for the roof of a shelter if you expect to stay in the shelter for an extended period of time. You'll need the skis for foraging for water and firewood. With all snow shelters, stick your skis outside the entrance – somebody might see them!

When inside your shelter, stay in the HELP position (Heat Escape Lessening Position). HELP was originally used by boaters forced to await rescue while floating in very cold water. It is the same fetal position used by mountaineers during forced bivouacs. With a sleeping bag, a person can use a prone HELP. Always use an insulating layer between you and the snow made with available materials such as Ensolite or Thermorest pads, backpacks, or even a thick layer of pine boughs. If you have two snow hats, put both of them on for added warmth. Bring your knees up to your chest and fold your arms across your chest to protect the core area of your body. Stay in your shelter to conserve body heat and lessen exposure. Urinate in your pants if you have to, but stay in your shelter. Eat snow for water instead of leaving shelter and warmth to go look for it.

Making Shelters

- DEEP SNOW PACK: Snow cave – Prepare to get wet when you dig a snow cave. Plus, it will take over an hour to make a good one. It's important to have a good solid snow pack when you dig a snow cave. There are many stories of snow caves collapsing, so always sleep with your shovel. Snowdrifted hillsides can be good places to build a snow cave. Dig your snow cave during the light of day while you have energy. Pace yourself so you don't get all your clothing wet from snow without and sweat within. Take turns digging with other people in the group. The entrance to any snow cave or shelter should be kept as small as possible and below floor level within the cave to prevent

Fig. 10.2: Kids love to make snow shelters. Encourage them to do so. It might save someone's life someday. Vivesphoto.

heat loss (see figure 10.3). Always vent the snow cave when using a stove.

- DEEP SNOW PACK: Trench shelter – A trench shelter is like a horizontal subterranean snow cave. It's best used when you are stranded on a large, flat plain. The problem is with cold settling into the trench. Dig down far enough to stand in it, then dig a snow cave sideways (see figure 10.4). The original hole can act as an artificial cold sink. Probe snow-pack depth before digging.

- DEEP SNOW PACK: Tree well shelter – Tree wells are great for shelter since the wind has done most of the digging for you (see figure 10.5). Enlarge the well with a shovel so you can stretch out and cover the top

225

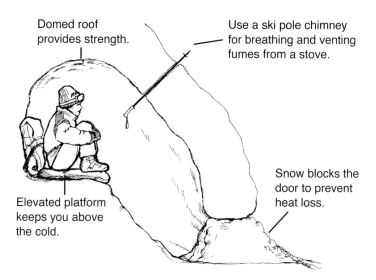

Domed roof provides strength.

Use a ski pole chimney for breathing and venting fumes from a stove.

Elevated platform keeps you above the cold.

Snow blocks the door to prevent heat loss.

Fig. 10.3: Snow Cave.

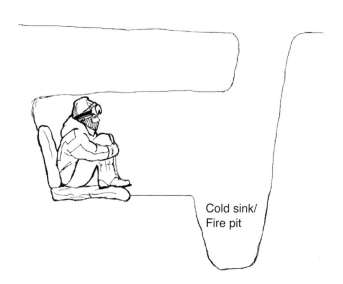

Cold sink/ Fire pit

Fig. 10.4: Trench shelter.

with branches and pine boughs. The Hug-a-Tree program designed for lost children uses trees as a place of shelter. In California, there once was a search for two children who were benighted in a snowstorm. The next day they were found in a tree well shelter alive and well, even though night temperatures had been below freezing.

Fig. 10.5: Tree well shelter.

- SHALLOW SNOW PACK: Lean-to shelter – Lean-to shelters can be made with tree branches and pine boughs against a frame supported between two trees or as a half-teepee with branches radiating out from a central tree support (see figure 10.4). A fire reflector can be situated in front of the openings for heat. Lean-tos can be drafty, so the ends should be closed off. Lean-to shelters can also be made against huge fallen trees or just a snow wall. If you have a tarp for a door, you can make a fast shelter.

- SHALLOW SNOW PACK: Tarp-igloo shelter – Make a ring of snow blocks and cover it with a tarp (see figure 10.5). A pole can be added to the center, which is helpful in keeping snow from gathering at the center. Without a pole, it still works well in light snow. It can be very comfortable.

Bivouac Strategies for Hut Skiers

All the strategies in this chapter can be used if you are benighted en route to a hut. It wouldn't hurt hut skiers to be more knowledgeable about snow camping techniques. Individual Gore-Tex bivy bags are more the norm in the United States, while multiperson bivouac sacks are still used in Europe. Bivouac sacks are best used inside an emergency structure whenever possible. A small two-person tent without fly or poles can act as a three-per-

227

Half teepee with fire reflector.

Lean-to with fire reflector.

Fig.12.6: Lean-to shelters.

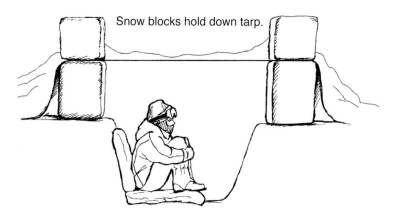

Snow blocks hold down tarp.

Fig. 10.7: Tarp-igloo shelter.

son bivy sack if it's windproof – this is basically what a European bivy bag resembles. A 10-foot (3-meter) square nylon tarp is also handy for making emergency shelters. One ski manufacturer shows how you can clip four skis together into a teepee – this is helpful if you have a tarp that will fit over them. Keep the teepee low to prevent heat from rising to the top of the teepee, where it won't heat anyone. Small lightweight Ensolite pads are invaluable for bivouacking and lunch stops. A small lightweight gas stove can also be carried for emergencies.

Step 2: Water versus Food

Dehydration greatly amplifies fatigue, impatience, and poor decision-making. It is well documented that you can survive by eating snow for water. You can last days without food, but remember that you will die from dehydration, so the choice is clear. James Scott, lost in the Himalayas, ate snow for 42 days while awaiting rescue (James Scott, Lost in the Himalayas). A man survived for 13 days in the Sierras after a plane crash by eating snow. Always avoid red snow, which is made of decomposing microorganisms. When eaten, even the "clean" snow underneath has been shown to cause severe stomach cramps and vomiting. Only use clean snow and clear off the top two inches (5 centimeters) to be safe. Melting the snow in your mouth makes it go down more easily.

Step 3: Regroup Psychologically

Group shock is a real phenomenon in which everyone knows something must be done, but no one knows what should be done precisely. One might encounter in this group silence blank faces, apathy, or high emotion. Do not take words spoken at these times seriously. You've made a mistake, someone got hurt, you have to spend the night out. Your first survival act is to make the conscious decision to survive. Fear, worry, self-rebuke, and guilt all must be ignored. You have only one job now – that is to survive.

A Psychology Lesson: Attitude

The average person has reserves of energy and endurance that are rarely used. You can endure it. There are several mental attributes that can make surviving a little less painful and frightening.

- HUMOR – It's important not to panic. Just relax and go with it. If indeed you must stay out overnight, you'll be miserable but you'll live.
- OBJECTIVITY – Really, how bad is it? Size up the situation and prioritize the solving of problems. Do you have enough water? Is there shelter? Do you really think the bears are hunting you down now as you wait to be rescued? No, they are sleeping. Stop imagining things.

- INGENUITY – Use your brain, be creative, remember what you learned in this book!
- PATIENCE – We have fast food, fast news, and fast travel. Survival takes time, so try to relax.
- HOPE – Rescue groups are relentless. Once they lock onto a rescue, they will continue to search until they find you. Your job is to stay alive and make yourself obvious.

USE YOUR MIND TO STAY WARM

Meditation can really help you stay warm and relaxed. If you are tense and scared, tight muscles squeeze blood vessels, decreasing the amount of warm blood going to the extremities. Survival literature contains many instances where meditation has been vital to survival. Here is a meditation that can help you sleep and rest in difficult situations: Calm your mind. Take several deep breaths. Picture the sun within your chest. Feel the heat going from the center of your body into your fingertips. Repeat the following in a soft, inner voice: "My hands are warm, I feel the warmth flowing into my hands. My hands are warm. Warm. I am relaxed and my hands/feet are warm." If you believe that this can work, it will!

Surviving as a Team

Every skier is different and all have varying levels of temperament, technical ability, and judgment. Whatever the mix, certain principles can be followed that will result in the best effort and outcome of a difficult situation.

- PRINCIPLE 1: Do not move. Do not move unless there is a very good reason to make the switch: a better site for an emergency shelter, a better tent site that is more protected from the weather, more available firewood, or a larger open meadow that can be used for ground-to-air signaling. Once you are there, stay put.
- PRINCIPLE 2: Stay together. Ski groups usually range in size from 3 to 10 or more people. Staying together means there is no major movement without everyone going. I'm not saying that one or two people may not go on exploratory patrols within a half mile in good weather, but if it is snowing no one should move. Ski tracks are easily buried

and can vanish in the fog. Having all the brainpower and muscle in one place makes survival easier.

- PRINCIPLE 3: Cultivate teamwork. Making decisions can result in leadership conflicts. Experienced skiers have a responsibility to make correct decisions to the best of their ability. Those decisions must be objective and always point toward one goal: the survival of the most members of the group. However, the group as a whole should endorse the final decisions together.

Step 4: Make a Fire

Fires are not a condition for survival. People survive all the time in the winter without fires. But the warmth and psychological lift of a fire cannot be ignored. They also add daytime smoke signaling possibilities.

Use a small earthen pit if barren earth exists. Or boot-pack a firepit in the snow about two feet (.6 meters) in diameter in a sheltered area. Make it

Fig. 10.8: Big kids sometimes need a snowcave themselves. It's not going to be warm, but it will be warmer than outside. Vivesphoto.

one foot (.3 meters) below the snow level to provide for a windbreak. Make a platform out of green tree bark to keep the fuel off the snow. Once the fire is going, it will create ash thick enough to insulate itself from getting extinguished from melting snow.

Around the bottom of trees you'll find dry pine needles and very small twigs and leaf debris that can be used for fire fuel. Save the wet twigs for later when they can be dried once a fire is going. Look for fire fuel in your pack: toilet paper, dollar bills, cotton socks, and pages from a book all will make good fuel. The biggest error in building any fire is using twigs and branches that are too big. The second error is using too many branches so that the fire is suffocated. Fire is a mix of fuel and oxygen. You need both. Try toothpick-size twigs first, then small drinking-straw-sized twigs. Have pen-sized twigs and larger wood standing by to take advantage of any flame that is created. Keep the fire small – it will keep you warm and won't keep you running for more firewood.

Butane lighters are an overlooked winter survival tool. Hurricane matches, flint, steel, and such don't even come close. Carry several butane lighters for starting stove and wood fires in the wild (remember the ones in your jacket?). They have long life, and can survive machine washing if accidentally thrown in there before your trip. I've even used them to dry a wet twig to the point of combustion! A headlamp can also be used as a fire starter. Inside the lamp's battery holder, carry a small amount of steel wool. Connect both ends of the battery with the steel wool. This completes the electrical circuit, causing the steel wool to burst into flame. Don't forget to wear your gloves!

Step 5: Signal for Help

Boaters have long used the alert/locate signaling system in emergencies. First you have to alert people that there is a problem. Use signaling that can be noticed far away: a cellular phone, headlamp, mirror, smoke, satellite beacon, or flares. Once a rescue is evident, you can bring rescuers right to you through locate signaling by using a headlamp, whistle, or strobe light. Those marked alert/locate can be used for both functions.

- ALERT/LOCATE: PATTERN SIGNALING/SOS – Search pilots report that the land becomes a hypnotic blur beneath their wings. You must make your position obvious! Use the letters SOS or even a simple X that is big enough will tell someone you need help. These markings are known as

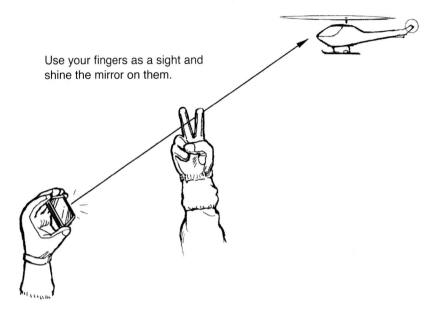

Use your fingers as a sight and shine the mirror on them.

Fig. 10.9: Use a mirror to signal for help. USAF pilots can see mirrors from great distances so this method should not be discounted.

pattern distress markings to pilots. It must be big enough to be seen by a pilot. Think about the size of a swimming pool, about 25 yards (23 meters) in length. Deep snow is the best for making this signal. Walk (don't ski) through the snow to make the letters. Neatness counts, so it won't look just like animal tracks. Make the letters at least two feet (.6 meters) wide and two feet deep. Fill the letters in with pine boughs for better visibility. You can use an arrow to indicate travel direction as well.

- ALERT/LOCATE: MIRROR SIGNALING – According to military survival experts, a signal mirror can knock a pilot out of the cockpit! Skiers are surrounded by mirrors – a compass mirror, sunglasses, camera lenses, tin foil, metal pots, plastic bags, and so on. One man was rescued after using a piece of ice as a mirror! Mirroring should be done slowly over the edge of the horizon (see figure 12.9), moving the mirror side to side using the fingers of one hand as an aiming sight. This should be done even if no aircraft can be seen or heard, because mirror signals have been seen over 100 miles (161 kilometers) away even with mountains.

- ALERT/LOCATE: DAYLIGHT SMOKE SIGNALING – A smoky campfire can be seen from many miles by air. Setting a tree on fire would be the last resort. However, smoke doesn't work in all conditions. High mountain winds can flatten out smoke instead of allowing it to rise so it can be seen.

- ALERT: SATELLITE RESCUE STROBES – Some satellite EPIRBs (Electronic Position Indicator Rescue Beacons) weighing 2.2 pounds (1 kilogram) not only transmit data concerning where you are, but who you are, because you must fill out a user questionnaire upon activation. They are so popular in Canada that the normal certification process was dispensed with. For larger groups and for people with chronic health problems, such a beacon could provide fast rescue. The 406 MHz satellite radio frequency eliminates false alarms, because the user can be identified immediately. Pinpointing location using GPS technology speeds rescue, reducing the chances of injury or mishap to rescuers as well.

- ALERT: CELLULAR PHONES – Over the last few years, many climbers and skiers have initiated rescues using cellular phones. Worldwide cellular coverage via satellite is just a few years away. Plus, new technology now allows cellular phone calls to be traced using GPS technology. It is up to the outdoor community to use these devices responsibly. Range varies widely in the mountains, and hilltop transmission is always better than in a valley. Be sure to charge your phone and then turn it off. Save it in case you need it. A rescue may be in the palm of your hand– but you still have to survive.

- ALERT/LOCATE: RESCUE STROBES – Rescue strobe lights are better than rescue flares because flares only provide a three-shot opportunity for signaling. Once you've used your three flares, that's it! A rescue strobe light such as the ACR Firefly can penetrate heavy snow and fog, is visible at night up to 5 miles (8 kilometers) in the line of sight, and lasts up to eight hours. They are used by military and civilian pilots, weigh 4 ounces, and use alkaline or lithium batteries. They give off a flash of 250,000 peak lumens per flash per second for eight hours. A camera flash can be used as well.

- ALERT/LOCATE: HEADLAMPS – Headlamps are not as bright as rescue strobes, but they're bright enough to be seen from a search plane or by viewers in the valley below in good weather. Multiple flashes will get anyone's attention. Continuous flashing will get them moving toward you. Repeating three short flashes then three long flashes is the international SOS signal. Always carry extra batteries and bulbs!

- LOCATE: TENT AND CLOTHING COLOR – Safety must come first when choosing colors for the backcountry. Bright clothing can help a skier be spotted while an avalanche is still in progress or after a long fall. Waving a bright jacket at a pilot will make you stand out. A yellow tent can be seen from a half-mile (.8 kilometers) away.

- LOCATE: WHISTLE SIGNALING – A whistle is always better than the human voice for distress signaling. A whistle takes much less energy than yelling. Whistles can cut through wind and forest noise and cannot be mistaken for another rescuer's voice. A plastic coach's whistle is loud, and won't freeze to your lips like a metal one. Eight sharp blasts should be used every 15 minutes, in case a rescuer is close by without the victim knowing it.

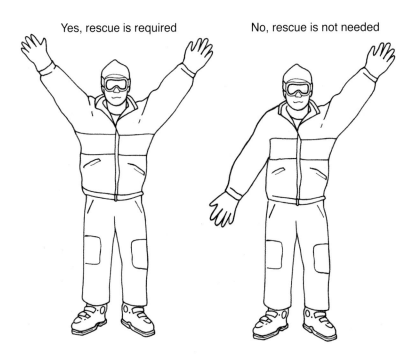

Fig. 10.10: International surface-to-air arm signals for a helicopter rescue.

Step 6: Prepare for Rescue

Once you've been rescued, don't give up. Rescue death occurs when the victim gives up after being reached by rescuers. The will to live is sometimes the only thing keeping us from going into extreme shock and death. Remember – it's not over until it's over. Don't let go of your defenses. Even if you are in good hands, you still have to make it back – then you can pass out!

Rescue by Air

The request for a helicopter rescue cannot be taken lightly. Helicopters are powerful yet sensitive beasts that can do amazing things. However, several fatal helicopter crashes during rescues have raised questions about determining need. Learn the correct surface-to-air arm signals so pilots will understand whether or not you need help (see figure 10.10).

Helicopters do not fly well in high winds or low visibility. Most helicopters, except high-altitude choppers, are strained to their limits during mountain rescues. A twisted ankle or broken arm is not a reason to call a helicopter. Those emergencies should be dealt with by the ski team. A head or back injury where any movement of the victim may result in death is appropriate for helicopter rescue. This may also include massive trauma to the leg, where excessive movement may result in nerve damage or uncontrolled bleeding.

Preparing a Landing Zone

1. The landing zone must be an open field, ideally sloping off at one end for takeoff. If you aren't in a place like this, an injured skier may have to be moved to a place where the helicopter can land. If the skier cannot be moved, wait for professional help to arrive.

2. Lake ice is good if late in winter with minimum thickness of 16 inches (41 centimeters).

3. A wind indicator such as a windsock (ski pole and scarf) is absolutely necessary for the pilot to see wind direction.

4. Scatter pine needles on the snow to help the pilot with depth perception.

Courtesy of MSgt. Jack Loudermilk, retired, U.S. Army

Fig. 10.11: Flight crew searches for signs of life in the forest below – could you be seen? You didn't wear your camouflage snowboarding suit today did you?

Moving Around a Helicopter

1. Do not approach the aircraft unless you are given permission by the flight crew.

2. Never approach the aircraft from the uphill side.

3. Always carry skis to the aircraft horizontally in your hands, not over your shoulders.

4. Always wear goggles or eyeglasses when near the aircraft.

Rescue by Ground

Make yourself obvious to people on snowmobiles or snowcats by making tracks radiating out from your shelter like a spiderweb. You can make arrows in the snow pointing back to your shelter. Break branches and brush to get attention. Keep a smoky fire going at all times so people can see smoke and smell it.

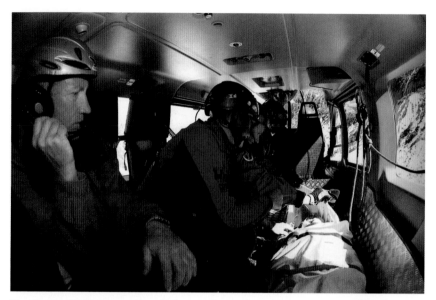

Fig. 10.12: PGHM Paramedics (Pelotons de gendarmerie de haute montagne) stabilize injured skier inside helicopter while en route to hospital in Chamonix. Photo by Philippe Poulet from his awesome book, "Secours Extreme" (Extreme Rescue).

Conclusion

Every skier should have the means and knowledge to be self-sufficient in the winter wilderness. All skiers should carry their own sleeping bags, shovels, and extra food. The lost skier is somewhat like a "man overboard" in a white frozen sea who must save himself while letting others know of his plight. By carrying just a few small tools in your clothing at all times, you dramatically increase your ability to survive. Brightly colored clothing and camping equipment can help rescuers find us. As helicopter rescues increase in the backcountry, we need to learn to use them only when we absolutely need them.

Ivan Getting conceived of the GPS system during the 1950's while acting as vice president of research at the aerospace firm Raytheon. Professor Bradford Parkinson helped to co-invent the system and ran the NAVSTAR GPS Joint Program from 1972-78.

Technical Appendix

Appendix A: Bibliography

Glacier Travel and Crevasse Rescue

Cliff, Peter. Ski Mountaineering. Pacific Search Press. 1987.

Cliff, Peter. Alpinism: A Guide to Safety in the Mountains. Cordee Publishers. 1998.

Cox, Steven. & Fulsaas Kris. Mountaineering: The Freedom of the Hills. The Mountaineers Books. 2003.

Doerry, Eck; Ojero, Ryan; and Strong, Michael. Glaciers, The Art of Travel and the Science of Rescue. The Globe Pequot Press. 2001.

Selters, Andrew and Selters, Andy. Glacier Travel and Crevasse Rescue. The Mountaineers Books. 1990.

Petzl Catalog, Petzl America. Crevasse Rescue: Use of Equipment 2006, 2007.

Smith, Blaine. A comparison of stretch and forces between low and high stretch ropes during simulated crevasse falls, 2005.

Avalanche

Temper, Bruce. Staying Alive in Avalanche Terrain. The Mountaineers Books. 2001.

Fesler, D., and Fredston, Jill. Snow Sense. Alaska Mountain Safety Center, Inc.1999.

LaChapelle, Edward. Secrets of the Snow: Visual Clues to Avalanche and Ski Conditions. University of Washington Press. 2001.

McClung, David., Schaerer, Peter. The Avalanche Handbook, The Mountaineers Books. 1993.

Weather

Renner, Jeffrey. Mountain Weather: Backcountry Forecasting and Weather Safety. The Mountaineers Books. 2005.

Barry, Roger. Mountain Weather and Climate. Routledge, Chapman and Hall Publishers. 1992.

Nelson, Mike. The Colorado Weather Book, Westcliffe Publishers. 1999.

Survival and Rescue

Davenport, G.J, Wilderness Survival . Stackpole Books. 2006.

Steven, G.J. Surviving Cold Weather. Stackpole Books., Mechanicsburg, Pa. 2002.

Graham, J. Outdoor Leadership: Technique, common sense and self-confidence. The Mountaineers Books. Seattle. 1997.

Wilderness Medicine

Houston, Charles. Going Higher: Oxygen, Man and Mountains. The Mountaineers Books. Seattle. 1998.

Backer, Howard D. Wilderness First Aid: Emergency Care for Remote Locations. 2005.

Schimelpfenig, Todd. NOLS Wilderness First Aid. Stackpole Books, Mechanicsburg, PA. 2000.

Forgery, William Wilderness Medicine: Beyond First Aid. Stackpole Books, Mechanicsburg, PA. 2004.

Ski Randonnée!

Navigation

Hinch, Stephan (2004) Outdoor Navigation with GPS. Annadel Press, Santa Rosa, Calif.

Burns, B. & Burns M. (2004) Wilderness Navigation: Finding Your Way using Map, Compass, Altimeter and GPS. The Mountaineers Books

Kals, W.S. & Soles, C. (2004) Land Navigationj Handbook: The Sierra Club Guide to Map, Compass and GPS. Sierra Club Press., San Francisco, Calif.

Skiing Technique

Flores, Lito Tejada. (1981) Backcountry Skiing, The Sierra Club Guide to Skiing off the Beaten Track, Sierra Club Press, San Francisco, Calif.

Crockett, Linda (2006) Alpine Skiing Technical Manual, Professional Ski Instructors of America. Denver, CO.

Fellows, Chris (2006) Tactics for All Mountain Skiing,

Professional Ski Instructors of American. Denver, CO.

Joubert, George, How to Ski the New French Way. Dial Press, 1967.

Alpine Climbing Techniques

Cliff, Peter Alpinism: A Guide to Safety in the Mountains, Cordee Publishing, London. 2006.

Cox,S. & Fulsaas K. Mountaineering: The Freedom of the Hills, The Mountaineers Books, Seattle, Wash. 2003.

Chavy, Jocelyn The Petzl Technical Catalog, FOT, France. 2006.

Chouinard, Ivon (1992) Climbing Ice, Sierra Club Press, San Francisco, Calif. 1992.

History of Skiing

Dawson, Louis. Wild Snow: A Historical Guide to North American Ski Mountaineering. 1997.

Lunn, Morten A History of Skiing, Oxford University Press, Oxford. 1927.

Randonnee Sports Science

Bigard, A.X. Ski de randonnee, cout et rendement energertiques d'une activite de haute montagne. Medicine du Sport. 62 (3),126-132. 1988.

Vives, J. R. The physiological responses of moderately active individuals to four modes of snow locomotion. Doctoral Dissertation. University of Northern Colorado. 1995.

Appendix B:
A Brief History of Backcountry Skiing

Like Stephen Hawkings " A Brief History of Time" this is a brief history of backcountry skiing. It is "brief" since one could write a book on just backcountry ski history. There are both North American and European entries. Much thanks to Louis Dawson and Peter Cliff for their research on backcountry history. Some entries are also from the famous ski historian Arnold Lunn. For more information check out Wildsnow.com, and alpenglow.org/ski -history for Northwest American entries.

2500bc Estimated date rock carving of skier found in cave at Rodoy, Norway

618   Reference made to skiing in the official history of the Tang Dynasty.

1521   King Vasa of Sweden escapes on skis from the Danes

1840   Era of Snowshoe Thompson (Jon Thorsteinson) who delivered mail between Placerville, California and Carson City, Nevada. a distance of 100 miles. Thompson is credited with saving his sick wife and child carrying them on his back and skiing to a doctor.

1870   Skis first introduced from Norway to the Alps through Norweigan and English contacts in Davos and Meiringen, Switzerland.

1880   School boys are riding the ore buckets up the Plumas Eureka Mine carrying their skis at Jonesville, California.

1887   Paulcke and company complete the first traverse of the Bernaise Oberland in four days in January reaching passes of 11,000 feet.

1889   Mathias Zdarsky is called the Father of Alpine Skiing but Telemarked down Mt.Blanc while racing the English ski champion Rickmers who paralleled. This was to determined which technique was superior. Rickmers won by a small margin. Each reportedly admired the others form.

1897   Dr. Payot reached the Col du Geant near Mont Blanc, French Alps.

1898   The first use of metal edges on skis was recorded by the Norweigan Nansen during a traverse of the southern part of Greenland. He and his team pulled sledges over 300 miles and reached an altitude of 2,700 meters.

1892   Wilhelm Paulke founded the Black Forest Ski School. He advocated that long skis and Telemarking and Stem Christi be used for turning on steep mountains.

1900   Sir Arnold Lunn,the famous ski historian, reports that a Golden Age of Ski Mountaineering is underway in Europe.The British are the leading force in ski mountaineering with the Austrians and the Germans close behind. The French aren't as active at this time.

1903   First attempt of The Haute Route from Zeermat to Chamonix, about 60 miles by Payot, Couttel, Simond and local guides.

1906   First aerial tram in the world at Montevers,Chamonix, France. Fastest vertical transportation in the world at the time.

1910   Vivian Caulfield in her book, "How to Ski" stresses the importance of the rudder action of the rear ski in Telemark skiing.

1911   South Pole is reached by Ronald Amundsen and team. Over 1,875 miles is covered in 99 days with a high point of 10,000 feet. It end on Dec. 16, 1911.

1911   Haute Route from Zermatt to Chamonix experiences first traverse by Roget and Kurz.

1912   Scott reaches the South Pole on skis.

1912   First ski lift in the world built at Truckee, California. A tobaggan was pulled up the hill by steam engine.

1913   Most of the main summits of the Alps were reached by this date on foot. Monte Rosa 1898, Gran Paradiso 1913.

1917   Lunn and Kurbel complete early traverse of Oberland glaciers.

1917   First ski descent of the Vallee Blanche starting from Aiguille du Midi.

1928   First ski lift built in Europe at the Brevent, Chamonix. The world's first rope tow.

1928   First ski traverse of the John Muir Trail from Mt. Whitney to Yosemite Valley, California by Orland Bartholomew. 280 miles in 100 days. He reportedly hunted for food and used a massive fur sleeping bag.

1930   Traverse of the Bernise Oberland. 400 miles by Walter Paulcke and team. This puts Paulcke into prominance as the ski touring expert of his time.

Ski Randonnée!

He co-authored the authoritative text "Hazards in Mountaineering" orginally published in German in 1885 by Helmut Dumler.

1933   The "Chemin a des Neiges" (The Road of the Snow) Traverse of the Alps from Nice to Innsbruck by Leon Zwingelstein of Grenoble. He covered 1200 miles in 3 months between February to May, 1933.Over 50 passes were crossed.

1934   Ski Traverse of Russia. 4500 miles were skied in four monthsbetween November 1934 and February 1935 from Nerchinsk, Skiberia to Moscow by Russian Army skiers Ityaksov, Baronin, Kurznetsov, Druzhinin and Leonenko. From Nerchinsk, the route went via the Siberian Taiga, the Bararba Steppes and the Ural Mountains. Twelver soldiers were selected but only five survived the expedition and they were decorated for the feat.

1936   First ski lift in US is built at Sun Valley, Idaho. Designed after banana hoist lifts used in South America. Built by the Southern Pacific Railroad.

1937   First ski traverse of the Central Causasus by Austrians Hromatke and Rossner.

1937   First ski lift built at Aspen, Colorado. Steam powered tobaggan type.

1940   The war years were not a great period of backcountry ski activity except for the military type. The formation of the German army mountain troops predates that of the 10th Mountain Division.

1942   Sierra Club publishes The Manual of Ski Mountaineering which introduced many American skiers to the backcountry. It was used as a training manual for US ski troops.

1943   Ski Traverse of the Coast Range of British Columbia, Canada by Watson, Beauman, White and Couttet.

1944   Tenth Mountain Division is formed by the U.S. Army with training near Leadville, Colorado. Marines form similiar training camp near Bridgeport, California.

1945   Historian Sir Arnold Lunn reports that most summit of the Alps have been skied by the end of WW II. He states that the early forties mark an end of the era of ski mountaineering and marked a divorce between skiing and alpinism which lasted until the appearance of "extreme skiing" around 1967 which according to Lunn is not a "mere variation of alpinism, but the result of the marriage of two sports: alpinism and skiing."

1950   The Sierra Club Bulletin briefly mentions a Haute Route that lies between Mt. Shasta and Lake Tahoe, California. There is some activity in the High Sierra and the Wasatch Mtns of Utah. David Brower and Allen Steck are personalities in mountaineering and ski touring.

1953   Bugaboo Mountain Traverse. Backcountry ski historian Lou Dawson reports in his book "Wild Ski" that Bill Briggs and Sterling Neil make the"first modern style alpine ski traverse in North America" on Head skis, cable bindings and flexible boots.

1954   Aiguille du Midi Tram is built in Chamonix transporting climbers and skiers to the base of Mont Blanc and skiers to the Vallee Blanche 15 mile run. The orginal cables were attached to climbers who climbed the vertical face of the Midi. The longest tram in the world (3 miles).

1956   Traverse of the Alps by the famous alpinist Walter Bonatti and fellow guides. Skied from the Italian Julian Alps to Colle de Nava in the Maritime Alps. 1,100 miles and 500,000 vertical feet were skied in 66 days of unsettled weather. In one instance 200 miles was covered in 82 hours while in another the entire Haute Route from Zermatt to Chamonix (70 miles) was covered in 24 hours (that's what he said! "Upon the Heights", 1964). Bonatti lamented the fact that Randonnee skiing was "unjustly neglected by the younger generation of mountaineers."

1965   Traverse of the Alps by Bertholet and guides. 621 miles in 22 days.

1965   June 10, First ski descent of the Whymper Couloir, Aiguille Verte by Sylvain Saudan.

1967   Great Divide Traverse , Canada. From Jasper to Lake Louise 190 miles by Canadian climbers Don Gardner,Neil Liske, Charlie Locke, and Chic Scott.

1968   October 16, First ski descent of the Gervascutti Couloir, Mt. Blance du Tacul by Sylvain Saudan.

1970   Traverse of the Alps by Kittl and other members of Austrian Army. Low altitude crossing of 1,242 miles in forty days.

1970   Descent of the South Col, Mt. Everest by Japanese skier Yichiro Miura. The resulting film exposes the world to ski mountaineering although the parachute descent and crash is criticized as a stunt.

1970   Denali First Descent by Japanese skier Tsuyoshi Ueki.

Ski Randonnée!

1970   Hut building begins in the United States. Fred Braun of Aspen begins building the U.S. Ski Association Hut System between Aspen and Crested Butte.

1970   A New Age of Ski Mountaineering? The seventies are a decade of tremendous wilderness activity. The use of light weight metal edged telemark skis use Alpine race ski technology. Crested Butte becomes a hub of Telemark activity and telemarking comes to the forefront in backcountry skiing.

1970   Ski Traverse of the John Muir Trail by Doug Robinson and Carl McCoy. 287 miles in 36 days. The route was repeated by David and Susan Beck.

1971   Maroon Bells, North Face descent by Fritz Stammberger of Aspen, Colorado.

1972   Denver to Aspen Traverse, Colorado by Jim Ward, Trish Nice and team.

1972   Rocky Mountain Continental Divide Ski Traverse from Marshall Pass, Colorado to Wyoming border 450 miles between April 2, 1972 to May 17, 1972 using Telemark skis by Don Jensen, Bill Wells, Billy Pugh and Bob Kemp.

1972   Ski Traverse of the Alps from Kaprun to Gap. British team led by Alan Blackshaw and Peter Cliff. Cliff went on to write his treatise on backcountry skiing "Ski Mountaineering".

1973   Mt. Moran Central Couloir Descent by Bill Briggs, Jackson, Wyoming.

1973   Middle Teton Descent by Bill Briggs and Tom McClure.

1973   Traverse of the Brooks Range, Alaska by a team led by Ned Gillette and Wayne Merry. 180 miles in Arctic conditions. The development of a leather double Nordic boot by Galibier, France was an important technical development which helps to further develop high performance Telemarking in the US.

1974   Eiger West Face Descent by Sylvain Saudan, Austria. Saudan will continue to influence the sport of extreme skiing with his contribution of the Wind Shield Wiper Turn for ski extremists.

1974   Denali Descent by Sylvain Saudan

1975 First Traverse of the Wind River Range, Wyoming, US by Dick Dorworth and team. 200 miles were covered n 17 days.

1977 Several ski descents were undertaken by extremists Anselme Baud and Patrick Vallencant including the North Face of the Aiguilli du Midi, May 17 with Daniel Chauchefoin and Ysves Dietry.

1977 May 17, First ski descent of North Face, Aiguille du Midi by Anselme Baud, Daniel Chauchefoin and Yves Dietry. May 31 First ski descent of Arete de Peuterey by Baud and Patrick Vallencant.

1978 Circumnavigation of Denali by Galen Rowell, Ned Gillette, Allen Bard and Doug Steins. 90 miles were covered using Nordic ski (Epoxe 88's). Lightweight equipment was chosen since the skiing was usually on flat glacial plains interspersed with difficult mountaineering.

1978 First North to South solo traverse of Greenland by Naomi Uemura of Japan. 93 days over 1400 miles between May 21 to Aug. 21.

1979 Pyramid Peak, East Face Descent,Colorado Rockies, US by Chris Landry who coined the difinition of extreme skiingas "skiing where if you fell, you would die".

1979 Grizzly Peak, North Face Descent, Colorado Rockies , US by Art Burrows. First Telemark descent.

1980 Mt. Logan, Alaska. First Nordic Descent by Art Burrows.

1980 Mt. Rainier, Liberty Ridge, First Descent by Chris Landry

1980 Mt. Mendel, High Sierras, California. First Descent by Chris Landry

1980 Matterhorn East Face by French skier Marc Boivin.

1980 Hut Building evolves in US with start of 10th Mountain Hut Association under Aspen architect Fritz Benedict. Robert McNamara, former Secretary of Defense under President Johnson helps to convince US Forest Service of hut system potential.

1980 French government states that there are 150,000 full time backcountry skiers in France.

1980 Broad Peak, Pakistan. First ski descent by Patick Vallencant

Ski Randonnée!

1982   John Muir Trail Traverse, Sierra Nevada's, California. 230 miles in 7 days by Brad and Randall Udall using Nordic racing skis. They camped using snow caves.

1982   Grand Teton First Nordic Descent by Rick Wyatt. June 10, 1982. On Telemark equipment useing Ramer self arrest grips.

1982   Mountain Skiing is written by Vic Bein and published by the Mountaineers. Wild skiing photos covers Telemarking and some Randonnee skiing.

1983   Mt. Rainier, Liberty Ridge, First Nordic Descent by Tom Carr and Eric Hendren.

1984   10th Mountain Hut System in Colorado reports 2,252 skier nights at their huts during the 1983-84 skiing season.

1985   First Apine ski touring competition in the Alps with the introduction of Le Grand Defi: 320 miles in 6 days.

1985   First Traverse of the Grand Tour, Colorado Rockies. From Saint Marys Glacier to Vail, Colorado by alpine ski touring equipment maker Paul Ramer, Steve Barnett, Charlotte McDuff, Peter Shelton, David Moe, Chris Noble and Bill Wildberger. 93 miles over a month due to bad weather. One of the first attempts to connect up Colorado ski resorts into a Haute Route system.

1986   Colorado Super Tour by Jean Vives and Patrick Griffin, ski guides from Aspen, Colorado. Longest randonnee tour in US from Winter Park to Crested Butte, Colorado (via Vail). 180 miles in 28 days in bad weather (authors note: the worst avalanche conditions in a decade were carefully avoided). The route connected up three importent tours: The Grand Tour, The 10th Mountain Hut System and the Fred Braun Hut System.

1987   Ski Mountaineering is written by Peter Cliff published by Pacific Search Press. Randonnée skiing with an excellent crevasse rescue section.

1990   1,000.000 skiers ski the backcounty on Randonnee equipment in Europe according to ski journalist and researcher Volodia Shahshashan of Le Skieur Magazine (personal communication,1992).

1991   International Committee of Ski Alpinism Competitions is formed in Barcelona by Volodia Shahshahani for development of Randonnee racing in the Alps.

1991   10th Mountain Hut and Trail System, Colorado reports 12,195 skier nights for their hut system during the 1990-91 ski season.

1992   Mt.Everest, South Col First Descent by French skier Pierre Tardivel. This the first real top down ski descent down the standard climbing route.

1993   American Louis Dawson II of Carbondale, Colorado completes his last 14,000 foot peak in his quest to ski all 54 peaks over 14,000 peaks in Colorado. The East Face of Pyramid Peak was his last.

1993   10th Mountain Hut and Trail System, Colorado reports 23,377 skier nights in its hut system for the 1993-1994 ski season.

1994   Denali, Wickersham Wall. First Nordic Descent of one of the biggest walls in the world. 14,000 ft. of vertical were skied on classic Telemark equipment by Tyson Bradly and John Montecucco on May 24, 1994.

1995   Mt. Robson North Face First Descent by Ptor Spricenieks and Troy Jungen. The 60 degree face was according to Lou Dawson North America's "ultimate prize".

1995   First Physiological Study of Telemarking and Randonnee skiing by Dr. Jean Vives Ed.D., University of Northern Colorado. Rare on snow study conducted at Arapahoe Basin, Colorado using middle aged skiers showed that Randonnee skiing was more efficient during climbing than Telemarking. This study helped to ligitimize backcountry skiing as an area of physiological study in the world scientific literature. It also emphasized the importance of the binding mechanism in the energy expenditure equation. (see Appendix G).

1997   WildSnow written by Louis Dawson published by AAC Press. First book to cover the history of North American ski mountaineering.

1999   Backcountry Skier written by Jean Vives and published by Human Kinetics describes backcountry skiing on Telemark and Randonnée equipment.

2005   Colorado Haute Route First Traverse East to West from Vail SkiResort to Winter Park Colorado by Jean Vives and Charlie Gray both from Winter Park, Colorado. 62.4 miles. 19,583 feet of ascent and 24,405 feet of d scent in 7 days between April 17-23. This route compares favorably to The Haute Route and actually has 3,000 ft. more climbing than the original.The final day had to be done two weeks later due to persistant spring storms.The skiers stayed in towns along the way after a European model. It is by an altitude standard one of the highest ski routes in the world. Is this the "American Haute Route" ?

2006   Doug Coombs, famous ski guide and steep skiing specialist dies at La Grave, France attempting to save another skiers life. Doug had exemplified a thoughtful approach to backcountry skiing and pioneered many innovative skiing and guiding technigues.

Ski Randonnée!

Sources:

A History or Skiing (1972) Sir Arnold Lunn. Oxford University Press, London, England.

Ski Mountaineering (1987) Peter Cliff. Pacific Search Press. Seattle, Washington. USA.

Wild Snow (1997) Loius Dawson, American Alpine Club Press. Golden, Colorado.

Appendix C: Weights and Measures

Volume and Distance

1 quart water	=	2.2 pounds
1 quart water	=	(32 fluid ounces)
		2 pints
1 pint	=	480 grams
1 pint	=	16 ounces
1 cup	=	240 grams
1 inch	=	2.54 centimeters
1 centimeter	=	.3937 inches
1 foot	=	30 centimeters
1 meter	=	39.37 inches
1 kilogram	=	2.2045 pounds
1 pound	=	.4536 kilograms
Convert F to C =		(F - 32) x 5 4 9
Convert C to F =		(C x 9 4 5) + 32

Temperature Conversion

Celsius (C)	Fahrenheit (F)
-40	-40.0
-20	-4.0
0	32.0
1	33.8
5	41.0
10	50.0
15	59.0
20	68.0
25	77.0
30	86.0
35	95.0
40	104.0

Shoe Size Converter

Metric Size	U.S. Size
35	3.5
36	4.0
37	4.5
38	5.5
39	6.0
40	7.0
40.5	7.5
41	8.0
42	8.5
43	9.0
44	10.5
45	11.0
46	11.5
47	11.8

Appendix D: Daypack List

Skis
Poles
Climbing Skins
Ski Repair Kit (see winter camping list)
Anti-Glop Skin Wax
Anti-Glop Ski Wax
Ski Boots
Backpack
Climbing Gear (optional)
Rubberized Equipment Stap (at least one)
Sunglasses
Goggles
Anti Fog Cloth/Spray
Swiss Army Knife
Water Hydration System 16 oz minimum
Thermos of Hot Tea (optional)
Power Bars™ / Lunch
Quantity Duct Tape
First Aid Kit (includes Pocket CPR Mask)
Snow Saw
Snow Shovel
Snowpit Kit
Avalanche Probe Pole
Avalanche Transceiver (keep under clothing) and extra batteries
Extra Gloves
Extra Wool/pile Hat
Small Headlamp
Sunscreen
Camera
Map of Area
GPS with extra batteries
Cell Phone (fully charged) keep in inside pocket
In Jacket (Never Leaves Jacket): whistle, butane lighters, small compass)

Appendix E: Winter Camping

Unless otherwise noted, "quantity" depends on the size of the group, amount used, and days spent out.

Ski Gear

1	expedition backpack
1	pair skis
1	pair ski boots
1	pair climbing skins
1	tube climbing skin adhesive (optional)
1	pair ski poles (metal/avalanche probe)
1	pair crampons (optional)
1	climbing harness (see glacier skiing list)
1	ice axe (optional)
1	avalanche transceiver (with fresh batteries)
1	avalanche shovel

Ski Repair Kit

1	Swiss™ army knife
2	binding screws
2	drywall expansion sleeves
1	pair of adjustable ski pole inner bushings
1	quantity duct tape (25 feet – stored on ski pole or in pack)
1	pair of pliers or composite tool (optional)
1	binding adjustment tool
1	sewing kit (leather needle with dental floss ok)

Clothing

1	pair gaiters
1	top synthetic underwear (expedition-weight)
1	bottom synthetic underwear (expedition-weight)
1	top synthetic underwear (medium-weight)
1	bottom synthetic underwear (medium-weight)
1	Dry-Lite™ T-shirt
1	ski hat (pile fleece or wool/nylon)
1	balaclava (or extra hat)
1	neck gaiter
1	pair heavy gloves/mittens
1	pair glove liners
1	pair lightweight cross-country gloves

Clothing continued

1   cotton handkerchief
1   pair heavy ski socks
2   pair ski sock liners
1   pair cotton socks
1   Gore-Tex™ storm suit top
1   Gore-Tex™ storm suit bottom
2   pair briefs
1   pile fleece vest
1   pile fleece jacket (optional)
1   pair camp booties (or use ski boot liner)
1   pair orthotics

Snow Camping Gear

1   water pump/tablets
1   sleeping bag (-20 degree F. minimum rating)
1   sleeping bag cover (optional)
1   compression bag for sleeping bag
1   tent (with vestibule)
6   stuff sacks
1   Thermorest™/Ensolite™ pad

Cooking

1   15-inch square Ensolite™ pad (to insulate stove)
1   camping stove
1   quantity stove fuel
1   Lexan™ spoon, knife, fork
1   cooking pot and lid
1   quantity dehydrated food
1   Power Bars™/Gue™
1   camp towel
1   quantity coffee filters/french press
1   quantity alcohol wipes
2   water bottles (32-oz., wide-mouth)
1   thermos drinking mug
1   1/2 roll of toilet paper or 5 kitchen towels, in plastic storage bag
2   extra plastic storage bags
2   small butane lighters
1   headlamp
4   extra batteries (lithium batteries optional)
2   extra light bulbs (1 high intensity, 1 regular intensity)

Sun Protection

1   crushproof sunglasses case
1   bottle sunblock (SPF 45)
1   stick lip balm (SPF 45)
1   sunvisor or baseball cap
1   pair sunglasses
1   set sunglass retainer straps
1   pair prescription glasses
1   extra pair prescription glasses (optional)
1   pair goggles (with fog lenses)
1   antifog cloth or antifog spray product

Survival Equipment

1   compass (with mirror)
1   map of travel area
1   altimeter
2   butane lighters (kept in jacket at all times)
1   plastic whistle (kept in jacket at all times)
1   quantity duct tape (25 feet – this is already in your ski repair kit)
2   athletic bars
1   space blanket
1   Ensolite pad

First Aid Supplies

1   quantity latex gloves
1   CPR mask
1   quantity steristrips

Medical Kit

5   antacid tablets
5   antidiarrhea tablets
5   throat drops
5   aspirin tablets
5   ibuprofen tablets
1   bottle eyedrops

Blister Kit

1   quantity moleskin
1   quantity second skin
1   quantity bandaids

Personal Camping Gear

1   book (optional—for leisure)
1   notebook
1   pencil
1   tube toothpaste
1   toothbrush
1   washcloth

Appendix F: Conditioning

Backcountry skiing is a physically demanding sport, and conditioning away from the slopes can help prevent injuries. You don't train for the good days, you train for the cold and long ones. People generally hate to "train". The outdoor athlete is usually, well, outdoors! Staying in shape comes naturally to the experienced, but not to beginners. When you are stronger you increase your survivability and are safer as a result. You are most injury prone during the first hours or days of a ski tour. Ski touring has its own training effect that is more sport-specific than any exercise you could do in the gym. Conditioning before a trip prepares you for the initial exercise stress of the trip, reducing muscle soreness, increasing ski performance and speeding your adjustment to higher altitudes. Losing excess body weight and doing cardiovascular training improves power and endurance.

Training for backcountry skiing is not like training for cross-country skiing. Strict aerobic training like long-distance running is not enough! Not only do we travel long distances, which requires aerobic training, but we also must carry heavy packs and climb hills, which require anaerobic training. Building an aerobic base with long runs, swimming and biking helps to build a foundation for harder training such as running wind sprints, running stadium stairs and doing swimming one lap sprints.

The North American Skiing Training Center at Truckee, California identified five areas of conditioning important for skiing: Strength, speed/power, balance, flexibility and endurance.

- SPEED/POWER: The stereo type of skiers training is the skier who is jumping back and forth over a box. This is basic Plyometrics or "jump training" developed by eastern bloc-Russian trainers. Plyometric is best described as "explosive-reactive" power training. We can also develop this fast reactive training when we run mountain trails since that also develops reaction speed by jumping up and over obstacles. One legged squats

- STRENGTH: Nothing develops strength and muscle size like weight lifting. Most alpine ski teams, including the U.S. team, have strength trainers who emphasize overall body training. Exercises that include core body muscles are the best, such as : Squats, Bench Presses, Pull ups, Lunges, Inclined leg presses are the best at building whole body strength. Three sets of 12 should be done three days/week when aerobic training is not being done since that may interfere with weight training strength gains. Another one: lie on your back and squeeze a gym ball between your lower legs. Raise your legs to a 45 degree angle with the floor and lower slowly. Keep your back pressed against the floor. Do three sets of 12.

- ENDURANCE: Running and biking are great for developing over all endurance which in turn will help the body faster adjust to higher altitudes by increasing the efficiency of aerobic pathways. Swimming is also a great conditioner for this purpose. Keep your heart rate at 60% of your age adjust maximum. (220 beats per second - your age = max. heart rate x 60% = training heart rate).

- FLEXIBILITY: The gym ball and medicine ball have become popular for exercises that stretch leg and inner leg muscles. Stretching should emphasize the hamstrings, hips and back. Place your foot on your desk and lean over your leg keeping your back straight. Hold this and all stretches for 20 seconds.

- BALANCE: Holding a medicine ball with both hands, pick up your right leg a few inches above the ground while squatting a few inches with your left knee. Repeat with the opposite leg. See how low you can squat comfortably. Strength and balance work together to stabilize your body during ski movements.

Training for Altitude

As we ascend in altitude the maximum volume of oxygen ($\dot{V}O_2$max) that we can utilize decreases along with our potential for exercise. An altitude of 7,000 to 8,000 feet (2,133 to 2,438 meters) seems to be the threshold altitude at which the body starts to make physiological adaptations. If you live at sea level and cannot train at altitude, your best preparation is to train the metabolic pathways that are most involved in physical work at altitude: train anaerobically. At altitude the body prefers anaerobic pathways for metabolizing energy since there is less available oxygen at altitude. By preconditioning those pathways, they are primed for maximum strength gains once you are at altitude. Wind sprints (50- to 100-yard running sprints or one-lap swimming sprints) and weight training are all variations of anaerobic training. When we train anaerobically, we feel a burning sensation in our muscles. This is caused by the accumulation of lactic acid – a muscle metabolite that results from hard exercise. This is different from the pain of a muscle injury that is accompanied by the total failure of the muscle to continue working. Sport breathing (discussed in more detail in chapter 4) will also maximize efforts at altitude, which is why it is so encouraged throughout this text. To maximize physical performance on a ski tour follow the long-accepted advice: climb and ski high but sleep low, for best recuperation at night. Be sure also to follow a high-carbohydrate diet – a good example is presented in the nutrition chapter.

Periodization

Ski training can fit into a year long fitness schedule. Periodization is the practice of timing conditioning so that you are at your physical peak at the optimal time. In the past, elite skiers would design their training so that they would be in peak condition just before a major competition. You can adapt this idea to be in the best shape possible when the ski season begins or just before a major ski trip.

Summer is a great time for aerobic training, which forms an aerobic base that prepares the body for harder training. Studies have shown that without an aerobic base, strength and muscle mass gains are reduced and more difficult to achieve. Most skiers like mountain biking, mountaineering, swimming, and backpacking, and these are great training modes year-round. Running up hills and stadium steps (within the parameters of knee health) will help form your aerobic base. In the fall, focus conditioning to include more ski-specific training. This means weight lifting three days/week until December, when you enter a maintenance phase during the ski season. During the season, if skiing on weekends, you may lift two days per week. This continues until April, when you may wish to train for summer sports again such as mountaineering or mountain biking.

Appendix G: Nutrition

As the old saying goes "an army marches on it's stomach". Well, skiers ski on theirs! Mealtime is a time to recharge physically and psychologically. Proper nutrition increases stamina and alertness, and therefore safety. Many athletes are confused about their nutritional needs. Yes, backcountry skiing can be termed an endurance sport and because of that may require higher amounts of carbohydrates as exercise fluctuates. However, it must be based on sound nutrition. You can't live on power bars and athletic gels! You need fat, proteins and carbohydrates. Today's skiers should resist fads and build a solid and disciplined approach to nutrition.

Nutrition and Altitude

At altitude, nutrient absorption is not impaired, but the hunger sensation is dulled. Accompanying weight loss is often referred to as high-altitude anorexia. Even well-trained individuals may lose weight at altitude even though caloric intake remains the same as at sea level. This phenomenon may be caused by a combination of both neurological and biochemical imbalances due to reduced oxygen pressure at altitude. Physiologists consider any altitude changes exceeding 6,000 feet (1,829 meters) a physiological change in altitude. Any such gain can decrease the appetite for food and water between 40 to 60 percent of normal. Whatever the reasons, the bottom line is that you need to eat while at altitude even though you may not feel like it.

Present Issues

Two areas that need attention are the amount of water that should be consumed and the ratio required between fats, carbohydrates and protein.

Water Intake

The figures for water intake are all over the place. Some say that you should be drinking 8 oz/1 cup per hour while others say just drink when you are thirsty. The common wisdom "drink 8 glasses of water a day" has no scientific basis. Dartmouth physiologist Heinz Valtin (2002) reviewed 30 years worth of hydration studies. The daily intake was approximately 4 glasses per day. One nice thing about the new "camelback" hydration systems is that you can take in many small amounts over time. This is the same way you should be eating as well. I like to prehydrate before I go skiing, since I drink coffee which I feel dyhyrates me. I feel better if I match my coffee intake cup for cup with plain water. Coffee is OK if you are already a coffee drinker. Coffee is one of the few true ergogenic drinks (work enhancing) since it is a mood elevator and stimulates fat metabolism during exercise. More water intake information can be found at the Gatorade Sport Science Institute web site: www.gssiweb.com. including a water intake calculator.

Fats, Protein, and Carbohydrates

Some climbers tell the joke that "cliff bars (energy bars) should be a food group". As much as I like energy bars and energy gel, they are not a substitute for good nutrition and real food. The problem with these energy products is that they require a lot of water for their assimilation. If you don't do this you can really get dehydrated. There is a story of two climbers (I won't name names) who climbed the Polish Route on Denali and ate cliff bars and gel for two days. When they got to the medical camp at 14,000 after the climb they were greatly dehydrated and required intravenous rehydration.

Recent research shows that you need 25% fat, 15% protein and 60% carbohydrates for strenuous exercise at low to high altitudes. This ratio has been used on Everest climbs and at sea level during the Steger Arctic expeditions. After a hard day of exercising outside peanut butter and cheese really tastes good. That because our fat stores are decreased and fat is really brain food. Exercise demands mental work as well as physical work. Chocolate is also like coffee in that it is a stimulant that effects the same neuro pathways. Carbo loading like eating a big pasta dinner the night before a big ski day is a good idea and it works well.

There definitely is a place for carbos and energy bars and that is right during exercise when you are really in it. I like the newer packs that have the small pocket right on the belt just for energy bars. Theres is nothing wrong with adding energy powder to your water. But don't make it too strong since your stomach can absorb it. In fact your stomach will suck water from your body to dilute it so it can absorb it and in the process make you drier which negates the whole reason you drank it in the first place.

You can't eat all you need in three meals. You have to eat like a bird, eating several mini meals spaced over the whole day. The body can also absorb more nutrients from smaller meals than larger ones, because the body's blood flow is concentrated on the muscles during skiing rather than on the stomach. It's important to actually schedule food and water breaks ahead of time because altitude and exercise blunts your hunger and thirst.

Adding Up The Numbers: Nutritional Demand

The energy demands of Randonnée or Telemark skiers while climbing are identical. In my own research, it was shown that a 170-pound male skier burns approximately 785 kilocalories per hour when climbing full-time. This shows how more efficient Randonnée equipment is since the Randonnée gear was 35% heavier than the Telemark equipment! To get calories needed for Randonnée skiing multiply, in kilograms, body weight by .17 kilocalories per kilogram to get a kilocalorie-per-minute rate and then multiple that by 60 to get an hourly rate). Including resting, and climbing only 60 percent of the time, the figure totals 3,769.92 kilocalories in a eight-hour touring day

Ski Randonnée!

(4.8 hours flat skiing and climbing). Factors such as skill level, slope angle, weather, and pack weight will further affect this figure (actually there are 30 variables). For comparison, a Tour de France cyclist may consume 6,000 kilocalories a day, while an Arctic skier may use 5,200 kilocalories a day.

For those scientists out there the following equation by Bigard (1987) and Vives (1996) shows the different components that account for total work being done during Randonnee skiing:

$$Wtotal = Wg\,(Wr2) + Wm + Wr1 + Wf + Wi$$

where:

Wg	= work to displace center of gravity
Wm	= work to accelerate and decelerate segment mass
$Wr1$	= work to overcome air resistance
$Wr2$	= work to overcome resistance of boots and bindings to forward movement
Wf	= force needed to overcome snow resistance to sliding
Wi	= work of internal metabolism

Appendix H: Mountain Health

You are the Ski Patrol!

Knowledge and a cool head are important in backcountry emergencies. All skiers should take a first aid course dealing with mountain emergencies. Several excellent mountain medicine texts are listed in the bibliography. This book cannot be a complete treatise on first aid, but it will emphasize some areas needing attention. If you have a chronic condition, don't forget to take along the medicines that you need (such as insulin or asthmatic inhalers).

A little red bag with a white cross might help you fix small cuts and bruises, but it won't help you fix a broken leg. Some will be disappointed by my medical kit, which stresses minor stomach and blister medications (see the equipment list on pages 264-265), but keep in mind that almost everything you carry can be used in a first aid response. Handkerchiefs make fine bandages, and duct tape is a good skin tape. On a attempt to ski the Colorado Haute Route, I crashed into a tree on the Commando Run on the backside of Vail ski area. There was excruciating pain and I knew I had blown out my ACL. But we still had to go three miles to our hut and it was 6 pm! At least the weather was good – it was clear with no wind. My knee joint was a mess. I slid down on my butt to a road cut. I then wrapped my whole knee in a duct tape cast and was able to ski the remaining miles to the hut by 11 pm. Don't forget your duct tape!

Protective Devices

Always use the appropriate protective devices during skiing. Knee pad protectors have longed been used by Telemarkers and are now being used by parallel skiers. Those with a history of knee injury should definitely wear their knee braces to protect the knee joint. Lower-back braces should be used by those with a history of back injury.

Treating Athletic Injuries

With any twisting injury (whether to the knee or the ankle), one might experience severe pain and swelling. Fracture pain differs from other pains – it is more severe and persistent and will not allow weight bearing. Pain from a twist may subside somewhat with continued skiing, but it should not be ignored. The faster you care for the injury, the sooner it will heal. Use the RICE formula – Rest, Ice, Compression, and Elevation. In camp/hut – get off your feet and Rest. Elevate the whole leg and use a large freezer bag full of snow held in place with an elastic wrap for an Ice pack. Cold has tremendous healing power. Apply the ice pack for 20 minutes every half hour for the first 72 hours. An anti-inflammatory drug such as ibuprofen, aspirin, or naproxen should also be taken (with food or milk, if these drugs upset your stomach). You should wrap the knee or ankle in a Compression bandage for the next days ski even if it "doesn't hurt that much". I've heard that before. Massage is good therapy for most general aches and pains.

Blisters and Foot Care

Blisters are always a problem in outdoor sports. Slippery sock liners don't prevent blisters; they actually cause them by increasing sliding and friction inside the boot. Always use dry, clean socks. Pretape nuisance spots with white medical tape or duct tape before skiing. Treat blisters promptly, before they get too big. Deflate blisters at their edge with a sharp pin that has been sterilized with a flame. Carry a "blister kit" that contains second skin, moleskin, and medical tape or duct tape. Apply in the following order:
1.   Second skin – gelatin padding that reduces pain
2.   Moleskin – tougher outer padding
3.   Tape – keeps other layers on

Also, before skiing don't forget to clip your nails and spray your feet with antiperspirant to reduce wetness. In camp, take your socks off and allow your feet to dry. Foot massages are always good for general pains and can eliminate cold sensations within a few minutes.

Hypothermia and Frostbite

Severe hypothermia occurs when the body temperature falls below 90 degrees Fahrenheit (32 degrees Celsius). With severe hypothermia, shivering stops; the person usually cannot ski; and the person may be unconscious. Mild hypothermia involves shivering, apathy, and loss of coordination. A body temperature just at 90 degrees Fahrenheit causes mild confusion to occur (a dangerous time to be making navigational decisions). Because there is a danger of hypothermia and frostbite when air temperature is below –20 degrees Fahrenheit (29 degrees Celsius), exercise should be limited. Many mountain emergencies evolve due to the loss of judgment and ability to reason that occurs with this condition.

Hypothermia is often accompanied by frostbite. Frostbite was once thought to be caused by the freezing of inter cellular water resulting in cell rupture and tissue death, but it is currently thought to be caused by the obstruction of blood vessels in the affected area. Frostbite begins as the freezing of the skin – something that can occur even on a sunny day, when cold and wind exist together. The skin appears patchy white (especially on the nose and ears) due to a constriction of blood vessels. After the blood returns, the skin becomes red and swollen. In severe frostbite, the skin becomes purple and then black after rewarming. Always rewarm affected areas after returning to shelter where re-chilling cannot occur. Immersion in warm (not hot) water should be done gently, and the affected area should not be massaged. Seek medical advice if severe frostbite is suspected.

The best defense against hypothermia and frostbite is smart skiing – avoid fatigue and bad weather, use the proper clothing, and stay hydrated. Since metal conducts cold, avoid wearing earrings during periods of extreme cold as this will promote frostbite. It's not uncommon for a whole group to be hypothermic without even knowing it. You can usually ascertain a group's comfort level by the amount of talking in the group; on the trail, quiet people are frequently cold people. Strike up conversations to keep people talking and to keep their minds off the cold. Some skiers might never admit being cold in front of a group, so periodically ask individuals how they are feeling and make sure everyone is eating high-energy food and drinking plenty of water (dehydration leads to hypothermia in cold conditions). Thermos containers filled with hot Gatorade™ are also good to take on colder day tours, and chemical heat packs last four to six hours and are fantastic for heating up cold hands and bodies while providing a great psychological lift. In stormy conditions, keep everyone moving. If a map stop is necessary, find a spot in a dense grove of trees where wind protection is available – don't do it in the open. In severe cases of hypothermia or frostbite, those affected may need medical care upon returning.

Acute Mountain Sickness

Altitude illness doesn't occur just in the Himalayas. People occasionally get ill at ski resorts that lie between 8,000 and 12,000 feet (2,438 to 3,657 meters) above sea level. The effect of altitude depends on the degree and rate of the change in altitude. Illness can occur when there is a change in altitude of 6,000 feet or more, where the normal healthy body can take up to two weeks to acclimatize.

Acute mountain sickness is not a specific disease, but describes several symptoms caused by high altitude. Symptoms may include extreme fatigue, headache, dizziness, breathlessness, and hyperventilation. Tourists usually feel these symptoms above 8,000 feet (2,438 meters), while high-altitude inhabitants most often feel them above 14,000 feet (4,267 meters). Conditioning won't prevent the onset of mountain sickness, but it may increase the ability to deal with the debilitating symptoms. A past history of altitude problems may mandate a slow ascent to altitude and a stay of a few days close to the trailhead before a major ski tour. For example, many people stay a few days in Denver (5,260 feet [1,603 meters]) before ascending to the ski resorts at higher altitudes. Alcohol consumption usually makes the symptoms worse. Symptoms tend to worsen at night with reduced physical activity and usually decrease in 24 hours. If they don't, the victim should descend to the lowest possible altitude immediately. Always be sure the person is hydrated and resting. Those with heart conditions should always get a physical before going to high altitude.

Heat Exhaustion

You can get hot while mountain skiing, especially in the spring. Sunstroke and heat exhaustion, basic overloads of the body's cooling system, are marked by very high body temperature; red, hot, dry skin; abnormal breathing; and mental confusion. Both should be treated with rest, stay cool out of the sun, and drink lightly salted liquids. From an athletic standpoint, for every 10 degrees that the air temperature rises, the body must double its effort to produce the same amount of work. Reduce clothing before you get too hot. Don't cover your calves in hot weather, because they release a lot of body heat (you can wear shorts or knickers, or unzip your ski pants for ventilation). Wear lightweight gloves to allow heat release at the wrists. While visors allow heat to escape from the head, keeping the skier cooler, caps will protect the head from sunburn. In very warm conditions, wearing a polypropylene or Dry-Lite™ running shirt will keep you cooler and drier than a cotton T-shirt. Be sure to rest more often and drink more liquids in hot weather – this will also help keep you cool.

Ski Randonnée!

Sport Vision

Sunglasses and goggles are safety equipment for your eyes – if you can't see, you can't ski. High-altitude radiation can damage the eyes as easily as tree branch collisions and other accidental impacts. Coated plastic lenses work best – they are more scratch resistant than polycarbonate, and they cannot break. Mountain sunglasses or goggles should provide 100 percent protection from UVA, UVB, and IR (infrared) rays, and they should also be impact resistant. A brown-yellow tint is best for bright light, whereas yellow-brown goggle lenses should only be used for cloudy days where flat light, or no shadows or depth perception, exists. Yellow driving or shooting glasses are excellent for those who sweat profusely and have problems with their glasses fogging. Side panels can protect the eyes from incidental radiation that causes subconscious irritation that can greatly increase both fatigue and your temper! A sunglass-retaining strap can prevent accidental loss and breakage. Use an anti-fog cloth for cleaning, or apply a commercial anti-fog product to the inside of lenses to minimize fogging. Natural Tears eyedrops are an excellent remedy for eye irritation. If you do get "snow blindness", i.e. your eyes are so "burned" that you cannot open them and they feel like they have glass in them – you will recover – I have had it. Wet cool compresses to the eyes are great for this type of inflammation. But don't use eye drops that vaso-constrict. Neutral eye drops such as Natural Tears are OK.

Skin Protection: The Sun and Altitude

UVB rays – the ones that tan and burn you increase by 5% percent every 1,000 feet (University of La Paz, Boliva, 1997). That means at 9000 feet you are getting 45% more UVB than at sea level. And at high altitude, it doesn't have to be hot for you to get a sunburn. In fact the cool air can fool you into thinking the sun isn't that bad. New snow reflects up to 80% of the sun. Most wilderness medicine specialists advocate the use of sunblock with SPF 30 to 45. Suntan creams with SPF 50 made for kids work great since they are waterproof and won't sting your eyes. Second-degree burns are common among those whose skin is not sun conditioned. Sunburned arms and shoulders are not fun when you are carrying a 50-pound pack! Calves are also important to protect during spring ski tours. For dry, cracked skin from the sun and the dry mountain air, use a lip balm with a high SPF factor of 20 plus. (The concept of the Sun Protection Factor was invented by Franz Greiter of Piz Buin, Switzerland in 1950's).

Serious Injury and Evacuation by Sled

A very well respected mountaineering text states "a snow evacuation can be as simple as placing the patient in a bivy sac or blanket and sliding the patient down the slope". Not true. Evacuation by sled should only be used as a last resort. It can be appropriate for skiers suffering from fatigue, altitude sickness, hypothermia, or frostbite. However, moving a critically injured person is different from moving one who is tired. Order air or ground evacuation (that is, helicopter or snowmobiles) if you suspect neck or back injury. Those not showing signs of neck or back injury such as numbness or tingling in the feet, legs, or back can be moved short distances

(1 to 2 miles [1.6 to 3 kilometers]), but the route should be as smooth as possible; you should scout it out thoroughly before attempting transport because rough handling can cause a victim to go into shock.

It is better to make camp at the injury site if the site is safe from avalanche or rockfall. Keep the victim warm and comfortable, and let professional rescuers do the moving. If, however, the injured person must be moved before professional help arrives, you can construct an emergency sled.

Backcountry skis used to have holes in their tips and tails for sled construction but not anymore. Emergency sleds built from skis are not as solid as a rescuer's fiberglass toboggan, but if the victim's chances of survival are slim if he isn't moved out of a dangerous avalanche zone or to a place of shelter, an emergency sled can be considered. If you are prepared with a few minimal supplies, you can build one. Four aluminum bolts with wing nuts and washers can be used to hold two skis together on two large avalanche shovels. Wire can be used instead of bolts. No decent portable sled system is available on the market for such emergency use. Usually with enough rope a sled can be built out of tree branches, skis and ski poles.

Conclusion

Preparing your body for backcountry skiing is as important as preparing your equipment. A well-conditioned body can handle the exertion of skiing and the effects of altitude more efficiently than a nonconditioned body; as a result, you can learn faster, fall less with fewer ski injuries, and have more fun skiing. In the field, the use of proper precautions related to environmental hazards such as altitude, sun, and cold is just plain common sense. Take care of your body out there – it's your most important piece of equipment.

Pain can signal that an injury is coming. Listen to your inner voice. Stop yourself! Remember that you could put yourself out for the winter. Tomorrow is another day, and rest is as important as training. You shouldn't train when you are overly tired and can't exercise properly.

Appendix I: Internet Sources

This is just a small sampling of the Web sites that are available to the Randonnée skier. Many of these sites have their own links as well. Since the internet is so well used, I tried to include some unusual sites that you may not have heard of. Typically, if you add ".com" to a word it'll turn up a website. Such as "marmot.com" but it's not always the case, Black Diamond is "www.bdel.com".

Clothing

Polarguard	www.polarguard.com
Mountainhardware	www.mountainhardware.com
Marmot Gear	www.marmot.com
Patagonia	www.patagonia.com
Arcteryx	www.arcteryx.com

Gear

Petzl	www.petzl.com
Atomic Skis	www.atomicski.com
Black Diamond	www.bdel.com
Fritschi Bindngs	www.fritschi.com
Backcountry Access	www.bcaccess.com
Sterling Rope	www.sterlingropes.com
Mammut Rope	www.mammut.com
North Face Tents	www.thenorthface.com/na/gear

Avalanche

Ortovox	www.ortovox.com
Survival on Snow	www.survival on snow.com
USFS National Avalanche Center	www.fsavalanche.org
Swiss Istitute for Avalanche Research	www.slf.ch
Backcountry Access	www.bcaccess.com
Avalanche.org	www.snowpit.com
Worldwide avalanche conditions	www.avalanche.org
American Avalanche Assoc.	www.americanavalanche association.org

Life Link Safety Gear	www.lifelink.com
World Avalanche Conditions	www.csac.org
Snow Crystals	www.snowcrystals.com

Weather

weather forcasts	www.wunderground.com
weather worldwide	weather.com

Navigation

Garmin GPS	www.garmin.com
TOPO Maps	www.topo.com
Magnetic Declineation Correction	www.ngdc.noaa.gov

Expedition

Centers for Disease Control	www.cdc.gov
Travelers Insurance	www.travelex.com
US Ski Mountaineering Associaton	http://basinhome.com
American Alpine Club	http://www.americanalpineclub.
org/	
British Alpine Club	http://www.alpine-club.org.uk/
Alps Information	http://pistehors.com
Amar Andalkar (interesting)	www.skimountaineer.com

Survival / Rescue

Search and Rescue	www.sarinfo.bc.ca/sarlinks.htm
Sterling Ropes	www.sterlingropes.com
Petzl (crevasse rescue)	www.petzl.com
Rescue Respons	www.rescueresponse.com
Knots and Rope	www.knotandrope.com
Maps	www.maps.com

Information

Wildsnow/Louis Dawson	www.wildsnow.com
Couloir Magazine	www.couloirmagazine.com
Powder Magazine	www.powdermag.com
Mountain Gazette	www.mountaingazette.com
Skipressworld	www.skipressworld.com
Mountainzone	www.mountainzone.com
Skirandonnee.com	www.skirandonnee.com

Appendix J: Ski Route Grading

The TopoNeige System by Volodia Shahshashani

Ski route grading is in its infancy but develop into a future method of comparing ski routes to one another that can be used universally. The TopoNeige System was developed by Volodia Shahshashani, a Grenoble based ski mountaineer who pioneered many extreme ski routes in the 1970's in the Dauphine mountains of France. He is still very active (Pistehors.com, 2006). It attempts to grade ascent, descent level of difficulty and exposure (.1-.3 sublevels). The gradings are split into five levels each with three possible exposure levels (for instance level 5 could go to 5.1,5.2,5.3). Critics suggest that this system is too simplistic and will not adapt to future gear developments. It is still used extensively in Europe. Grades assume spring conditions. Letter grades correspond to each level:

R   Excursion (low angle,crampons/ice axes not need under any condition.
F: Easy (glacial routes without challenging sections)
PD: Not Very Difficult (slopes up to 45 deg)
AD: Fairly Difficult (difficult, possible short couloirs up to 50 deg)
D: Difficult (couloirs and snow/ice faces up to 55 and 60 deg)
TD: Very Difficult (undefined)
ED: Extremely Difficult (undefined)

Level 1: Beginner routes on mountain terrain. Slopes do not exceed 30 deg.(black runs in France). Forest trails are wide enough for turns. Less than 800 m (2600 ft). Low danger from avalanches and falls. (R)

Level 2: No real technical difficulty. Slopes do not exceed 35 deg. Dangers from high altitude possible. (R)

Level 3: Start of ski mountaineering. Technical sections, long slopes of 35 deg. short sections of 40-45 deg. Dense woodland, steep forest tracks. (F)

Level 4: Couloir skiing of steep slopes. Extended sections of 40 deg with possibility of 50 deg. Very technical routes on mid-mountain areas. Dense woodland with moderate slopes. (PD)

Level 5: Very steep slopes, long sections of 45-50 deg. Significant sections of 50 deg. (AD-D)

The D System by Louis Dawson and Andrew McLean

This system rates how difficult a slope is to ascend and descend. The term "D" is code for words such as "descendre, difficulty, descente, etc" (Dawson, wildsnow. com, 2006). The D System has three parts: D Scale for difficulty, R Scale for risk or danger, Grade Scale for time needed for route. Glacier skiing can automatically increase the R rating. More detail of this system can be found at wildsnow.com. In short, the following applies:

D Scale

Dawson suggests that most backcountry skiing occurs between D3 and D12 although the scale goes from D1 to D23:

D3: Above 25 deg. and may include narrow sections, transitions.

D4: Like an easier Expert run at a resort. Slope at 30 deg.

D5: Like an easier Expert run at a resort. Slope at 35 deg and more terrain obstacles.

D6: Similiar angles but with more obstacles such as rollovers, trees, ridges,etc.

D7: Increase in slope ange to 40 deg. No terrain obstacles, easy tree skiing.

D8: Terrain,angle or longer crux section make it harder than D7.

D9: Slopes increase to 45 deg. Crux sections are short.

D10: Slope angles at 45 deg. Complicating terrain features increase. This is where true extreme skiing begins.

D11: Slope angles at 45 deg. Complication terrain features more continuous.

D12: Steeper and /or complicationg terrain features.

Grade Scale:

Length of time needed by an party of skiers under average conditions:

Grade I: Few hours
Grade II: Half day
Grade III: One day
Grade IV: Long day but no overnight
Grade V: Big day and possible bivouac
Grade VI: Bivouac required
Grade VII: Multi-day

Ski Randonnée!

R Scale

This scale covers more objective dangers such as rockfall, crevasse danger, rocky areas that can be hidden by thin snowfall, etc.

- R1: Average backcountry ski route. Danger increase with avalanche conditions.
- R2: Slightly more inherent danger.
- R3: More sliding fall potential if snow if firm, moderate amount of features that can cause injury, rockfall exposure, tributary avalanches.
- R4: Plentiful hazards such as fall potential, rockfall, crevasses, etc.
- R5: Most hazardous routes.

Examples:

- D3: Big Emma, Snowbird Resort, Utah
- D4: South Slopes, Cardiff Pass, Utah
- D5: Standard Route, Ski Hayden, Aspen,Colorado
- D6: Avalanche Gulch, Mt.Shasta, California
- D7: Highland Bowl, Highlands Ski Resort, Aspen, Colorado
- D8: Main Baldy Chute, Alta Resort, Utah
- D9: Little Chute, Alta Resort,Utah (Alta mentionned for ease of reference)
- D10: Aussie Couloir, Joffre Peak, British Columbia
- D11: Snake Couloir, Mt. Sneffels, Colorado (rappel into chute)
- D12: North Face Cable Route, Longs Peak, Colorado

Further examples:

- D18: North Face, Mt. Robson (V D18 R4)
- D19: Great White Icicle, Little Cottonwood Canyon, Utah (rappel)
- D20: Landry Route, East Face,Pyramid Peak, Colorado (IV D20 R4)
- D21: Le Nant Blanc, North Face Aiguille Verte, France (V D21 R5)
- D22: Horbein Couloir, Mt. Everest
- D23: Mahogany Ridge, Crested Butte,Colorado (VII D23 R5)

Appendix K: Colorado Haute Route

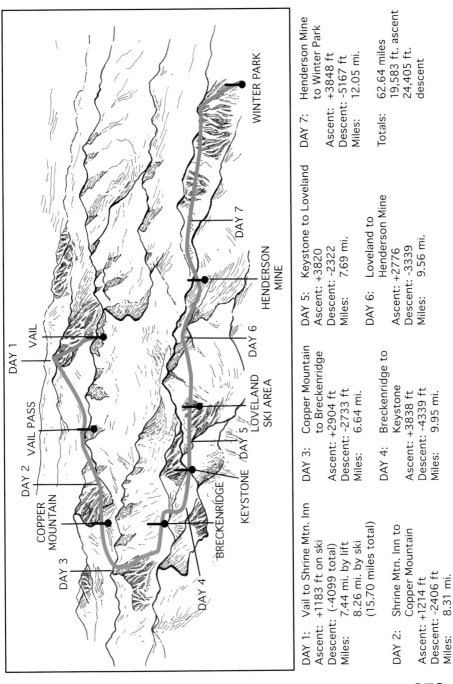

DAY 1: Vail to Shrine Mtn. Inn
Ascent: +1183 ft on ski
Descent: (-4099 total)
Miles: 7.44 mi. by lift
8.26 mi. by ski
(15.70 miles total)

DAY 2: Shrine Mtn. Inn to Copper Mountain
Ascent: +1214 ft
Descent: -2406 ft
Miles: 8.31 mi.

DAY 3: Copper Mountain to Breckenridge
Ascent: +2904 ft
Descent: -2733 ft
Miles: 6.64 mi.

DAY 4: Breckenridge to Keystone
Ascent: +3838 ft
Descent: -4339 ft
Miles: 9.95 mi.

DAY 5: Keystone to Loveland
Ascent: +3820
Descent: -2322
Miles: 7.69 mi.

DAY 6: Loveland to Henderson Mine
Ascent: +2776
Descent: -3339
Miles: 9.56 mi.

DAY 7: Henderson Mine to Winter Park
Ascent: +3848 ft
Descent: -5167 ft
Miles: 12.05 mi.

Totals: 62.64 miles
19,583 ft. ascent
24,405 ft. descent

Index

Appendix A - K: A-A, A-B, A-C, etc.

About The Author

Jean Vives is well qualified to write this book. He has more than 30 years of backcountry skiing and mountaineering experience. Plus, his unique doctoral research on alpine ski touring won him the Charles Houston Award from the Wilderness Medical Society. In addition to skiing the Haute Route in the Swiss Alps between Chamonix and Zermatt, he has twice skied the Colorado Super Tour from Winter Park to Crested Butte. The latter took 28 days to complete and covered 170 miles, making it the longest ski tour in the United States using Alpine touring equipment. Vives has published numerous articles on backcountry skiing that have appeared in Outside, Powder, and Ski magazines. A former co-director of Aspen Alpine Guides and past member of Aspen Mountain Rescue, he has climbed and trekked all over the world including Patagonia, the Alps and Ecuador. Jean received his doctoral degree in physical education with a speciality in exercise physiology from the University of Northern Colorado. As a professor at Kathmandu University in Nepal, he taught high-altitude exercise physiology. Jean recently designed and skied the Colorado Haute Route from Vail to Winter Park, 63 miles of route and with over 43,000 ft of ascent/descent. Vives lives in Fraser, Colorado.

Notes :

Notes :

Notes :